City Hall of Breslau
Dates back to the 13th century

The Other Side of the Coin

Autobiography
by
Hans J. Kunert

Revised Edition

HERITAGE BOOKS
2008

HERITAGE BOOKS
AN IMPRINT OF HERITAGE BOOKS, INC.

Books, CDs, and more—Worldwide

For our listing of thousands of titles see our website
at
www.HeritageBooks.com

Published 2008 by
HERITAGE BOOKS, INC.
Publishing Division
100 Railroad Ave. #104
Westminster, Maryland 21157

Copyright © 2002, 2008 Hans J. Kunert

Other books by the author:
The Other Side of the Coin: Autobiography by Hans J. Kunert

All rights reserved. No part of this book may be reproduced or transmitted in any form or by any means, electronic or mechanical, including photocopying, recording or by any information storage and retrieval system without written permission from the author, except for the inclusion of brief quotations in a review.

International Standard Book Numbers
Paperbound: 978-0-7884-4561-3
Clothbound: 978-0-7884-7568-9

*In Memory of
My Relatives and Friends
Who Lost Their Lives and Homeland*

TABLE OF CONTENTS

List of Illustrations	vii
Acknowledgements	ix
Introduction	xii
Growing Up in Breslau	1
The Labor Company	49
The German Army	64
Escape from Breslau	117
A New Life in Stuttgart	153
Coming to America	211
Epilogue	228

LIST OF ILLUSTRATIONS

City Hall of Breslau	Frontispiece
Hans with parents	2
Gerhard Weiser on the Oder River	36
Hans at the office	38
Jutta and Gerda Kunert	40
Hans as a recruit	64
Members of the driving school	70
Messenger duty	80
Crew manning a 50-millimeter mortar	82
Russian villagers	84
Russian village after a rain	86
Hans in Russia	92
Map of German Borders	152
Map of Eastern German Provinces	152
Elfriede Kunert, late wife of Hans	170
Hans, Hannelore and Gerald	200
Hans, Elfriede, Hannelore and Gerald	227
Kunert Family	230
Hans and Cindy	231

ACKNOWLEDGEMENTS

For many years I thought that my past seemed interesting enough to put down in writing, but I always found an excuse to delay. My wife, Cindy, deserves all the credit for the completion of my autobiography. She convinced me that I owed it to my children and grandchildren.

My special thanks goes to my son, Steven, and his wife, Amy, for their encouragement and help in amending my writing.

INTRODUCTION

Silesia is a beautiful piece of this earth with its mountains, rivers, lakes, rich farmland, endless forests and a great climate. Even though the winters have snow and ice, the rest of the year is sunny and mild. There was a saying that Silesia had six hundred and sixty six poets who mostly praised their homeland. A little larger in size than Denmark it used to have a population of six million. After being German Territory for hundreds of years it became a part of Poland in 1945.

Breslau, the capital, now known by the name of Wroclaw had before WW II a population of 650,000. The city is located on the Oder River, which originates at the Karpathian Mountains and flows into the Baltic Sea. It probably had its beginning at the present location on account of an island in the middle of the river which provided a safe crossing. Officially Breslau became a city in the year 1242. The inner city, once surrounded by the Oder and a wide moat for defensive purposes, consisted of many historical buildings and churches with some of them dating back to the 13th century. Later, In addition to the many existing parks, the moat was turned into parkland with beautiful promenades along its way. With its history and culture, Breslau was one of the most impressive cities of Germany.

GROWING UP IN BRESLAU

The long corridor that led from the front door to the rear, where we lived, was dim in daytime and pitch dark at night. Heart pounding, I always raced down that gloomy hallway as fast as I could. Eerie shadows loomed everywhere and I eventually resorted to carrying a stick, jabbing at the darkness in the hidden corners along the way. What increased my fears even more were my mother's ghost stories about that spooky place.

The house I was born in was located in the oldest part of the city, just a stone's throw from the Oder River. It was hundreds of years old and there was a rumor that the house had once been a monastery. Over the years, it had been converted into an apartment building, with apartments in front and in the rear. It even had a tunnel leading to the river. The tunnel wasn't used anymore and was full of large white mushrooms. Interestingly, the apartments had no toilets and everyone had to empty their honey pots into an opening in the basement, next to the tunnel.

The only part I liked about this house was the view I had from our windows onto the street and neighborhood below. At the time of my birth, in 1922, Germany was reeling from its defeat of WW I and Breslau, my hometown, was no exception. There was a lot of turmoil and as a child it was fascinating to observe the propaganda marches of the major parties, usually accompanied by bands, and the occasional fights among adults.

My father, Erich Kunert, was well educated and an amicable person. He was the vice president of a bank that exclusively handled the finances of a large slaughterhouse. His job took him frequently to Berlin and I always looked forward to his return, because I knew he would bring me a toy or sweets. Sadly enough he became addicted to alcohol and our happy family life would never be the same.

My mother Elfriede, a born Heimlich, was a homemaker. She was very strict, and even though I didn't appreciate it at the time, I'm grateful for the way she reared me. Moreover, still today, I admire her strong will and determination that enabled her to prevail over the severe hardships in later years.

I have little knowledge about my father's lineage. My great-grandfather was born around 1850 in Trachenberg, Silesia. He served in the German Army during the Franco-Prussian war of 1870/71. Later on the Kunert family moved to Breslau, Silesia. As far as my grandparents are concerned I only know that my grandfather, Karl Kunert, owned a butcher shop. Both my grandparents died before I was born.

In contrast, the Heimlich family came originally from Jutland, Denmark to Silesia. They settled in the Silesian mountains and it was from there where my grandfather, Alfred Heimlich, relocated to Breslau. I possess the very interesting Heimlich family tree dating back to 1590 and coat of arms dated 1427.

Overall I had a happy childhood until I was about six years old. We were members of a country club, which was a lot of fun. The club covered quite a large area; it had an oval shaped clubhouse with a restaurant, bowling alley and shooting gallery. There was a lake for fishing and swimming and many old trees that gave shade and were great for hammocks. For us children there was a playground and lots of white sand to play with. We had big lockers where we stored our swimsuits, toys, etc. because we spent most of the summer there. I believe that the earliest memory of my life is at the club when I looked up and wondered about the moving leaves of a tree.

I also learned how to swim there. The lake had a white beach and I could observe swimmers against the bottom. My parents bought me a swim girdle made of cork and I tried to imitate the

Hans (age two) with parents, Elfriede and Erich
Breslau 1924

movements of the swimmers with my girdle on, lying more on the sand than being in water. One day I couldn't believe it, I was swimming free. I swam a short distance out in the lake when my mother saw me and almost fainted.

Breslau had a beautiful opera house and my parents went there quite often. They acquired the librettos of the different operas and we had a large collection. My mother liked to sing many of the arias and this started my interest in opera that continues today.

Many times my mother and I visited the zoo that was located picturesquely along the Oder River. They had started to remodel the zoo after the Hagenbeck Zoo near Hamburg, the kind of zoo where animals could be seen in their natural habitat and not behind bars. What I remember the most, from our visits, was the ape exhibit. There was a particular ape that had fun by throwing his excrement at people. I suppose he liked to hear them scream. Since he had to throw that stuff through a chain link fence, it really scattered. I believe a warning sign was there, but people either didn't see it or didn't take it seriously.

I had many toys to play with but I preferred a box full of paper money. To describe it I have to explain that sometime before I was born the craziest thing happened to the German Mark. It devaluated so rapidly that workers were paid every day. For instance, a loaf of bread could cost five thousand Marks on one day and ten thousand marks the next. Naturally, at the end there was a total collapse, but not before billion and trillion Mark banknotes went into circulation. Later I always wondered how the little store keepers were able to handle that. For me playing with all the money was fun; somehow I realized at this time already the importance of money. I also played with my parents' bankbook, using it as a coloring book. A few years later, they reevaluated a small percentage of savings and my mother had to take that mutilated book to the bank.

We belonged to a Lutheran Church with the name of St. Elisabeth. The church was very old, beautiful inside and its steeple was three hundred feet tall, the tallest steeple of all the churches in Breslau. When I was about six years old, something happened which left an everlasting impression on me. The church had a Christmas party for us children and they charged twenty-five cents for each child. It was very festive with candles and evergreen decorations. We sat on long tables and had hot chocolate, cookies and an apple. From where I sat, I could see the entrance door and some poor children seemingly half-frozen looking wide eyed at us. Well, someone shooed them away, maybe because they didn't belong or most likely because they didn't have the twenty-five cents. I could not understand what happened here and thought Jesus would not have chased these children away.

I didn't know that my pretty little world was coming to an end and that I was going to join the poor kids on the street soon. It was 1928 and Germany was in a deep depression with a great number of people out of work. One day my father came home with the bad news that he had lost his job too. No doubt, this probably had to do with the bad economic situation, but in my father's case, it was mainly his excessive drinking. He probably didn't want to admit it to himself and blamed another man in the bank for backstabbing him and for his dismissal. I remember a terrible scene, my father gesticulating with a big butcher knife vowing to kill the man and my mother trying to calm him down. Fortunately, nothing came of it, but we had started our downslide. What I have to say here sounds funny even though it certainly wasn't, but we finally began to fit into the neighborhood.

To shed a little more light on this subject I have to emphasize that where we lived all the houses were very old and many run down. There were plenty of bars and prostitution. Since prostitution was legal, the girls, I'm using this term lightly, paraded around on the streets swinging their little handbags propositioning passersby. With few exceptions, the people around us were poor and there were beatings and even killings. My father used to earn a lot of money with his job at the bank. Both my parents had fur coats; we had costly furniture, oil paintings, fine china, expensive books and so on. In other words, we didn't have to live in this neighborhood. My mother was very unhappy there; she had grown up in the mountains and in a small town where life had been serene. My father was the one who didn't want to move. It was his home; he and his father were born there and he knew almost everyone in the neighborhood.

With no more steady income and my father's drinking habit, practically everything we owned went down the drain in a relatively short time. One of the last pieces to go was our sofa. My mother had taken me for a walk so I wouldn't be there when they came to pick it up. Unfortunately, we came back too early and I saw when they carried it out. I remember saying to my mother: "Mama, they are taking our sofa away." After that, we had to manage with the few leftover belongings for a long time to come.

At about the same time I started school and I remember my first day. My mother came with me in the classroom and there was a woman my mother knew, with her boy. His name was Rudi. My mother said to me "Why don't you sit next to Rudi," which I did, and right away felt a lot better. I guess misery likes company.

The school was located on a wider street but just as old and run down as our neighborhood. The schoolyard in particular was depressing. The yard was rectangular shaped and surrounded by buildings. The ground consisted of cobblestones and there wasn't a speck of green anywhere. In addition, the paint on the buildings was peeling off, making the courtyard even more despicable. The classrooms looked somewhat better, but the floors were made of boards that were blackened from oil. I began to hate these floors later on when I had to attend school barefooted because the black stuff stuck to the soles of my feet like printing ink.

It was an all boys school, which was typical at this time. Discipline was very strict-this was Prussia. Spanking with a cane was a daily occurrence. Fortunately, it happened to me only a few times, many of the other boys weren't that lucky. In all honesty, I have to say we studied and we learned.

I had about a ten-minute walk to school and through another

red-light district. I saw some interesting and funny things, also educational ones. One time a naked girl was chasing a man down the street. He was running like mad and she gave up and ran back to her home. Another time I saw a cat fight. It was scary to watch these two women going after each other rolling around on the sidewalk.

One afternoon I could see a group of people on the street looking up to the second floor window of a house. When I came close, I saw an old guy sitting by the open window pulling his own teeth. He was obviously drunk and when he pulled a tooth with a pair of pliers, he showed it to his audience and dropped it in a coffee can. The people applauded him each time and he seemed to be very proud of himself. I thought I wouldn't want to be in his shoes the next day.

The prostitutes who lived to the right of our house visited regularly the bars to the left of us and the shortest way was the street below our windows. One Sunday morning in summer and before sunrise, one of the ladies sat on the curb opposite our windows and sang, if anyone could call it singing. It woke all of us and my mother decided to shut her up. She took a raw potato, threw it at her and hit her right on the forehead. I would say it was a one in a million shot. For a moment, it was quiet and then came a barrage of obscenities; words I didn't know existed. Since most of the windows in the building were open in summertime, she couldn't have known where it came from and we certainly didn't show ourselves.

Some of the prostitutes liked me and once in a while they would call me to go and get cigarettes for them. They usually gave me a quarter which was a lot of money for me. Since I was always hungry, I bought myself something to eat. I liked raw sauerkraut and could get quite a bit of it rolled in newspaper for a nickel.

One time my father was drunk again and went into a rage. He was yelling and screaming and broke the only full-length mirror we still had by hitting it with a skillet. My mother called an ambulance and the orderlies tied my father to a stretcher and carried him away. All this was very upsetting for me.

They had taken my father to a sanitarium near Breslau. We went to see him on a Sunday afternoon and he was allowed to leave with us for a while. We went to a garden restaurant, sat under trees and everything looked so perfect. I found a lot of kids to play with and had a good time. Then some of the children lined up for a foot race and I joined them. To my own surprise, I won a big box of chocolate. I went over to my parents happy as a lark and started to dig into the chocolate. It didn't take very long and a man came over to us and wanted the chocolate back. He said I couldn't have it because I didn't belong to their club. My father told him that this was too bad, but he wasn't to get the chocolate back because this wouldn't be fair. So I was allowed to keep it.

Later my mother talked to the doctor at the sanitarium and inquired about my father's health. He told her that in his opinion, based on my father's symptoms, my father wouldn't get very old. I think that my mother considered a divorce at the time and that she didn't leave my father based on the doctor's assessment. Well, my father lived another thirty years. So much for medical science.

After my father's return it seemed like he had straightened out a bit. He started to do some accounting work on the side for a restaurant. My mother could go there with a shopping bag and empty pots and they would put meat, potatoes and vegetables into them. That helped quite a bit. However, it didn't mean that my father had given up drinking. One night he came home drunk and fell down the stairs. He chipped off part of a front tooth and scattered the contents of a package of potato salad and wieners all over the stairs. My mother couldn't save the potato salad but was at least able to salvage the wieners.

My father was a friendly, outgoing and soft man. He never spanked me, not even once, despite the fact that I deserved it some times. However, when he was drunk he changed into a completely different person. He turned nasty and obnoxious and I started to dislike him more and more for what he did to my mother and our whole family life.

The Other Side of the Coin

I think my mother must have loved my father or just tried to be a good wife, I don't know, in any case, she became pregnant and in June of 1930 gave birth to my sister Jutta. Anyway, it couldn't have happened at a worse time. One morning I could hear my mother crying out and I was worried and afraid to come out of my room. After a while, the moment arrived when the midwife came in and said to me: "Here is your little sister." I was stunned and couldn't believe what had happened. When I looked closer at my sister I was somewhat disappointed because she looked so pink and I said: "I don't like her." That, of course, changed completely later on. I don't remember too much else of this day except that at night my father came home stone drunk. He threw himself backwards on a bed with his feet in the air and acted like an idiot. I am sure that my mother had to get up and take care of things. I always tried to help but there was just so much I could do.

I began to venture outside my immediate neighborhood more and more. Uncle Emil and Aunt Elfriede, my father's brother and sister, owned gardens on the outskirts of town. These gardens were very popular and the idea behind it was to give city dwellers a place to relax. In the 1800's, a man named Schreber introduced this concept. Therefore, they were known all over Germany as Schrebergartens. My uncle Emil and aunt Elfriede had their gardens next to each other and each had a little wooden cabin. My cousin Ruth, Aunt Elfriede's daughter, and I walked there together quite often. Ruth had grown up into a very pretty girl and I enjoyed her company. The distance we had to walk was approximately two miles one way, but we had so much fun that time just flew by. We had to cross three bridges over the Oder River and there was always so much to see. Especially from the last bridge we could look down on locks and watch the boats being raised or lowered.

In our house lived two boys who didn't mingle with our bunch on the street. One of them lived in the apartment below us. He was about a year younger than I was and his name was Erich. I played with him occasionally and found out that his home life was, in a way, worse than ours. His mother was a small, frail looking woman and always seemed depressed. I learned that Erich's father beat her all the time. One day Erich showed me a dagger and said next time his father would beat his mother he was going to plunge the dagger in his back. Fortunately, it never happened.

The other boy lived in front above my aunt Elfriede's apartment. He was about three years older than I was and kind of a quiet guy. His name was Heinz. During a conversation I had with him one day he asked me if I'd like to learn how to play chess so we could play together. I felt flattered that an older boy lowered himself to my level and agreed. I remember we used to sit with our board on the stairs and play. I was caught up in it and played with him every time I had a chance.

The economic and political situation in Germany had gone from bad to worse. Practically everyone we knew was out of work, my uncles, the men in our house and so on. There were at least twenty different political parties; even the Catholic Church had their own party, and they were all fighting each other. Naturally, all this affected us children in many ways. It became a common occurrence, when we went to school in the morning, to see blood pooled in the street.

Not far from our school, there was a store named Amelung that sold nothing but Nazi merchandise, such as uniforms, boots, medals etc. One day the Communists marched by the store, broke the windows and threw everything on the street. The police, who were usually on horseback, tried to break up the melee and the shooting started. I found all of this out later. Some of us kids had just come out of school when we saw this herd of people rushing toward us. It looked like a stampede. We made the mistake of not going back into the school and instead started to run in front of them. Fortunately, we could outrun them and made it into the doorway of the All Holy Hospital. It didn't take very long and they were carrying wounded people in right in front of our eyes.

It seemed to be typical for the Communists to knock out store windows. In the center of town, a store named Bielschofski, was a favorite target. The owner finally made a deal with the Communists in which he would buy them the instruments for a band if they would leave his store alone. It worked. However, after that we had to listen to their music quite often, which consisted mainly of the same tune, "The Internationale." To this day, I still don't know the origin of this song or who the "Internationale" were.

The three parties that staged most of the marches were the Social Democrats, the Communists and the Nazis. I don't remember anything special about the Social Democrats except for a certain incident. One evening my parents went to see a propaganda march by the Social Democrats. My sister Jutta, who was one year old, was with them and my father carried her on his arm. Some spectators near my parents started to heckle the marchers and it quickly got out of hand. My father sent my mother and Jutta home and, apparently not a moment to soon, because fighting started. Police on horseback moved in, striking people indiscriminately with their long nightsticks. My father was hit on the shoulder, the one where he had held Jutta moments before. He was hurting for a long time, but we were glad that things didn't turn out any worse.

I don't know where the communists started their marches, but eventually they came down the street under our windows and ended their march in a market square. Announcing the start of the parade was a police vehicle that resembled a large pick-up truck and had a searchlight and loudspeaker as well as policemen with rifles. While letting the searchlight wander along the windows they warned people over their loudspeaker to keep their windows closed or they would shoot. A similar car followed at the end of the parade.

The first of the marchers were two rows of women pushing baby carriages, I guess for extra protection, followed by a fat woman carrying a red flag. Next came the band playing *The Internationale,* of course. After that came two rows of their leaders, most of them wore black leather jackets and sports caps and looked like people one wouldn't want to meet in a dark alley. Then followed a bunch of men and women yelling slogans like: "We want work," "Justice and bread," "We are hungry." The last group was made up of teenagers who had their own slogans. I don't remember any, just that they were plain dumb. All together it was a sight to behold.

In contrast to the Communists, the Nazis looked sharp, marched in military order with their boots shined and their brown shirts and ties looking neat. When they marched at night they usually carried torches that looked quite impressive.

By the way, whenever passing a Communist or Nazi on the street us kids got a big kick out of greeting them with either a clenched fist or a stretched out right arm.

I have to give my father credit for being persistent in his political beliefs. He was a one hundred percent Democrat and never wavered. He despised Hitler and called him all kind of names. The name "painter's apprentice" was one of the milder ones. The real danger with that came later on when he was drunk in public.

My father had been a soldier in the German Army during World War I. He never saw any action and believed that the regiment's Jewish doctor saved his life. The doctor liked my father, perhaps as a person or for his ability to keep records and for his neat handwriting. Since nobody ever questioned a doctor's diagnosis, he was able to keep my father for medical reasons at home during the whole war. My father told me that his regiment went to the western front and that most of them drowned when the Dutch opened their dikes. I sometimes wondered later on if what this doctor did for my father had something to do with my father's dislike of Hitler.

Life was getting harder and harder. We received twenty of unemployment money per week. This was the bare minimum to live on but by the time my father brought it home, there were maybe ten left; the rest had gone down his throat. I really don't know how my mother managed. Of course, there were enough arguments all the time. One time it was so bad that I feared the worst. My father was hanging out the open window backwards and my mother was hitting him with a bundle of keys in the face. I couldn't blame her but I was terrified.

I had to go to my Heimlich grandparents quite often to borrow five to keep us going. Sometimes we had to scrape store coupons, bottle refunds and the last few pennies together to buy a loaf of cheap bread. The bread always felt like a rock in my stomach. Since we couldn't afford to buy meat we ate herring, which was inexpensive. A great help were the street vendors, selling mostly vegetables at a very low price. They pushed their carts by hand and yelled with a loud voice what they had to offer. My mother usually sent me down to get potatoes, cabbage, onions, etc. One thing I have to say, as meager as our meals were, they were healthy.

My life on the street was my main entertainment. At one time, they were painting an apartment house on our street and they had scaffolds all the way up to the fourth floor. There was a pulley with which the workmen pulled up buckets of paint or plaster. One evening after the workers had left, one of my friends sat in the bucket and the others pulled him up. He was passed the second floor or so when one guy yelled, "Somebody is coming." The others let go of the rope and he came down like a bomb. No one came and he wasn't really hurt; they just couldn't get him out of the bucket because he was wedged. Somebody took him to the hospital and left him there, but he didn't like it in the hospital and took off. It was kind of funny when he came home clad in only his pajamas.

The University of Breslau was founded in 1811 and was located along the river not far from where I lived. There was an open area between buildings with a bronze statue of a nude man holding a foil. The statue was very cleverly named "The Naked Fencer." I went once in a while to one of the buildings to watch the students fencing. I couldn't get inside and had to pull myself up to a window to see the action. Most of the time the fencers wore face masks but a couple of times they were fencing without masks. I never saw anyone get cut, but I once saw a washbowl and bloody towels on a table. Apparently these fencers wanted to get cut. They didn't want the cuts properly sutured and even put salt or poured beer into the wound to get a nice scar. The purpose of this insanity was to become a member of an exclusive brotherhood, which usually paid out handsomely in their future.

Visiting my grandparents was something I had to do and not what I liked to do. My grandparents showed no love or affection toward me, the other grandchildren or even their own children.

One time their son George came to visit them, out of work and probably hungry.

My grandfather was eating a big piece of salami and George said, "This looks awful good."

My grandfather answered, "If you can't stand it, then you better leave."

I was there once on Christmas and a table in the living room was covered with chocolate and other goodies. My grandmother knew how poor we were and that we couldn't afford anything of that sort, but she didn't give me a morsel. She died when I was about fifteen years old. I didn't go to her funeral and it didn't faze me at all. I sometimes thought that my mother would have had a chance to break away from my father if she would have had some support from her parents.

I had made friends with a boy by the name of Willie who was a little older than I was. Willie asked me one day if I wanted to go with him on a Hitler Youth night march. At the time I didn't know the Hitler Youth existed and later on I wondered how a guy like Willie became involved with them; he certainly didn't fit in. I agreed to go with him, but I still don't understand why my mother gave me permission. We left at sundown and headed for a village called Sponsberg. We were about twenty-five boys and we marched in military order. Some had uniforms and others like myself were in regular clothing. Since I was the smallest of them I had to march at the end. After a while, it grew very dark and we were passing some houses whose light fell out on the road. When passing the houses we sang a Nazi song. I shouldn't say "we," because I didn't know any. The people in those houses didn't like Nazis for some reason. They shouted at us and threw some objects; I didn't know if it was potatoes, rocks or what. I thought I had made a mistake to go along with Willie's idea.

We arrived at midnight in Sponsberg and ended up at an estate. The leader told us that we should address the owner as Contessa.

She came then and said, "Heil Hitler, boys."

We answered dutifully, "Heil Hitler, Contessa."

We got some boiled potatoes with salt and artificial coffee. After that we slept in the barn on straw, which didn't matter, because we were dead tired. The next day we were served hot soup and bread and actually had a lot of fun jumping into the straw or hay from beams above. After all, this was new to us city kids. In the afternoon we went home on a different route. We came to a river with fast flowing water and a few of us went in. Even though the water wasn't deep, I should have seen what was going to happen. I went in and it swept me away. I was lucky that there was a big boulder in the middle of the river and I was able to hang on. After regaining some strength I made it back to the bank. I knew I learned a valuable lesson there. I was also very happy to make it home safely.

At about the fourth grade every school class had to take swimming lessons. All students had to participate regardless if one could swim or not. When our turn came, we went to a protected pool in the river. After completion of our lessons and some practice we had to pass a final test. The test consisted of diving, swimming a certain distance in pants and shirt and a twenty-minute continuous swim. I had no trouble passing the test but the funny part was that after I finished I had a streak of black grime across the lower part of my face. No doubt there were no environmental concerns at this time.

The Oder was a big river that had many tributaries, mainly coming from the mountains. In school we had to learn each of them by name and I still remember them today. The part of the river upstream from the city was called upper water and downstream from the city was lower water. Most people preferred the upper water because it was cleaner. Unfortunately, every year up to thirty people drowned in the river. One of the biggest dangers was the whirlpools. They said if you were caught in one, don't fight it, let it pull you down to the bottom and then push yourself up. I don't know if anyone ever had the nerve to do that. For one thing, the river was very deep.

Every summer I spent as much time as possible at the river. Even though it could have cost me my life, I am glad it was part of my youth. I spent some of the happiest years of my life there. The tug boats pulling barges loaded with coal became a big attraction for my friends and me. The barges were also peoples' homes. We liked to swim up to them and to pull ourselves up on deck, take a little ride and jump back in the water. I learned very quickly not to jump on the anchor that was barely visible under the water surface. Getting up on the barges wasn't all that easy; the water rushing along was so strong it could strip one's swimming trunks off. The boat people didn't like us to come uninvited on board, so to speak. They usually chased us with a broomstick or threw coal at us. Maybe they were afraid someone might steal from them, but I guess mainly to protect their privacy.

Later, when I was older, I made a big mistake. I swam up to one barge to get on when another tugboat with a barge passed in the opposite direction. I ended up caught between the waves coming from both sides and every time I wanted to take a breath, a wave swamped me. I really thought this was the end. Fortunately, I was able to catch a breath of air at the very last moment.

Another time three of us swam up to a barge and climbed on. We were surprised to see an old man sitting on a chair grinning at us. That was the complete opposite of the reaction we usually received. Well, we found out quickly the reason. The boat had been freshly painted with tar. I had tar all over my body from my chin to my knees. The others didn't look much better. We swam back to the bank and tried to clean ourselves with sand but that didn't work. We had to go home by streetcar and everyone stared at us, we must have puzzled them.

By 1932 everything had gotten worse, unemployment, hunger and political fighting. My father was still out of work but at least he continued doing some bookkeeping here and there. For a while he worked for a company that made sugar candy. Occasionally, he brought some home, a rare delicacy.

At this most inopportune time, my mother was pregnant again. I thought when my sister Jutta was born things were bad, but it was even worse now. We had absolutely nothing. My mother was fully aware of it and I suspected that she tried to end her pregnancy prematurely. It didn't work. When my mother knew the time was here to give birth, she sent me to my grandparents overnight. The next day, Aunt Gertrude, my mother's sister, came and gave me the good news that my mother was fine, that I had another sister and I could go home.

My new sister was born in December and was named Gerda. I liked her right away. I remember she had a lot of black hair and was holding her two little fists against her cheeks. One sometimes wonders about life's mysterious ways. What seemed to be a calamity at the time turned out to be a blessing for my mother. After my father had died and the rest of us had left the country, Gerda took care of my mother for the last twenty-eight years of her life.

Gerda's birth brought a lot of pressure on me, namely that I had to take care of my sister Jutta more and more. Jutta was about two and a half years old and I used to drag her all over the neighborhood. She tells me sometimes that she still remembers that, which I doubt a little. Nevertheless, I took good care of her.

Two months after Gerda's birth, on January 30, 1933 Adolf Hitler became Reich Chancellor, an event, which would change the lives of all of us and to an extent, nobody could foresee at the time. To me it didn't mean anything; after all, I was only ten years old.

Spring was in the air. I could get back on the street again with my friends. Unfortunately, my fun didn't last very long. I came home one evening and sat in front of my house and everything looked like it was in a fog. I went to bed and didn't wake up for six days. I had been in a coma from a serious concussion. I never found out what had caused my injury. I suffered a complete memory loss. I know I spent a long time in bed after that. My parents had to walk in socks in my room because the slightest vibration hurt so much. Another boy named Hans came to visit me once in a while and brought me grapes and chocolate. That was very unusual because these gifts were very expensive. I always suspected he had something to do with my mishap, but I never found out. Sadly, I was not the same person anymore after my concussion. I had lost my spunk. My head was very sensitive and I frequently felt dizzy. I was also excused from physical exercise at school. I just know that I was very fortunate, and that except for a permanent bump on the back of my head, I didn't suffer any further damage from this bad injury.

My uncle Erich, my mother's brother, came quite often to visit me while I was recuperating. Maybe he came because he knew more than anyone else about the misery of a head injury. In 1920 there was an attempted overthrow of the powerless German Republic by soldiers under the command of an officer named Wolfgang Kapp. They came to Breslau and immediately forced military law on the population. There was resistance by worker's groups that resulted in quite a bit of shooting. Near my grandparent's house, a lieutenant was shot and killed and Kapp's soldiers were looking for the killer. My grandfather warned his sons not to leave the house, but my uncle Erich didn't listen. He went out to buy some cigarettes and was arrested. The soldiers took him to their headquarters and accused him of the killing. They beat him mercilessly to get a confession. They cracked his skull and broke almost every bone in his hands. Then they threw him into the basement and left him. Luckily, three days later Kapp's soldiers were chased out of town by some other forces and he was rescued. I had the feeling that he never recovered fully from this ordeal.

My father was a lot luckier during this episode. Citizens had been warned that anyone caught with a weapon would be executed. My father used to carry a pistol and when he walked across a bridge, he threw the pistol into the water. He told us that it wasn't an hour later that he was stopped and searched by Kapp's soldiers. If he still had the pistol, it probably would have cost him his life.

Not too much later, my mother finally had her wish fulfilled and we moved out of the inner city to a much nicer part of town. I thought; why couldn't this have happened before I was hurt so badly? I left our house with mixed emotions. In a way, I was sad to leave and on the other hand, I was glad. I hardly ever went back to the old neighborhood but over the years found out a few things. My friend Rudi from school was killed in Russia on his first day at the front when he stepped on a mine. Erich, the boy with the abusive father also was killed. My friend Willie, I heard, became a pimp. My cousin Ruth I saw only occasionally in town. The rest of the gang never crossed my way again.

Our new home was on the top floor of a two-story building and was located in the rear of a large apartment house. The building might have been a former warehouse. All the rooms in our apartment were huge and with the little furniture we had, they looked even larger. To tell how big it really was, later on I rode my bicycle in the apartment, which was fun. Only my mother didn't see it my way since I left tire tracks on the floor.

Quite a few of the boys in the neighborhood had bicycles and I wanted to have one too. I knew I could not expect one from my parents and that I had to take matters into my own hands. All bicycles had an identification number engraved on the frame, below the saddle. To avoid being caught, some bicycle thieves stripped the stolen bikes and threw the frames into the river. My mother's brother Kurt's favorite fishing spot was at the bank of the river and under a bridge. It just happened to be the location where one could find bicycle frames in the water. My uncle retrieved some of them, cleaned them and took the frames to the police station. If nobody claimed them within one year, the frames belonged to my uncle. He always had two or three frames in his storage room and he gave me a very nice looking one. I suppose thieves only steal something worthwhile. Anyway, I was off to a good start.

My grandfather had a brother named George who didn't resemble my grandfather at all. In particular, he was always in a good mood and willing to help. He was married and had two children, Charlotte and Herbert. "Uncle" George, as I called him, owned an automobile body shop. I had noticed two bicycle wheels there that no one seemed to want. My uncle gave them to me and even found a handle bar. Now things really began to look good, but I still needed a saddle and a chain.

At the time, the cigarette companies added photographs or pictures to each package, comparable to baseball cards. I collected these pictures for a long time. I always asked my uncles for them and also looked for discarded packages on the street. Some photos showed the places the Zeppelin had visited, for instance New York, the Pyramids, Rio de Janeiro and other interesting locations. Another group of pictures showed the expeditions by the Hagenbeck Zoo, catching animals all over the world. There were more sets of subjects, like medieval uniforms, etc. Even though it was hard for me to give up my pictures, my bicycle was more important. So I traded some of them for a saddle. I don't know anymore where I got the chain, but my bike was now complete and a new world was at my disposal.

My life had changed in many ways. It was the new neighborhood, the new friends and our new apartment. We now had electricity, a real miracle, and fully realized what we had missed all these years. The area around us was wide and open and a park was close by. Even life on the streets had changed; there was no more fighting among the adults. For the first time in my life I saw what it meant to have law and order. My father was still out of work and getting drunk and we were still dirt poor. However, he must have been bringing home some money, and at least we didn't have to scrape our last pennies together anymore to get some cheap bread.

Winter came and another change in our life was looming. We couldn't heat our apartment as it was just too big, and so we knew we couldn't stay. Winters had been a problem for us for many years, especially with clothing and shoes. I remember in particular my cold blue fingers sticking out of my torn woolen gloves and my cold and wet feet. As far as heating went, we had managed before, but to heat this apartment was impossible.

We survived the winter, but it was rough. I spent every moment I could in bed. This could have been pretty boring because there was no radio or television. I was glad that I had my bicycle, and whenever the streets were free of ice, I rode to the library and loaded up with books.

Reading became an eye opener. I read books by German, French, Russian and other authors. It might sound a bit strange, but my favorite books remain the same today *What There Crawls and Flies*, *My Green Book* and *My Brown Book*. Hermann Loens, a forest ranger in the Lueneburger Moor in northern Germany, wrote them. Sadly enough, he was killed in France during World War I. He loved the moor and everything about it. He described it all in such a vivid and loving way that one could almost see and feel it. No matter if it was a blade of grass, the heather, a little field mouse, a mother bird and her young or just a sunny, beautiful day. The latter he called "A day like God had made it just for you." When I visited my relatives in Kiel at the Baltic Sea later on, I had the chance to spend a day in the Lueneburger Moor. It gave me an even better understanding of his writing.

With the end of the winter the ice broke on the Oder River. This was always a real spectacle and the best spot to watch was on the bridges. I would guess the ice was usually close to a foot thick. The big pieces piled up on top of each other and broke up with a thunderous noise. What followed after the ice was quite different in nature. The snow in the mountains melted and the water coming down from the many tributaries resulted quite often in the flooding of the river. Again, standing on the bridges, one could see almost anything rushing by, like dead animals, furniture and so on. One time I saw a cradle floating along like a little boat.

By resuming the visits with my relatives, I found out who liked to play chess. One of them was Uncle Walter, my mother's brother. He belonged to a chess club and I learned a lot from him. In the beginning I lost most of the games but after a while we broke even. I think because I didn't play by the book worked to my advantage. It threw him off. He later was drafted into the Air Force, and since he was already in his forties ended up with some antiaircraft batteries at the Atlantic Wall. Apparently, he and his comrades sat around a lot and played chess. One time, when he came home on leave, I played five games with him and lost all of them, which proves that practice makes perfect.

Under the Nazi Regime different welfare programs had started. One of them was to send poor children from the cities to rural areas for recreation. Without my knowledge, my mother signed me up. I was certainly qualified but wasn't all that eager to go. Anyway, I went along with the idea, since I knew my mother meant well. The day came when a group of us children went by train to a small town named Winzig. I was supposed to stay with the druggist's family, but they wanted a girl, and I ended up with the doctor and his wife. The doctor already had taken a boy, but took me as well.

The two of us were put in a room on the second floor of the house. I remember the room, and especially the bed, were very luxurious. All of it could have been the beginning of a nice vacation. Unfortunately, it turned out to be the opposite. First, the other boy had absolutely no personality whatsoever. I tried to have some conversation with him but it was useless. Secondly, the doctor's wife didn't like me. I had no idea why. The doctor was a very quiet man who hardly said anything. He took me a couple of times with him in his car to see patients. I assume he wanted to do me a favor, but it wasn't much fun for me waiting in the car. Well, to be honest, one time it was. I was sitting in the car when I saw this little girl across the street. She was looking at me as if I came from Mars. She kept on walking slowly backward and all of a sudden fell in a ditch behind her. I felt sorry for her but I still had to laugh.

After a few days, I made friends with a boy and his sister who lived behind the doctor's house. We really liked each other and I began to spend most of my time with them. Sometimes we went swimming in a small lake or played hide and seek in their garden or even in the potato field. Their parents liked me too and quite often invited me to eat with them.

I might have spent the whole four weeks if it hadn't been for the doctor's wife. She seemed to get nastier by the day and I decided to go home. When I found out that my friend's father was going to the railroad station one morning with his horse and wagon, I decided to go with him. When the time came I grabbed my few belongings, climbed out the back window, down on a patio roof, down a trellis and took off. I knew this wasn't the right thing to do but I didn't care. The railroad station was in a town named Wohlau, which was located about twenty miles away from Breslau. My getaway had worked fine so far, but then I ran into trouble. I found out I didn't have enough money for the train ticket. I was in a bind and must have looked pretty desperate. A man, who was standing nearby, noticed and gave me the rest of the money I needed. When I showed up at home, my mother was quite surprised but I knew she was glad to see me.

I couldn't believe it, but my father actually got a full-time job with the City of Breslau. It made my mother and me very happy, but we couldn't help wondering how long he would last. We were lucky. As far as I remember, he kept this job for about two years. With him working it not only meant that finally some money came in, but also that we could afford to move out of our "Ice Cellar."

We moved to the outskirts of town and into a brand new apartment building, one of about eight buildings joined together.

Behind the houses were lawns and a playground for children. We even had a maintenance man named Krueger who took care of the grass, sidewalks, garbage cans, etc. Often there were parties for the children with ice cream, cake and lemonade as well as games. The whole neighborhood was very neat too. I felt like I had entered a different world.

My school was not far and had a soccer field. Close by was a pond with promenades on two sides. At the pond was a small building where one could buy a glass of carbonated spring water for a nickel. Next to the building stood big, old trees and there were tables and benches under the trees. Some people just sat on the benches to relax and watch the birds on the pond, but mostly elderly men came to play chess under the trees.

It was easy to make friends at the new apartment because all of the boys were new to the area. We eventually became a group of seven who hung out together. In our free time we mainly played soccer, either among ourselves or against other groups. While we played mostly on the soccer field, we sometimes played behind our houses, which was forbidden.

In winter when the pond was frozen we played ice hockey. We got walking canes from our fathers and sawed the end part of the handle off, making them into nice hockey sticks. I could skate pretty fast going forward, but never managed to skate backward. Maybe it had to do with the lousy skates I inherited from my Aunt Erika, my mother's sister, but I don't really know.

Breslau was practically flat except for two hills on the opposite sides of town. Both of them had been garbage dumps that had gotten too big. The city had them beautifully landscaped with grass, pine trees etc. and nobody would have known what they consisted of before. On top of the hills were many benches for relaxation. At night it was especially nice to be able to look over the city and all its lights.

One of the two hills was only a few minutes away from our house and was a great place for sledding in winter. However, it was not without danger, especially when two or three sleds were tied behind each other. Their combined weight and speed was enormous and one had better get out of their way.

I didn't own a sled, but when on top of the hill I usually could catch a ride with someone. Later on when I was a little older, I took advantage of the young maids who worked in big homes in the area. They showed up with their sleds around nine o'clock in the evening, probably after they had done the dishes. I waited until one of them was ready to take off and hopped on the seat behind them. After a little scream and pretending some resistance, they appreciated my skill in sledding. I also pulled the sled up the hill for them, something they definitely liked. There was a little shack near the bottom of the hill that was operated by an old woman. She sold hot drinks for a dime. The drinks consisted mainly of hot water and some berry juice. Sometimes I generously invited one of the girls for a drink.

Saturday nights our group liked to go to wrestling matches that took place in a former circus building. The wrestlers came from different European countries and we knew all of them by name. In particular, our local hero was Max Waloschke. After the matches, many of the wrestlers could be found at a bar and restaurant nearby. We followed them and asked them for their autographed pictures.

They always asked us first, "Did you guys boo us tonight?"

And we always answered, "Of course not, we applauded you like crazy."

The funniest part of the evening was the band. They were all old men and played terribly. I still have to laugh today when I think about the leader of the band. At the beginning of the evening all the wrestlers walked in one behind the other to be introduced. At this point, he played the "Entrance of the Gladiators" solo on his trumpet and hit about every wrong note possible.

One afternoon my father embarrassed me so much that I could have killed him. I was standing in front of our house door with some friends when he came home drunk. He fell down right in front of us and wet his pants.

I went over to him, pulled him away from the puddle and helped him back on his feet.

My friends asked me, "Who is this?"

I had to tell them, "My father."

I could see it was just a matter of time before he would lose his job again.

In school they started to pressure us to join the Hitler Youth. I found out that once all the boys in school had joined, the school could fly a special flag. I didn't like the idea of joining for different reasons, mainly that I never liked to take orders and had no interest in marching around with a wooden rifle on Sunday mornings. Finally, there were only three of us holding out and the leader of the Hitler Youth in our district came to see my parents. He made it clear to them that it would be in my best interest to join if I wanted to get anywhere in life. So the other two boys and I joined and the school received their silly flag.

One night my father didn't come home, something he had never done before. We didn't know what to make of it and my mother sent me to school the next day anyway. At around eleven o'clock I saw my mother talking to the teacher. He called me and told me and I could go home. My father had been drunk and was hit by a streetcar. While I took care of my sisters my mother went to the hospital to pick him up. He had a crack in his skull over the left eye and his head was all bandaged like a turban. Even though the blood was seeping through his bandages, he took off the same evening to drink some more; the way he put it, was to do something for his pain.

Summer was near and I think my mother wanted to do me a favor again by getting me out of the house. She knew I wouldn't go to strangers anymore, like in Winzig. However, she found out that the same welfare program took children, free of cost, to relatives out of town. My mother wrote to her aunt Anna in Kiel, a city at the Baltic Sea, and asked her if I could visit her for four weeks. She answered that I was welcome and that actually made me very happy.

There were quite a few children on the train to Kiel and we had a great time together until our arrival. Before I left home, I had asked my mother how I would recognize her aunt and my mother told me, "You will know her when you see her. We resemble each other." That wasn't quite the case and they had to get us together with the help of a loudspeaker.

After that, everything went very smoothly. Anna was a fine person with a great sense of humor. I called her "Aunt" Anna even though she was my Heimlich grandfather's sister. Her husband was kind of grouchy, but later I could understand the reason. He was about sixty years old and had served in the Merchant Marines and in the German Navy. After leaving the navy he had taken the job of a prison guard. The prison where he was employed was located on a quiet street and there were two nice looking apartment buildings on each side of the actual prison. My uncle and aunt lived in one, on the same floor with the prison doctor, his wife and a daughter by the name of Irmgard.

My uncle still suffered from malaria, and he looked somewhat yellowish. I could see that this probably had something to do with him being moody, but what truly affected him were the times when he had night duty, because he had trouble sleeping in daytime.

Irmgard wasn't there when I arrived, and after I had been there for a few days she was about to come home. My aunt told me that she was my age and very pretty. She wanted me to look my best when I met her. I had straight hair and my aunt got the idea to make my hair wavy with a curling iron. I thought what the heck, this could be fun. Well, my aunt hadn't exaggerated; Irmgard was blond, tall, and slim; at the tender age of thirteen I was in love. I had the feeling that she liked me too and I spent most of my time with her. We went to the movies, the beach and other places, but then one day when we were in town it rained and my hair straightened out. At first, I felt embarrassed but she didn't seem to notice and I relaxed.

We also took two trips, one with her father, to see relatives of theirs who lived near the Lueneburger Moor. I was really happy to see the moor since I had read so much about it. I found out that Hermann Loens, my favorite author, had his grave there and that they brought his body home from France to the land he had loved so much.

On the other trip we went with my uncle to visit some friends out in the country. The man worked at an airfield and told us they were testing airplanes that came down almost vertically from a great height. He said the planes usually couldn't pull up and crashed, leaving a deep hole in the ground. It became clear to me later that these planes were Junkers '87, the Stukas.

One Sunday, my uncle and aunt took me to the harbor to watch the arrival of a large cruise ship carrying hundreds of Swedish gymnasts. Seeing a ship, first as a small dot on the horizon, then getting bigger and bigger and finally so large and impressive in front of me was a new experience. I remember vividly the "Kieler Kayak Club," mostly young men and women, who had come in their kayaks to welcome the Swedish guests. They underestimated the huge waves this large ship would make. As a result, many kayaks were literally thrown against the harbor walls and the kayakers were pulled out of the water with their wet shirts and shorts clinging to their bodies. I have to admit, for a young man, looking at the girls was a lot of fun.

My uncle had a nice sailboat that he called a Jolle. The boat had one mast, a deck with a curved bench at the stern and two beds below deck. He was an experienced sailor and he told me that he could make it in about two hours to the nearest Swedish Islands. All of this was very exiting for me, since I had never been on a sailboat before or for that matter on the open sea.

All good things come to an end, and so did my vacation. As much as I wanted to see my mother and sisters, I still wished that I could have stayed longer. In any case it was a beautiful and memorable vacation. I said goodbye and never saw any of them again. My aunt died during a bomb attack and I don't know what happened to my uncle. I corresponded with Irmgard for a while, but this also ended; I guess the distance had a lot to do with it.

I had to go back to school, and hated the thought of getting slapped in the face or being hit with the cane again. Unfortunately, it started almost immediately. During gymnastics I was sitting on the parallel bars and my foot wasn't in perfect alignment with my shin when the teacher hit me so hard in the face that I almost fell off the bars.

Worst of all was a teacher by the name of Tschirsch, and unfortunately, we had him most of the time. When dictating he walked up and down between the benches with a cane and hit us over the back when someone made a mistake. One day when he was about to hit a boy over the back, the boy straightened up and he hit him accidentally across the neck. The kid let out a loud scream, jumped up and ran out the door with two other boys right behind him. That caused quite a commotion and when the teacher ran after them we jumped on our seats and cheered. It didn't take long and the boys came back with one father and two mothers and they went straight to the principal's office. We had a good idea what went on in there because the caning stopped. It was too bad that this didn't happen earlier because this was our last year in school. Again, I have to say at least we learned a lot and I was able to lay a solid base on which to build my education.

The Nazi Regime had been in power for three years. The effect of it was evident; almost every one had gone back to work, and as a result, people dressed better, ate better and in general felt better about themselves and about Germany. What impressed me the most was the order and safety on the street. There was practically no more crime because criminals came to expect swift and severe punishment.

Many Americans have asked me why Hitler came to power. I only can say that in my opinion it had to happen. The foundation for it was laid by the Treaty of Versailles in 1919 after World War I. England and France, with the blessings of the United States, "negotiated" this peace treaty which forced Germany to pay one hundred thirty billion in gold Marks, ships, livestock, natural resources, etc. In addition, Germany had to give up thirteen percent of its territory to France, Poland, Czechoslovakia and other European countries, as well as its four colonies. This "War Debt" finally brought on the total collapse of the fledgling German government. As a result, life in Germany became more chaotic by the day and eventually out of this quagmire emerged Adolf Hitler. Hitler definitely had an oratory talent and he used it well. He told the masses what they wanted to hear, namely "No more Injustice and Humiliation." He kept his word by putting Germany back on track and restoring German pride. It is just sad that so many people who supported him at the time had no idea what price they would have to pay later on by living under a ruler with absolute power.

By watching film clips of the Nazi era I can understand why many foreigners believed that all Germans were Nazis. I can honestly say this wasn't so. There were very few people one could have called a real Nazi and they were sprinkled throughout the community. One of them by the name of Haesler happened to live one floor below us. We got into a serious confrontation with him later on.

It didn't come as a surprise that joining the Hitler Youth would have its consequences. Along with the other boys on our street, I got the order to come to one of their meetings. When we arrived, late on purpose, there was the leader of the troop and approximately twenty other boys. The leader was about eighteen years old and seemed to be a fairly decent guy. I had always thought that the kids from the inner city were rowdy, but I found out the ones from our street were even more so. The meeting continued and we didn't pay any attention to what the leader was telling us. We even had the other boys laughing. The leader thought that taking us outside and chasing us around would restore his authority. The house had a backyard with big trees and was very dark. He ordered us to run to the rear of the yard and back.

Well, the other boys did follow orders, but we didn't; we

stayed at the rear.
 He called, "Come back."
 We yelled, "Come here if you want us."
 This pretty much was the end of the meeting.
For a while it seemed the Hitler Youth had given up on us but were we ever wrong. We received the order to report to a military compound where we had drill sergeants chasing us around. My brain worked overtime to find a way out of this situation. Fortunately, the opportunity came soon. It was very hot one day and the sergeant had us standing at attention, which seemed like forever. I felt a little woozy anyway but I mainly thought here is my chance, so I collapsed. The sergeant called me a sissy, which didn't bother me a bit, and sent me home. I don't know why but they pretty much left me alone after that. I think that maybe I fell through the cracks. I remember somebody came to our apartment a couple of times to inquire about me, but my father told him that I was sick. I have to say this about my father; it took guts because trying to fool the Nazi's could have dire consequences.

When I played chess with Uncle Walter I always admired his aquarium of tropical fish. I didn't have any money, but I wanted to have an aquarium too. By looking around I was lucky enough to find the frame of one. I cleaned it, found some glass and my uncle helped me put it together using a watertight putty. In addition, he gave me some guppies and black and red snails. For anyone who doesn't know, these snails stay in the water and go up and down the glass keeping it clean. I gathered some white sand from the river and added some small rocks that looked red in the water. Together, with a few water plants it looked beautiful, and I was very happy with my creation. Later on I was able to install lights behind the aquarium that made it look even better, especially at night. Two other boys in my class had tropical fish, and with their help, I eventually acquired a nice variety.

It was getting close to graduation from school and I had to start looking for a job. Going to a job center for counseling and registration was the first step to take. To my surprise, my father went with me, but he might as well have stayed at home. Throughout my school years I had excellent grades in drawing and mathematics and I hoped to find a profession in which I could use my talent. The man at the job center didn't have anything available in this field at the time, only jobs in manual labor. My father said, "Well, then you have to take one of those." I looked at him and thought, "You have to be crazy." Nevertheless, the important part had been accomplished, as I had been added to their register. I was also glad that neither the job center nor my parents put any pressure on me to accept a job I wouldn't have liked.

The day of graduation came and I ended up in a tie with another boy for the best student in class. The two of us each received an expensive book and were congratulated by the principal in front of all the boys in school. It felt great to be out of school and not be treated like a slave anymore.

I had a casual friendship with a boy by the name of Guenter; we used to attend the same class in school. He was in a similar situation as me, waiting for the right job to come along. Since we anticipated starting work soon, we thought we should take a vacation while we had time. We decided to go to the mountains and stay there for at least a week. After loading our gear on the back of our bikes, we took off and made it on the first day to a small farm in the mountains. The farm belonged to his uncle and he and his family were happy to see us. The surroundings were beautiful and reminded me of the state song of Silesia, which begins with the words "Blue mountains, green valleys." I felt we had a nice vacation ahead of us.

The following day we left in the afternoon and told his uncle where we were heading. He told us to be very careful at a village named Ketschdorf because the road there was very dangerous. If we had only listened to him. When we reached Ketschdorf we saw several warning signs, in particular one warning cyclists. Maybe young people think they are indestructible; in any case, we didn't heed the warning and kept going. There were big, old trees on the side of the road, which blocked the view. Guenter was in front and when I came out of the first curve, my heart almost stopped. I had never seen such a steep slope on a road before. I tried to slow down but couldn't; maybe all the weight of my belongings had something to do with it. I was riding in the middle of the road but was worried that something might come up from the opposite direction. I tried to get over to the right side of the road which was my big mistake. I ended up in gravel, my handlebar shook violently and I was unable to hang on. I sailed over the handlebar and landed about two feet in front of a big tree. If I had gone a split second faster, my fall could have been fatal.

I was pretty messed up anyway. My face looked like it had been sandpapered. I had a deep cut in my chin, a hole in my left forearm and my right knee looked like a blue grapefruit. A man came out of a house and said something like "Stupid kids." He took me inside and gave me a bowl with water and a towel so I could clean myself. There was only a nurse in the village, and she bandaged me and put Vaseline on my face. It took Guenter quite a while to come back up the hill. He couldn't believe what he saw and I could tell that he was very disappointed to see our vacation coming to a sudden end. He found one of my shoes on the other side of the road and helped me get the bent front wheel of my bike back in shape.

It was getting dark by the time we started on our way home. We had about thirty miles to go and I hoped for the best. My knee was really hurting and I was bleeding from my chin. The road sloped downhill for quite a few miles, which helped, but I was very glad when we arrived. It was still dark and I woke my whole family. They couldn't believe the way I looked, my face covered with a mixture of blood and dust. A few days later I took a closer look at my bike and saw that the fork above the front wheel was cracked. That made me shudder, because if the fork had broken off on the way home I would have taken another spill.

It started to look like my plan for the future was beginning to become reality. An offer came from the Breslau Electric Company for a job in their engineering office. Unfortunately, I had to turn it down because the work required going to the top of high buildings or towers occasionally. I had a tendency to get dizzy very easily, probably from the head injury I had not too long before.

About a month later I received an offer from Junkers Aircraft Works in Dessau, Saxonia, which would have been a great career opportunity. They wanted to train me in aircraft design and also they provided housing and other amenities. This was a very hard decision to make. I wanted to go but I just couldn't leave my mother and sisters. So I turned this offer down too. This was another time when I really hated my father for what he had done to our family.

I was beginning to worry that for refusing these offers the people at the job center might take me off their record. Then one day our neighbor, by the name of Seidel, called me over to his apartment. He told me he had received a questionnaire concerning a job for me. He said that he actually knew very little about me except for listening to the boys and me playing soccer below his window.

Somehow I had the feeling that bothered him and to smooth things over I told him, "I don't think this is so bad."

He had to laugh and said, "Come over here to the window and listen."

My friends were playing soccer and I had to admit that they used a lot of foul language. We continued to talk for a while afterwards and I told him about my hopes for the future.

Mr. Seidel's reply must have been of a positive nature because a short time later the State of Prussia, Office of Land Management, contacted me. My interview went well and my parents signed a three-year contract by which I would be trained as an Engineering Technician. My training was going to consist of a combination of working and going to a technical school. After completion of my training, I had the choice of either staying with the State of Prussia, or I was free to leave. However, they let me know that they would prefer to see me stay. I could understand that; after all, they had invested in me.

I was elated that I was going to start in the profession I had dreamed about and where I could use my talent. At the time I didn't fully realize how lucky I was. Over the years I saw how many young people either didn't know what to do with their lives or never had the chance to do what they wanted. I can say that I never changed my mind and worked in the engineering field until my retirement.

I really had to buckle down when I started working. Along with work and school, I had a lot of studying to do. At fifteen years old, I was the youngest in the office and had the least education. The reason I was the least educated was that in Germany, when a child reaches ten years of age, the parents have to make the decision to either let the child stay in Grade School for another four years or to send them to a Middle School or High School. To go to the latter cost money, which we didn't have.

There were four other young men in the Engineering Department. They were all very congenial and helpful. After a while I got together socially with one of them named Kurt and another fellow by the name of Rudi who worked in the accounting department. My supervisor was an older man who had the unusual first name of Wunibald. Behind his back everyone referred to him as Wunnie. He had to be addressed as Mr. Inspector and he was a typical bureaucrat. It took me a little while to get used to him and his quirks.

Despite that everything was new to me, it didn't take long to feel comfortable in my job. I liked the fact that my office was only ten minutes from our apartment and I could go home during my lunch hour.

Miraculously, my father was still working and I could only guess that he must have had a broad-minded supervisor. With some money available we went out to eat once in a while. One time we went to an outdoor restaurant with tables and chairs set under big trees. It was very enjoyable. There was also a little red wagon, which was pulled by a goat. That was a lot of fun for my sisters. There were loudspeakers attached to some of the trees and on this day Goebbels, the German Propaganda Minister, was making a speech which was broadcast over these loudspeakers. In the course of his speech Goebbels said, "And if the Western Allies don't believe me, they can come here and ask the German People." My father was drunk as usual and said loudly, "Yes, let them come here and we will tell them what we are really thinking." My mother ushered all of us out as fast as possible and we were very lucky that we didn't get into serious trouble.

At school I met a student by the name of Gerhard who was my age. He was working for the State of Prussia also, but for a different office. We had a lot in common, including alcoholic fathers. The only difference was that his father managed to keep his job, but to "balance things out" he cheated on his wife.

Spring came and Gerhard told me that there was an opportunity to buy a kayak inexpensively. The boy who had owned it and his friend both drowned during a flood. Apparently they put the kayak into the river just upstream of a weir but were unable to continue going upstream; the force of the water pulled them back over the weir and they capsized.

I told Gerhard that I was all for buying the boat and we went to the boy's house. His mother was there and we told her why we came and that we had very little money. She was in tears and she said that she didn't want to see the kayak anymore. She took the fifteen Marks we had scraped up between us and gave us a receipt. We went to the boathouse where the kayak was stored and found that the monthly rent of three Marks had been prepaid for the next three months. That was great news because it meant we actually bought the boat for six Marks. The kayak itself was in good shape except the rudder and paddles were missing. The owner of the boathouse was very helpful and he gave us what we needed without charge. We painted the boat light green and changed the name from "Blitz" to "Typhoon."

Then the big day came when we put the kayak in the water to check if everything was one hundred percent in order. We were lucky; the boat was fine, except Gerhard and I needed some practice using our paddles in unison. However, it didn't take us very long adjusting to each other and we were soon moving along like one heart and one soul.

The boathouse was located at a small lake, which was actually part of a narrow river, by the name of Ohle, which flowed into the Oder River. The lake was beautiful and peaceful with its quiet water and large weeping willows. Nobody would have expected to find such an idyllic place within a big city. There was a cantina next to the boathouse that sold sandwiches and soft drinks, and sometimes the owner played the accordion for us.

Getting out on the Oder River for the first time was an experience I will never forget. It was just an incredible feeling. I sensed I had a great time ahead of me but didn't know how much enjoyment, excitement and just plain fun I would have in the coming years. I didn't realize at the time that Gerhard would become the only true friend I would have in my entire life.

I was getting a fine education because everything I learned at school I could practice at work. I just think how much easier my work would have been with today's calculating machines and computers, instead of slide rules and the calculating machines we had to crank by hand.

In school the main subjects were mathematics, in particular geometry and trigonometry, along with cartography and surveying. We also took field trips to practice surveying, including the use of a theodolite and leveling instrument.

When I thought things were going great for me, a few unpleasant events came up. In a way, not everything that happened came unexpectedly. To begin with, my father lost his job with the city. I had been expecting this for quite a while. The previous four weeks he had been throwing up every morning. Sometimes I thought he must be made of iron because it made me sick just listening to him. The day he was laid off, he had one of his fits again. He yelled and screamed so loud one could hear him a mile away and he threw things around. I felt like grabbing and

Gerhard Weiser on the Oder River
Breslau 1938

shaking him. A few days later he had the bright idea to sue the city. Again, he didn't want to acknowledge that it was his own fault that he lost his job. He was lucky that he had taken an honest lawyer who talked him out of a lawsuit. He had absolutely no chance of winning.

I don't know how it started but I had a lot of nosebleeds that went on for a long time. Our family doctor prescribed nose drops and other medication. When this didn't help, he sent me to a specialist. This so-called specialist examined me and told me that I had a growth on my adenoids, which caused the bleeding and that they had to be removed. I arrived at the hospital the following Saturday at nine in the morning. The doctor came and rushed me into the operating room. He wore a white coat covered with large blood spots, which was something I certainly didn't want to see. I had to sit in a chair and he gave me a shot in the back of my palate. Since he was obviously in a hurry I don't think he waited long enough for the shot to take effect, based on the pain I had to endure. Then the operation was about to start. I was given a bowl to hold under my chin and a nurse was holding my forehead from behind. The doctor sat in front of me with my legs between his legs. He showed me the instrument he was going to use, which looked like a pair of pliers. He told me in order to clip off the adenoids he had to go down into my throat and then up. When he stuck the instrument in my throat I had to gag and he yelled at me, probably for wasting his precious time. On the second try it worked, and all I can say there was no clipping. He tore, tore, and finally pulled out a bloody clump. The pain I felt was awful and blood oozed out of my mouth.

Then came the icing on the cake when he said to me, "You can go home now."

I could barely talk with that blood in my mouth, but I told him, "I am not going anywhere. I am going to stay right here."

They kept me for three days in the hospital and gave me a lot of applesauce and ice cream, which felt good. However, this wasn't the end of the story. My nose continued to bleed. I wondered if a doctor or a butcher had treated me. I never returned to this doctor and went to see another one who told me that a small vein in my nose needed to be cauterized. It took only a few minutes for the procedure and I never had a nosebleed again.

On a day during the summer of 1937, it was announced that Adolf Hitler was coming to Breslau. I don't remember what the occasion was; maybe he came for some ribbon cutting ceremony. I was curious and wanted to see what he looked like. I went to the route he was supposed to take and climbed up on one of those old cast-iron street lamps. Then he arrived in an open, black Mercedes, standing up in it with his right hand raised. He had his cap pulled down to just above his eyes, but I could see his face clearly and he looked very stern. This was the only time I ever saw him in person.

I was so happy that I had met Gerhard and that we bought the kayak. Every chance we had we went out on the river, particularly on weekends. There was always a lot to see, like other kayaks, sailboats, racing shells from the university and pleasure boats with dancing and music. This was fun to watch but what we preferred was the quiet part of the river upstream. It was so peaceful and one could enjoy the fresh air. It was a great location for swimming and sun bathing along the white, sandy banks. In fact, we had been lucky that the Ohle River and our boathouse were located upstream from the city; this made it so much easier to reach the places we liked the best. On our way upstream there were many jetties, and we found out that once we made it around the tip of a jetty, the water was actually flowing upstream to the next jetty. Nevertheless, it usually took us two hours to get to our favorite spots. Going home in the evening required a lot less effort. We let the boat float down the river and hung our legs over the side of the boat into the water. Many times we saw the sun sinking on the river and it was such a beautiful sight that will always remain in my memory.

It happened very seldom that my inspector sent me out surveying. This was fine with me I preferred the office to the

Hans at the office
Breslau 1938

field. To give an example, I had to go out surveying for a few days with a young engineer by the name of Fogger. When we arrived at the survey site, I felt I was in the middle of nowhere. On top of it, the weather was lousy, mostly fog and rain. When it was starting to get dark, Fogger told me that he had a place to stay overnight but that I had to find my own lodging. What a character, to tell me this so late in the day. I was just glad that I had my bicycle with me. It was already dark when I finally found a little inn down the road. The owner was an old woman who looked like a witch. She offered me room and board for a very reasonable price and said she could fix me a sandwich to take out. I was glad to have found anything at this point. With her looks, I didn't trust her completely and barricaded myself in during the night, which probably wasn't necessary.

The next morning something funny happened. I was sitting by myself in the guest room having breakfast when a cat came running out of the kitchen with a piece of sausage between its teeth. The old woman came running like the devil behind the cat and retrieved the sausage. Later, when I looked at my sandwich I could have made a bet that it was the same sausage the cat had stolen in the morning. Since I was hungry, I didn't care and ate the sandwich anyway. We finished our work the next day and I was glad to go back to the office again.

I am not sure how it came about but my father was ordered to report for work at Gotenhafen at the Baltic Sea. I assume that the employment office had told him to accept this job or he wouldn't receive any more unemployment money. We found out that the Battleship Bismarck was being built there and my father was going to work as an accountant in the payroll section. Since there was not enough housing available in Gotenhafen he had to live with the other workers on a permanently anchored ship by the name of *Tanganyika*. All of that was good news for the rest of the family because we finally could look forward to some peace and quiet. I was surprised that the whole arrangement worked so well for nearly a year. I don't know why, but when my father returned home he had changed for the better. As a matter of fact, I didn't think that he was the same person.

During my father's absence something very unpleasant happened. All over Germany the old greetings like Good Morning, Good Day etc. had been replaced by the greeting, "Heil Hitler." Not everybody followed up on this, but in government offices and the like, it was mandatory.

My two small sisters were well behaved, friendly, and greeted people the way they had been taught. One afternoon they returned from the playground and both were crying. My mother found out that Mr. Haesler, the Nazi in our house, had yelled at them because they didn't greet him with "Heil Hitler." My mother was so upset that she made a big mistake. She wrote Mr. Haesler a letter in which she told him to stay away from her daughters and what was the difference anyway if they said "Heil Hitler" or not. What happened next was that Mr. Haesler came to our door and waving the letter in front of my mother's face said, "And with this letter I will get you into a concentration camp." However, he didn't know my mother very well and what she was capable of. She snatched the letter out of his hand, slammed the door and flushed the letter down the toilet. Luckily this was the end of the incident, and I am sure that my mother learned not to tangle with a Nazi.

Fall had come faster than I wanted. Gerhard and I had so much fun with our kayak that we were sad when we had to store it away for the winter. We had started to visit each other at home and even our mothers had gotten acquainted. I guess they had a lot in common, in particular, both having alcoholic husbands. I had found out that Gerhard liked to play chess too and so did Kurt from the office. Playing with my uncle Walter had come to a trickle, mainly because now he had four children and there was too much distraction. So Gerhard, a friend of his, Kurt, and myself formed a little chess club. Kurt had neither a father nor brothers and sisters and his mother liked to have us around. That worked out fine and we played regularly at Kurt's house. Kurt's mother

Sisters of Hans: Jutta and Gerda Kunert
Breslau 1939

was a gracious hostess; between games she served us coffee or cocoa and cake. We couldn't have asked for more.

In fall of 1938 there was no more doubt in my mind that war was on the horizon. Hitler had already annexed Austria and invaded Czechoslovakia. He further demanded the return of the Danzig Corridor to Germany. The Danzig Corridor, formerly West Prussia, had been handed over to Poland under the provisions of the Treaty of Versailles in 1919 and it separated the Province of East Prussia from the rest of Germany. While all of these territories contained ethnic Germans and everyone in Germany felt they should be returned, very few people wanted to risk a war over it. Unfortunately, Hitler stayed on his course and eventually war became reality. I remembered at the time that after WW I, Marshal F. Foch, Chief Commander of the Allied Armies in France, had predicted that "The Treaty of Versailles is not a peace, it is a 20-year truce."

For my sixteenth birthday my mother had the biggest surprise waiting. She took me to a combination men's clothing store and tailor shop. When we arrived there the owner and my mother hugged rather passionately. I had the feeling they must have known each other quite well from way back. For a while they talked and then he called for samples of material. I was allowed to look at them and select material for two suits and a topcoat. After I had made my decision, the tailor came and took my measurements. I couldn't believe what happened here-I felt like a millionaire. When I picked everything up, I felt even better; all of it fit perfectly and looked great.

I tried not to think too much about war, but rather how to enjoy my life while I still could. Something came up which not only added so much fun to my life then but still does today, namely ballroom dancing.

My friend Rudi from the office was two years older than I was and went dancing regularly. One day he asked me if I wanted to join him. That sounded pretty exciting. With the exception of Irmgard, I had never been close to a girl. My all boy schooling did not provide opportunities. Also, my drunken father embarrassed me. However, my main reason was that I never had any money.

Despite my money problems I went with Rudi. On the way he told me that I could buy just one beer and let it sit there all evening. I liked this arrangement. There were public dance halls in different parts of the city and we had two of them close by. After we arrived and found a table, Rudi took me to the men's room and showed me some dance steps. I still have to laugh today when I think about this first dance lesson. Close to our table sat two nice looking girls and Rudi said to me, "Let's go over to them, I'm going to ask the one on the right and you ask the one on the left." That worked fine for Rudi but not for me. My heart was pounding like a hammer and I couldn't go through with it and went back to my table. Rudi saw my cowardly behavior and told me that was it. He wasn't going to take me again. First, I sat there feeling disgusted with myself but then I decided that I was going to dance no matter what. I looked around and found the least attractive girl and asked her for a dance. As I had hoped, she didn't turn me down and seemed to be glad that anyone had asked her, even if it was a klutz like me. She was a nice person and I should have danced with her again but my success with her had already gone to my head. The longer the evening went on, the more daring I became, and by the time I went home, I was hooked on dancing.

From then on I went dancing twice a week and I got Gerhard interested in dancing too. After that I always had either Gerhard or Rudi to go with me and sometimes all three of us went together. When I went with Rudi only, I ended up many times by myself at the end of the evening. Rudi was a lover, and he had money too. I personally just liked to dance, but occasionally escorted a girl home.

Show bands were still coming to Breslau and I loved to go and see them. The one I enjoyed most was Teddy Stauffer and his band from Switzerland. Not only did they play great music but also they were a very unconventional group, a welcome contrast to the rigid life under the Nazis. When they came on stage with their multicolored clothing, saxophones under their arms and guitars on their shoulders, the audience went wild. The Nazis just barely tolerated them but when Teddy Stauffer started to jazz up Beethoven and Brahms, it was the end for him in Germany. Many years later I was happy to hear that he had become the official host of Acapulco, Mexico.

My sisters were growing up fast. They were now six and eight years old and going to school. I felt more like their father than a brother. I was glad that we had moved to the new neighborhood where they had a nice playground and school. I couldn't imagine them growing up where I had.

A rare exception to this tranquility happened one day. I was at home for lunch when Gerda came in the door excitedly and told my mother that there was a man downstairs who had shown her "This," pointing at her groin. I jumped up, grabbed a blackjack we kept in the hall and raced down the stairs. I didn't see anyone in the house, and when I went outside, I saw a guy taking off on a bicycle about a block away. My mother reported it and had to go with Gerda for a lineup a couple of times, but my sister didn't recognize anyone.

My coming home for lunch came suddenly to an end. Some Nazi organization wanted our office building, maybe because it was located next to a small park. We had to move to another site downtown, which nobody liked. Instead of looking out on green trees and grass, we now looked at the back of an old apartment building. The only consolation was that there was a lot to see and to do around our new location. For instance, there was a unique cafe that belonged to a Spaniard by the name of Pedro Coll. On the street level he sold tropical fruit and on the upper level he served the most delicious fruit salad. What made the place even more enjoyable were the small booths that seated not more than four people and were separated by aquariums with rare tropical fish. In the evening the room was kept in a low light and to sit there between the lighted aquariums was a real delight. Since I had tropical fish myself I admired the owner, not only for the beauty of the aquariums but also that they always looked spotless.

I visited my grandfather once in a while. Even though he had never shown any kindness toward me, I still felt sorry for him. With his wife gone he was very lonely. Later on, after my uncle Erich was drafted into the army, his wife Annie looked after my grandfather.

Spring had arrived and Gerhard and I went to spruce up our kayak. The lake and area surrounding the boathouse was the prettiest at this time of the year. There was the aroma of trees in bloom and the distinct smell of tilled earth in the air. We didn't waste any time getting back on the river, even though it was still cool. We now paddled in perfect rhythm and could maneuver our boat expertly. Sometimes that made us a little too daring. We made it a challenge to paddle between the barges and their tugboats, which were connected by a heavy steel cable with a small space in between. Sometimes the barges came so close that we had to push our kayak away with the paddles. I am surprised that we never capsized.

There were quite a few racing shells on the river and one had to be careful when swimming. They moved swiftly and either they might not see a person or, even if they did, couldn't change direction fast enough. I didn't pay too much attention to them until we had a thrilling encounter with the crew of one.

On a Sunday afternoon we were again at our favorite place away from the crowd when we heard some girls laughing farther downstream. We became curious and swam along the bank of the river as quietly as possible. We came to a small jetty covered with high grass where we were hidden from sight. There were four girls who had come in a racing shell. We watched them for a while and then something happened we hadn't expected in our wildest dreams. Two of them shed their shirts and shorts and went swimming in the nude. That was the first time that I saw a girl undressed from close up and it was quite exciting. We left without them seeing us. Later, we stopped at their spot with our kayak and chatted with them for a while. They were nice girls and I felt guilty, but not too much!

My father had returned from Gotenhafen and, as I had mentioned, he had changed quite a bit. He still drank but not excessively. Fortunately, he found another job. This not only kept him away from us most of the time but mainly meant money and a better life. He became the buyer for a company that built five-ton trailers. It was a challenging job, which required constant wheeling and dealing to acquire the different kinds of material needed. Apparently my father liked what he was doing and the owners, two brothers who had built up the company from scratch.

My father still cursed Hitler, I am sure at home only, and predicted that he was getting us into a war. As it turned out, he was right. In September of 1939 Hitler invaded Poland not long after he had occupied Czechoslovakia. Shortly after that, England and France declared war on Germany and World War II had begun. Also Hitler made a non-aggression pact with Russia stating they could occupy the eastern half of Poland while Germany would occupy the western half. This agreement was carried out and to this day Russia did not return their occupied territory to Poland.

Despite the fact that the war had started, my life remained about the same. Some of the younger men in the office had been drafted and food rationing had begun. We did not notice a difference with the food rationing. We never had much to eat anyway.

Gerhard and I enjoyed the last days of September on the river. We were more troubled by the thought that summer was coming to an end and that soon we would have to store our kayak away for the winter.

We still played chess but not regularly. By now Kurt had a steady girlfriend, and we had gone back to dancing.

Something new in our life had begun too. We started to go swimming every week. There were nice indoor pools in Breslau and we had hardly taken advantage of them because of the high admission charge. Then we found out we could get inexpensive tickets through a Nazi program called "Kraft durch Freude," which translated into, "Strength through Pleasure." People made many off-color jokes about this slogan. To participate we had to go on Monday and/or Thursday nights for two hours and follow instructions. We were at first a little suspicious about the instructions but discovered it was no problem whatsoever. There were two swimming teachers, a male and female, who were not much older than us. The first hour we had to follow their orders and did swimming relays, diving, water polo or games and the second hour we could do what we wanted. The fun part was that we were boys and girls together, which made it even more enjoyable. Ordinarily men and women had to go to separate pools.

Before we went home everyone had to stand for a few seconds, first under the hot shower and then under the cold one. This must have been very good for us. We generally walked home and many times my wet hair was frozen to my cap, but I don't remember catching a cold.

In early 1940 I had started my last year in training. I was getting forty-five Marks per month, a little improvement over the twenty-one Marks I was paid the first year and the thirty-three Marks the second year. I couldn't complain because I was aware of this from the beginning. This money was meant for school supplies and transportation and not a salary. I was very grateful for the education I was receiving; more money would have been helpful, but it wasn't the important factor.

Everything was quiet on the western front, to use this expression, but everyone knew it was the calm before the storm. I tried not to think about what might happen. It wouldn't have helped anyway.

At our favorite dance hall signs appeared which read, "Swing dance forbidden." Since the signs hung on little chains, we just turned them around and kept on dancing swing. That worked for a while, but then one evening two men approached Rudi and me and told us if they saw us dancing swing again they would throw us out.

Rudi didn't have to worry about that for long. He was drafted. He sold his tent for practically nothing to Gerhard and me; maybe he sensed he wouldn't need it anymore. I never saw him again and found out later that he was missing in Russia. It made me very sad; he had been so much fun to be with and such a good friend.

Shortly after Rudi's departure, my friend Kurt was drafted. That gave our chess club the final blow. Before he left he married his girlfriend, which I thought was a mistake.

In May, the quiet on the western front ended. Hitler invaded France. Fortunately, the actual fighting lasted only a few weeks but, of course, there were casualties. I lost one of my buddies from our street. I was very glad that Gerhard was still around. Sometimes I had the feeling that we both were trying to fool each other by acting as if nothing was going to change.

We were happy to have Rudi's tent and that it fit into our kayak. That made it possible to spend the whole weekend at the river. This was great; now we could do some real camping with a fire in the evening and also had protection from rain. Once in a while we joined another group of campers. There was always some kind of music, quite a few girls and a shortage of men. When looking back I can say we had a wonderful summer, and as it turned out, it was our last together.

Maybe autumn in general lowers one's spirits, but in my case, it was worse. I tried for so long not to think too much about my future, but I knew the time had come. I hated the thought of being drafted, and I had all kind of wild ideas on how to beat it. After awhile I realized it was useless. Then I figured that by volunteering I could get into the navy. That would have been better than the army, and besides, I loved the water. When I inquired I was told I would be accepted by the navy but was not entitled to pick any branch. That ruined it for me because I couldn't stand the thought of ending up in a submarine. When I was six years old, I saw a movie about a German submarine that sank during World War I. The situation was hopeless for the crew, who had no chance of being rescued. The scenes were shocking.

One man shot himself, another went berserk, and one man just sat there staring at a picture of his family.

Anyway, there wasn't anything I could do but wait and hope for the best. It didn't take very long to find out. Shortly after I turned eighteen, I was called for my military medical examination. I passed, because I was labeled, "kriegsverwendungsfaehig," meaning "usable for war!" A panel of officers asked me about my education and if I was able to compute distances and angles, which I could, of course. They told me I would be assigned as an artillery observer. I thought that doesn't sound too bad; unfortunately, this assignment never materialized.

My friend Gerhard was called for his physical at about the same time and was assigned to the Panzer Grenadiers, the infantry attached to tank units. I had the feeling we both had been hooked and cooked.

We had to wait now to be called to the Reichsarbeitsdienst, which translates into Labor Companies. Before going into the army, every young man had to serve in this outfit for six months. With the way the future looked, we went ahead and sold our kayak with heavy hearts. Also, I gave away my tropical fish since my mother thought she couldn't take care of them properly.

I was glad to finish my training at the office, and was now a Certified Engineering Technician. In addition, my monthly allowance of forty-five Marks had changed to a salary of one hundred seventy-five Marks a month. This doesn't sound like much, but for comparison, the price of a Volkswagen was one thousand Marks.

Maybe to keep up the morale at the home front, dancing was still allowed. Gerhard and I tried to enjoy ourselves as long as possible. I wished my life would have continued like this indefinitely, but wishes like that hardly ever become reality.

The Other Side of the Coin

THE LABOR COMPANY

In February of 1941 I was notified to report to the Labor Company in the town of Glatz, Silesia. I informed my office and said goodbye to Wunnie and the other mainly older employees who were left. I learned I would remain an employee of the state of Prussia and they would pay me a certain percentage of my salary during my absence. It was a lot more difficult to say goodbye to my family and to Gerhard. I knew the life I had known so far was over forever. What I didn't know was that I was about to enter the gates of hell.

I arrived in Glatz with several other guys. Some of them acted like this was going to be fun. I certainly didn't feel that way. One of the Labor Company troop leaders assigned us to different barracks and told us when and where to assemble. I took the time to look around and saw there was a big building with a parade ground in front, about a dozen small barracks and a large outhouse. Obviously, there were no toilets in the barracks. Each barrack was designed for fourteen men. They had bunk beds made of wood with straw mattresses. In the middle of the room were a cast-iron stove, stools and a table.

We assembled and they took us to get our uniforms, boots, etc. We soon realized what our life was going to be like. A maniac threw boots, uniforms and everything else at us. Nothing fit and we had to do a lot of exchanging among ourselves, which took time. However, they didn't allow us any time, which, I am sure, was done on purpose. When we appeared looking like idiots, our leaders cursed us and chased us around almost to complete exhaustion. This kind of treatment didn't change as time went by.

I would have understood if this would have been basic military training, but we were supposed to be laborers. To the very end of our duty with the labor company, there was never any communication with our so-called leaders. They treated us like dirt and we hated them.

Before we started our daily routine, we had our heads nearly shaved. Our hair was not allowed to be any longer than a match, and I was beginning to feel more and more like a prisoner.

After sports, marching and being chased around all day we had to clean our barrack, which included the stove. Our stools had to be perfectly aligned in front of our beds. Our garb had to be folded a certain way and in a perfect line. Somewhere between ten and eleven o'clock in the evening the troop leader showed up for inspection. Everyone was asleep by then except for one of us who had to report to him. About every other night the troop leader supposedly didn't like what he saw and either kicked all the stools around or stuck his finger in the stove and smeared black stuff on the face of the guy reporting to him. Then he yelled, "You call this clean? I'll be back in one hour and want to see everything clean and in order." By the time he or another of these jerks came back, things still didn't look right, as everyone was dead tired and couldn't see straight. Quite often after the second inspection of the night, we had to get dressed and run with mattresses on our backs around the parade ground. At this time of the year it was bitter cold in the mountains. It was bad enough if one had to run to the far away outhouse at night. The only thing that made all of this torment bearable was that everyone in our barrack was from Breslau. We had a lot in common and there was a great camaraderie.

Along the way we had the "pleasure" to meet the man in charge of the whole outfit by the name of Lenk. He was about 50 years old and ugly. His face looked red and puffy and his lips red and swollen. I thought he looked like someone who likes to eat raw meat.

Then something completely unexpected happened. One of the

guys in our barrack came down with scarlet fever. As sorry as we felt for him, it gave us a welcome breather. With our barrack declared off limits, nobody came inside any more. Meals etc. were left at the door. We were so worn out we slept the first two days. After that we played cards, wrote letters, told jokes and slept some more. It was almost too good to be true. Unfortunately, a fellow in another barrack came down with scarlet fever and then one more. Since the scarlet fever had spread, there was no more need to keep us isolated. That meant the end of our vacation and the return to our misery.

Through the grapevine we heard that we would be sent to Poland. I was wondering about going to Poland with scarlet fever looming. The answer came soon. We were inoculated against scarlet fever with a new drug from Sweden. To be exact, three big shots two days apart. This was unpleasant enough but not nearly as bad as what followed. Shortly after, I woke up at night with my scalp itching like crazy, and then the itch moved to my chest. When I looked at it I saw an enormous blister over my entire chest. In addition, I began to feel sick. They took me to the infirmary where I joined a few more patients. We had a reaction to the inoculation. Later I learned that we could have gotten seriously ill.

The rumor we had heard about Poland was true and the day of our departure came fast. All of us were glad to leave that depressing place even though our torturers were coming with us. We packed up our gear, were loaded on freight cars and left for Poland. After a short trip we ended up at a cigarette factory near Krakow. We moved into one of two large buildings; in the other one they were still making cigarettes. We noticed a lot of pretty girls working at the factory. Of course, we were not allowed to fraternize, but still it was enjoyable seeing some females.

I believe our outfit consisted of about eighty men, excluding our leaders. There was only one big room in the building and we put our bunk beds and upright lockers in a row, alternating beds and lockers. Each one of us had an aluminum washbowl that we had to put upside down on top of the lockers.

We were told that we had been assigned to the German Air Force. The airfield was approximately three miles away from our quarters and there was no transportation. That meant we had to march an hour in the morning and another hour in the evening. I would like to add here that we had to get up every morning at five o'clock and start the day with twenty minutes of sports.

Our first assignment was to build protective walls of sandbags for fighter planes, to be exact, Messerschmitt 109's. We split up in three groups, one worked at a sand pit, another laid tracks and pushed lorries, and the last group filled sandbags and piled them up. Eventually I ended up with the latter group. The sandbags had to be placed in a horseshoe shape with a camouflage net on top. After that the planes could roll in backwards and be ready for take off.

In the meantime, I got an unexpected break. They found out I was the only one in the whole outfit, including our leaders, who could do surveying work. I picked two helpers and was furnished the necessary equipment, like a leveling instrument and rod, measuring tape, etc. I surveyed the predetermined spots for the planes and set all the stakes. This aggravated one of our troop leaders by the name of Jaeger. He was constantly harassing me, even after work. I had a feeling he couldn't stand seeing one of us doing a job that went above his mental capacity, equal to the IQ of sixty.

It was early in May, but already very hot, and they worked us like slaves. The sandbags were very heavy and seemed to get heavier and heavier the higher we had to lift them. Then the most ridiculous event took place. Konstantin Hirl, the head of all the labor companies in Germany, came to visit us. He drove up in an open Mercedes and stopped at the sand pit. We were ordered to run toward him enthusiastically, singing at the same time! While all this was going on, his film crew had their cameras rolling. I couldn't believe what I saw here and wondered if the people back home would buy this baloney.

One Sunday it was my duty to sweep a part of our room. It took me a long time, and I disposed of all the dirt I had swept up. I had actually finished my job and sort of swept a little leftover dirt aside. I know I probably shouldn't have done this, but this is no excuse for what happened next. Our top leader, Lenk, saw what I did and charged at me like a raging bull. He grabbed me by the ears and shook me so hard that I thought he would pull them out by the roots. I can't describe the pain. I still can see his ugly face right in front of me like it had happened yesterday. If I ever had a wish in my life, it was to meet this bastard after the war and pay him back.

Also, there was a troop leader by the name of Kraemer who was on the top of our black list. To give one example, one night we came back from the airfield worn out and tired as usual. We were almost too tired to eat and everyone hit the sack with the exception of the guy on clean-up duty. After his report, Kraemer couldn't find anything wrong, so he climbed on top of the lockers and started to look under the washbowls. Wherever he found anything underneath, like food, a brush or whatever, the washbowl came flying through the air and landed with a loud crash on the floor. This would have been bad enough, but then we had to get up, get dressed and he chased us around in the yard in the middle of the night. Quite a few guys couldn't go on and collapsed. I believe everyone was ready to kill him. We didn't know that we would soon have the opportunity.

We had finished our job at the airfield. Our next place of work was at an old Polish fortress. The fort was built in a square with a yard in the middle. Every space within the fortress walls was full of bombs and anti-aircraft shells. Our job was to get all of the munitions out of the fortress and load them on trucks. Then the trucks took their cargo to a train depot, where everything had to be loaded on to railroad cars. This time we split up in two groups, one at the fortress and the other at the train depot. I was assigned to the group at the fortress and had the feeling it wasn't the better of the two.

The bombs were packed in heavy wooden boxes held together with metal straps. Five hundred pound bombs were packed one per box, one hundred pound bombs two per box. The shells came three to a braided container. The bombs were stacked on top of each other all the way up to the ceiling in each room. We had only kerosene lamps, and one couldn't see too much, which made things harder. Getting the heavy boxes down was back-breaking work; also, carrying them out through the narrow hallways was extremely painful. Many times we scraped our shoulders on the rough rock walls. What really made us mad was the constant yelling by the troop leaders. We were working like dogs in the dark, bleeding and sweating. What else did they expect from us?

Once we had the boxes in the yard, we had to pile them up on top of each other again to a height of about eight feet. Later on, the trucks backed up to the stack of boxes and were loaded. Fortunately, the trucks were not enclosed, which made this task somewhat easier. The two hundred pound boxes had rope handles on the short ends, which helped. One day a box was accidentally dropped from the top of the stack. The box broke and the two bombs rolled out. We thought this was the end, but when nothing happened, we started to get somewhat casual, swinging and throwing them on the trucks.

One morning at roll call, we found out that someone had deserted. I couldn't blame the guy; we all were about ready to give up. In this depressing time came at least one bright moment. Troop Leader Jaeger was in the yard standing close to the stack of boxes, cursing as usual, when a two hundred pound box dropped from the top onto his feet. In all the excitement, nobody ever found out exactly how it happened, not that any of us would have told. No doubt, everyone was glad not to have him around anymore.

On June 22, 1941 Hitler broke the non-aggression pact with Russia and the German Army attacked. Even though our work for the Air Force should have told us something, it came as a surprise. In addition, at the time none of us realized what grave consequences this event would have on us young men in particular and on Germany in general.

I didn't know why, but sixteen of us were sent to a shooting range. That was fine with me; anything was better than the slave labor at the fortress. They gave us Austrian World War I rifles, which were about five feet long, and ammunition. We were told that when we pull the trigger and see a blue flame, we should throw the rifle away. In a way, I thought this was funny, but on the other hand, I worried the gun could blow up in my face.

After some practice shooting, they took us to an ammunition dump for the Air Force, which was out in the open and not too far from our quarters. We learned that the Polish underground had tried to blow up the dump but didn't succeed. Our assignment was to reinforce the Air Force guards until more of their own men arrived. Unfortunately, Kraemer was in charge of this detail. An Air Force officer directed us to a certain part of the circumference and gave us the order to shoot without warning. Kraemer worked out a schedule of guard duty and rest periods and was acting almost human. I knew that some of us saw a chance to get rid of him permanently. I have no doubt that Kraemer knew our feelings toward him and was more than cautious. Even when we didn't see him we could hear him shout, "Don't shoot, Troop Leader Kraemer," over and over again.

Regretfully our guard duty didn't last very long and we had to go back to the fortress and to loading bombs. It was shortly after my return that I became very ill. First they tried to treat me at the infirmary, but they soon realized that I needed better treatment than what they could provide. I couldn't eat anymore and breathing became more and more difficult. I was transferred to an army hospital in Krakow where I was diagnosed with diphtheria. I was taken to the isolation wing of the hospital and given an injection that looked big enough for a horse. Even the nurse who administered the shot made a joke about its size. I must say the drug worked wonders because I felt better in no time. I was told I had to stay in the hospital for four weeks. This sounded terrific. I didn't need any more medical treatment, slept in a real bed and was served tasty meals.

My roommates were two young soldiers from the SS Division Adolf Hitler. I believe they were recovering from typhoid fever, but I am not sure. I have to say they were nice boys. We played a lot of chess games, of which I won the most. I was curious about their division and asked many questions. I don't remember much of what they told me, except that they never could retreat in battle. Their order was to either go forward or die. I had the feeling that they wouldn't get very old.

My hospital stay went by too fast and I had to go for my discharge examination. I dreaded going back to my torturous life with the labor company, and I was wondering how I could prolong my time at the hospital. I knew that the inoculation for diphtheria many times affected the heart, and thought this could be my chance. Before I went into the examination room I went to the toilet and did knee bends until my heart was racing. I found out later in what danger I had put myself with this foolishness. However, my effort was useless. I had to lie down for at least twenty minutes before the examination and electrocardiogram. When it was established that I was in good health, my fate was sealed and I was returned to my unit.

The work at the fortress seemed somewhat easier. The stacks of bombs had come down considerably. Also, the rest period at the hospital had given me more strength. Then one day, approximately thirty of the tallest of us were told that we would participate in a parade in Krakow. We joined about sixty guys from two other labor companies in the area. Each of us was given a new spade and for three weeks we practiced doing the goose step with the spade shouldered. We also had to learn how to do a spade presentation, which was similar to one with a rifle. Eventually we found out that the parade was in honor of Hans Frank, the Nazi Governor of Poland. I didn't even know that he existed.

The parade was scheduled for a Sunday. On Saturday we put a

shine on our black boots by rubbing them with a glass bottle and water. Every nail on our soles had to be in place. The uniforms had to be in perfect order. We had to scrape the wood handle on our spades with razor blades. Also, the metal blades had to be polished to a shine. That was followed by instructions on how to march. First of all, we had to pay strict attention to the beat of the band. When approaching the reviewing stand commands would be given, but we still had to pay attention to the pennants that told us where to start the goose step and to turn our heads to the right. The same procedure applied in reverse order past the reviewing stand. We had practiced all of this to exhaustion, but I could understand this time it was going to be the real thing and nobody wanted to goof up at this point.

On Sunday everything came together. In the stands were Hans Frank, the Governor, Dr. Ley, an important Nazi, generals, high-ranking Nazis and other dignitaries. Along with our outfit there were units of the Army, the Waffen SS, the SA (Brown Shirts), the Air Force and others. We all waited at different side streets until it was our time to turn into the main marching route. Our outfit marched in the following order, Lenk in front by himself, after him in one row, the troop leaders, followed by our group. I believe we marched nine in a row, a total of ten rows. Everything went like clockwork and we received a lot of applause. I have to admit we felt pretty good about it. After all, this was the first time we had gotten some recognition.

Afterwards we were served a big meal that we really needed. In addition, we had the chance to talk with Herms Niel. He had composed quite a few marching songs over the years, many of them glorifying the war. He was a nervous wreck and smoked one cigarette after the other. I assume he was under pressure, possibly from Hitler himself, to produce more of the same.

We were told that our outfit made the biggest impression at the reviewing stand. Maybe for this reason we were taken in the evening to the Krakow Castle, the Governor's seat. There, in the courtyard, we had to present our spades and Frank walked past all of us. To our surprise, we were given the following two days off. We assumed that Lenk had gotten a pat on the back from the governor to show us such generosity, something I never expected from this character. Incidentally, after the war, Hans Frank was hanged in Nuremberg and Dr. Ley committed suicide.

Back at our quarters something funny happened. Some of our men never had to leave the cigarette factory. They were the cooks, drivers and others. One afternoon when coming back from the fortress, we saw one of them, dressed in an undershirt only, running around in circles in front of our building. At the same time the Polish girls were going home from work taking a good look at him and laughing. Lenk saw what was going on and was mad as hell. He sent two men to catch the guy. What made the whole situation even funnier was that the two were carrying a stretcher. The scene looked like one from the Keystone Cops. After one or two more rounds they caught up with him, knocked him out, put him on the stretcher and covered up his private parts. We found out that he had made a bet that he could drink a whole bottle of liquor within three hours. He won the bet, but I believe that winning cost him dearly.

I knew that our six months of service with the labor companies was over, but it was a good thing that I didn't get too jubilant. The German Army had advanced into the Ukraine and we were about to follow. Even though there were still some bombs left in the fortress, we were ordered to pack our belongings. We boarded a freight train and left another sorry place behind. We didn't know the exact destination or what they had in mind for us. Sleeping in a freight car wasn't fun, nevertheless, I was glad that it didn't last more than two days.

We unloaded in the town of Lvov in the Ukraine, a fairly big town with old but well-preserved buildings. Our new quarters were in a school building in the downtown area. Each troop was assigned to a classroom. We liked this part because our old troop from Glatz was back together again. One difference was that we didn't have any beds. We had to sleep on the floor like sardines in a box.

The Russians must have retreated from Lvov in a hurry. I based this assumption on what the incoming German troops found in the Lvov prison yard. The big, square yard, as well as the basements of the surrounding buildings, was full of corpses. I was able to obtain photographs that showed a truly gruesome scene. The bodies were those of men, piled on top of each other. Some were partly dressed, some were nude, most of them had been bayoneted and all were badly bloated.

Sometime later I walked through the prison. It was all cleaned up, but a strange odor lingered in the air. I noticed too that the basement windows had been closed up with bricks and mortar. I wondered if some of the corpses were still there. In one wing of the prison was a small courtroom next to a row of cells. The cells were so small that a person could not stand up, lie down or even sit down. I thought that being in a cell like this, even for a short time, would make one confess to anything.

Our new assignment was at an airfield. I never found out what we were trying to accomplish. It seemed like we were doing prison labor. One group would load rocks of various sizes on pick-up trucks and then take them to another area. There another group broke up the rocks into small sizes with hammers. This not only became very boring after a while, it also started to get colder by the day. There was no protection from the icy wind on the open field.

In addition, we didn't have enough to eat. Fortunately, luck was with us. Some guys from our troop found a big wooden box in the basement of our building. When they opened it they saw it contained a solid block of a beige substance that looked like explosives. They called the rest of us to look at it and after some fruitless deliberations; one wet his finger and tasted it. It turned out to be dried soup that the Russians had left behind. We shared it with anyone who wanted it. I know today I wouldn't touch this stuff, but at the time it meant a lot. A little chunk of the soup with some hot water filled my stomach.

The Other Side of the Coin

We also ended up with a new troop leader whose name I've forgotten. I'll just call him Kraemer, Jr. I don't know where they found all of these troop leaders because he fit right in with rest of the morons. He tried to give us the same treatment we had been subjected to in Glatz and Krakow. Luckily there was no parade ground or yard anymore where he could chase us around. What he didn't seem to realize was that we were not the same kids we were a few months ago. He was going to find this out pretty fast.

One morning we were loading rocks on a flatbed truck with Kraemer, Jr. in charge. He was standing near the truck, on the opposite side from us, when someone threw, full force, a rock the size of a coconut over the truck just past his face. I saw it and held my breath. I thought it would take his head off. He didn't say anything; he might have been in shock. I know I would have been. He couldn't make a case of it, as he shouldn't have stood where he did. "Accidents" happen. Things changed after that; he had gotten the message.

Not too far from our school was a cafe which had just opened and where they served artificial coffee and delicious fruit tarts. I always loved cakes, and I had my eye on these fruit tarts but couldn't afford enough to satisfy my cravings with the little money we received. I saved up my tobacco and cigarette rations with the thought that if I could sell them, I would be able to buy more of these tarts. In the area nearby, I had seen some shady characters hanging around who I hoped might be interested in my cigarettes. They looked weird in their long dark topcoats and caps, but I was determined to go through with my plan.

One dark evening I went to their hangout. I was alone and didn't feel all that secure, but things worked out better than I expected. They gave me quite a bit of money for my rations and everyone seemed to be happy. Thinking about it later, I couldn't believe the risk I took just to get my hands on some pastry.

After the Russian retreat, there was a period of complete lawlessness. For example, one day we came home from work, riding in the back of our truck, when we saw the body of a man in the gutter. A light rain was falling and from where his body was lying, bloody water was flowing down the street. Apparently nobody seemed to care about it.

Nevertheless, I was now in the money and close to fulfilling my desire. On the next Sunday I went back to the cafe and saw to my delight that there were plenty of tarts. The cafe was filled with well-dressed natives, German officers and so on. In my Labor Company uniform I was definitely the lowest one on the totem pole. However, I didn't let this bother me. When the waitress came I ordered ten tarts. She looked astonished and asked me if she had understood correctly. When I told her, "Yes, ten tarts," everyone seemed to look at me. This gave me a real feeling of superiority. I enjoyed every one of my tarts; needless to say, they were a big improvement over the Russian soup or that slop we were served every day. Later, when I pulled out my roll of money, I noticed how some of the German officers stared at me. It had been a long time since I had felt this happy.

On a later visit to the cafe I became acquainted with an older gentleman who was a native of Lvov. He was a chemist by profession and married. He told me quite a few interesting stories. I found out that the murdered men in the prison had been marked by the Soviets as enemies of the state. He told me he lived in a big apartment house and that the Soviet Secret Police used to come in the middle of night to arrest people. The arrested were mostly intellectuals like engineers, professors, etc., and they were never seen again. He said to quell their fear, he and his wife were drunk most of the time. I sometimes wondered what happened to him after the Soviets returned. I know that the Russians killed everyone who had collaborated with the Germans.

A rumor started to make the rounds that we were going home soon. I hoped it would become reality. The work we were doing seemed senseless. I still didn't know if we were laying the base for a runway, a road or something else. Added to this was the awful cold of Russia in November. In addition to my socks I stuffed rags in my boots, but even then I never could keep my feet warm. I found out later that I had frostbite in the two smallest toes of each foot. I was glad that I came away with just this, but the toes itched for many years.

As they say, there is always some truth to every rumor, and we received the orders for our departure. Maybe somebody somewhere felt sorry for us or had some common sense, but mostly likely the army needed us. At any rate, we moved out of Lvov fast. I knew everybody was elated. We arrived back in Glatz and went through the formalities of our discharge. I was very happy but at the same time angry that I had to serve in this godforsaken outfit for ten months, instead of the standard six.

We all had become good friends in our troop and there was a certain sadness that our togetherness was coming to an end. With the war going on and us being prime cannon fodder, we knew that we might never see each other again. For the last night our leadership had a party planned, which I considered almost an insult. Since I had my discharge papers, I said goodbye to my buddies and, avoiding the guardhouse, I took off through the forest and on to the railroad station. It felt good to be home and with my family again. I never appreciated a bed and shower as much as I did then.

After the war somebody wrote, "Konstantin Hirl should have been hanged too for turning loose a horde of idiots and criminals on the German youth." I couldn't agree more.

It took me a little while to get used to leading a normal life, like sleeping undisturbed, spending a leisurely day, eating a home cooked meal and especially being treated like a human being. My sisters looked at me kind of curiously sometimes, I guess because they hadn't seen me in almost a year. My father was still working at the same company and our family life seemed normal on the surface. Later on I found out that I had been fooled and my parents had been in at least one serious fight. Apparently my mother hit my father with a glass pitcher. I couldn't blame my mother because I wanted to do it a few times myself. My sister Gerda told me that she had to remove the glass splinters from his head.

One of my first visits was to Mrs. Weiser, Gerhard's mother. She was really glad to see me. Gerhard was already in Russia and had been wounded. A bullet had grazed his head but it hadn't been serious enough to send him home. They just treated him in the field hospital. I had no idea that this had happened. I had lost contact with Gerhard because of the overall situation. I tried to be as cheery as possible with Mrs. Weiser, but it wasn't easy. I felt depressed myself with all of my friends gone and my own future clouded.

THE GERMAN ARMY

The army didn't give me much time to enjoy civilian life. The order arrived to report to the 8th Cavalry Regiment at Mulhouse, Alsace-Lorraine at the end of December. I was glad that at least I could celebrate Christmas at home with my family. The day of my departure came fast and it was more difficult to say goodbye this time. My father took me to the railroad station. There we joined a group of other young men, most of them with either their father or mother. All of us were going to Mulhouse. My father was very quiet. I think he was more aware than me of the fact that this could be the last time we saw each other.

When we arrived at Mulhouse I knew something had gone awry and that I was not going to be an artillery observer. Probably some clerk had been either too lazy or too dumb and had eliminated the word "Artillery" from my assignment. This meant I still ended up as an observer, but with a reconnaissance outfit. I soon learned the severity of my situation.

I had to go through more or less the same procedure as in Glatz, like getting my uniform and the rest of the gear. In addition I ended up with a rifle, ammunition, bayonet, gas mask and, to my surprise, a bicycle. While I didn't enjoy the whole process, I was still pleasantly surprised about the professional treatment by the sergeant in charge. The difference between the Labor Company and the army was just astonishing.

My fourteen man platoon was housed in a brick building, one of several which circled a riding hall and horse stables. In the riding hall, a large inscription on the wall caught my eye. It read, "The greatest happiness on this earth is on the back of a horse, at

Hans as a recruit
Mulhouse, Alsace-Lorraine 1942

the bosom of a woman and in the health of the body." I liked that saying; however, there were no horses or women around.

The drill sergeant, by the name of Kott, was also from Silesia. He was a big guy with hands almost the size of shovels and apparently was a watch repairman in civilian life. I wondered how he could repair a watch with those enormous hands. I liked him because he had a good sense of humor and didn't act like a typical drill sergeant.

First we had to learn to march in formation and to salute correctly. Next came the oath to our Fuehrer Adolf Hitler. Except for the latter, I was well acquainted with the rest. Our military training consisted of learning to use a rifle, bayonet, pistol, machine gun, hand grenades, gas mask and how to ride a bicycle. I certainly wasn't interested in learning how to kill human beings. Nevertheless, I became proficient with the rifle.

One time we had to shoot at targets at a distance of 100 yards, with our gas masks on and lying down. With three shots, I hit 33 rings out of a total of 36 rings. I must have made an impression because the lieutenant called me and handed me two Marks, told me to buy myself some beer and gave me the afternoon off.

As it was the beginning of the year, the weather was very cold with a lot of ice and snow everywhere. I knew how to bicycle under these conditions from my experience in Breslau. However, some of the other guys had problems and took some nasty spills. It mostly happened when the snow had melted and then froze again. The trick was to stay in a groove, if possible.

It happened that I fell too and, strangely enough, it turned out to be pretty funny. On this particular day our whole squadron bicycled on an icy road with a slight incline. With us was a sergeant named Chuck, who led another platoon. He had a nose like a potato and was cross-eyed. After we had reached our destination we bicycled back on the same road. We were now going downhill and the ice made it nearly impossible to apply the brakes. Suddenly in front of me several guys fell and ended up on top of each other. I couldn't avoid running into this pile of men

The Other Side of the Coin

and bikes, but just before the impact I saw Chuck's head sticking out and looking at me in horror. Looking at him under normal circumstances was already something, but with this expression of fear in his face, it was hilarious.

Most of the guys in my platoon were from Breslau and I made friends with one of them, Guenter Schiewani. He recently had completed his studies as a stage designer and told me about his work, which I found very interesting. Both of us had similar feelings about the army and our dim future.

I made friends with another fellow by the name of Novack. I never learned where he was from or anything else for that matter. He spoke French, which was a great advantage in Alsace-Lorraine. He had a girlfriend in town and even went to her parent's home. He was more anxious to get away from the army than me. I have to say that one had to trust the other person considerably before opening up like this. One day he took me aside and asked me if I had the guts to escape to Switzerland. The border with Switzerland was only a few miles away and it was, of course, a neutral country. He had met someone at his girlfriend's house who took small groups of people across the border at night through a cemetery. We discussed the matter for a while and finally decided not to take that chance. The problem was that we didn't know if the Swiss border guards would turn us over to the Germans or not. If they did, it would have meant the firing squad. After the war, I read that it had been up to the individual Swiss officer in charge of his segment of the border to send deserters back or not. Also, during the war, I listened to a speech by the German propaganda minister Joseph Goebbels in which he said, "It is high time to puncture the pest boil Switzerland." Maybe we did the right thing or not, I'll never know.

After a few weeks we started to practice our mission in the field, namely to seek out the enemy. At this time I knew for sure I had to get away from this outfit if I wanted to live through the war. I had heard from some of the guys who had come back from Russia that the survival rate of a reconnaissance squadron was about 15 percent.

I tried desperately to come up with some ideas. Then I found out that the Air Force accepted volunteers who were willing to sign up for four years of service. In my desperation I went to see our commanding officer. He looked pretty bad; he wore an eye patch and walked with a cane, which reaffirmed my way of thinking. I made up the story that I always wanted to fly and how much it would mean to me to get into the Air Force. I must have been a good liar because he went with me to the personnel office. He told the sergeant in charge about my intentions and asked how he could help me in this matter. The sergeant recommended that I finish my basic training first and then transfer to the Air Force. The officer agreed and told me to stay in touch with the personnel office. After the officer left I wanted to leave too but the sergeant told me to stay. He was very angry with me for having bypassed him, he cursed me and made me clean the floor of the office with water and a mop. That ended my hope for the Air Force, but it did teach me to follow the chain of command.

During the past century, Mulhouse, and for that matter Alsace-Lorraine, had been part of Germany or France, depending upon who won the last war. We could tell that some of the civilians were friendly toward us and some were not. We had been instructed to treat the French with kid gloves and avoid a confrontation under all circumstances. This wasn't all that difficult, except for their teenagers. They knew about our orders and tried to get away with insults and sometimes, physical contact.

What was probably unknown to the general public was the fact that we were hungry most of the time. This always puzzled me; after all, we were the victors and should have had at least enough to eat. As a result of this we tried to buy or beg for food whenever possible. I was lucky. I became friendly with a girl in a bakery and occasionally she treated me to one of those long French breads.

Quite often teenagers heckled us, mostly from streetcars or busses. They would yell at us, "Give me a little bread" or other insults. Sometimes going to a restaurant or movie, we could expect to get an elbow in the ribs. One time we had a different sergeant for three days and found out that our sergeant had spent that time in jail. I don't know the details, but when he was in town someone pushed him and he didn't take this too kindly. I couldn't blame him for that.

I forgot the occasion, but one night we had wine with our supper and a lot of guys were pretty loaded. Later, a fellow from our platoon by the name of Schmidt went to the toilet and someone from another platoon smeared black shoe polish in his face. Even though it was only a prank, Schmidt got mad and knocked the guy out. We learned at this time that Schmidt was a boxer, which explained part of it. Nothing became of it, probably on account of our alcohol consumption.

There was a young man in our platoon by the name of Kursawe. He was a good-looking guy with his blue eyes and blond hair. He started to find love letters under his pillow. They went like this: "I love your hair and your beautiful skin, I would love to touch you, etc." The poor kid didn't know what to do and told our sergeant about it. He and another sergeant set a trap and caught the writer of the letters. To our astonishment it was Schmidt, the last guy we would have suspected. What followed was rather sad. The sergeants started to drill Schmidt until he couldn't take it anymore and deserted. Since this was wartime, anyone who deserted and either didn't return or wasn't caught within 48 hours after his leave ran out faced the death penalty. Fortunately, he was arrested after 46 hours in Karlsruhe, a city at the Rhine River. We never saw him again. What I didn't know at the time was that our platoon would have been the firing squad. Still today, the thought of that makes me shudder. I found out later that Kursawe was killed in Russia from a shot to the head.

Our squadron consisted of approximately 150 men, and one day the commanding officer wanted a photo taken of all of us. Everyone lined up about four rows deep on the parade ground. I don't know why, but a lieutenant, who was supposed to take the picture, asked me to do it. Either he wanted to be in the picture too or maybe he had seen me take photos with my camera. I never expected anything like this to happen. I was nervous even though he had set the shutter speed, lens opening and distance. To my amazement and relief the photo turned out perfect. I had the whole group right in the center where they were supposed to be. It made the lieutenant very happy and I'm sure he was relieved. This event started an unusual friendship.

Before World War II officers came from a military family, and had either a higher education or both. They were a cast of their own. The Nazis eliminated this prerequisite; anyone who passed certain requirements could become an officer. Even though the relationship between enlisted men and officers had become more relaxed, the dividing line still existed.

Despite this, the lieutenant and I started to have conversations. Among other things I found out that he was hungry too. That surprised me, as I always thought that only the enlisted men had this problem. He told me the commanding officer ate very little and the rest of the officers didn't dare to eat more than him. Besides the bread I secured on the side, I sometimes was able to get some cheese. I offered him some of my food and he gladly accepted, but he asked me to keep it out of sight. Something I would have done anyway.

I mentioned my concern for the future and he admitted he didn't feel too hopeful about his own either. To my surprise, one day he told me that he had managed to get me enrolled in driving school. He said it didn't mean too much, but at least I didn't have to go to the front right away. I was grateful for this and deep down I hoped that by becoming a driver I wouldn't end up on a bicycle later.

Driving school was fun and for a while I forgot about my worries. We were three students with an instructor, who was a sergeant. He was a nice guy and very well qualified. We learned how the engine and every part of a car worked. Then for the first time I had the chance to drive. The car was an old Opel with stick shift; maybe automatic transmissions didn't exist yet in 1942. This fact turned out to be painful for us students, because every time we killed the engine the instructor pinched us on the thigh. Sometimes we had to kneel in front of the car and say: "Dear motor, I'll never kill you again." Another time one of us ran through a stop sign. The instructor made him climb up the pole and clean the sign with a rag. I remember some French civilians looking at us like we were crazy. I must say the whole driving course was very memorable, and I'm still grateful to the instructor for everything he taught me.

March had arrived and I had the feeling that things were beginning to move. While my school was going on the lieutenant got transferred and my friend Guenter was sent off to Russia. Before he left we spent a pleasant Sunday afternoon together. We exchanged our addresses in Breslau, promised to stay in touch and wished each other good luck.

Our short basic training was over and most of the guys were sent to Russia. I had no idea what was going to happen next. The answer came quickly. I was given the order to report to another reconnaissance squadron at Mailly De Camp, a town near Reims, France. The group of men I traveled with was all drivers. One of them was my friend Novack. Apparently he knew how to operate a motorcycle and was going to be a messenger. I was glad he was still with me; it made me feel a little better.

When our train slowly rolled into the railroad station at Mailly De Camp, I was looking out the window to get an idea of what the town looked like. I noticed quite a few girls standing in front of an exotic looking building and waving at us.

I said to the guy next to me, "Boy, this is some friendly population here."

He answered, "That is the cat house, stupid."

Out of curiosity, I went later with a couple of guys to check it out. They served beer and the girls mingled with the customers in a very suggestive fashion. A few of us just drank and watched. That didn't please the madam and she yelled off and on, "Who

Members of the driving school
Hans on the left of the instructor
Mulhouse, Alsace-Lorraine 1942

doesn't f..., out!" Her German with a French accent sounded pretty funny. We just laughed at her and left after a while. I knew the whole thing wasn't for me, and made this my first and last time at a brothel.

Shortly after our arrival we were taken to a motor pool at Reims. The group of the drivers I had been assigned to, picked up four large trucks, two cars and a number of motorcycles, some with sidecars. I ended up with one of the cars. They were Bedfords, British cars, very heavy and resembled jeeps. I suppose the British forces at Dunkirk had left them behind. On the way back to our unit we stopped at a cafe in Reims for coffee. Naturally I had to turn the engine off before going inside. I didn't realize that this would create a real problem. When they turned the car over to me it was running and I was instructed to crank the engine in order to get the car started. When we left the cafe everybody took off. Frantically, I tried to get the car going but without success. Here I was in a hostile country all by myself and all kind of thoughts crossed my mind. Finally the damn thing started and almost took both of my thumbs off. Nobody had told me how to crank properly and not to wrap my thumbs around the crank handle. My thumbs looked dark blue and hurt terribly, but I couldn't pay any attention to them at the time. I jumped in the car and took off like the devil. Fortunately, when I turned the first corner I saw the last of the motorcycles making a right turn way down the street. It was all I needed to catch up.

The last time I saw Novack was at the motor pool. Sadly enough, we didn't even get a chance to say goodbye; he ended up with a different group. Later, when I had returned to my reserve unit at Oels, I found out that he had been wounded in the throat by shrapnel. He was still alive when they took him to a field hospital, but nobody knew what had happened to him after that.

I was given the order of driver for the master sergeant. He was about 40 years old, portly and not too bright. I didn't care for him but tried to hide my feelings. There wasn't a lot of driving; he mostly drove himself and even then not very often.

Our squadron wasn't at full strength and there wasn't too much going on, which suited me fine. One time about 20 additional young men arrived, all from northern Germany. Practically all of them were blond and blue eyed. They seemed to have a chip on their shoulder, because they looked like the kind the Nazis idolized. That didn't bother me. I had already decided not to get too friendly with anyone, under the circumstances. I expected that we would suffer heavy losses and I dreaded the thought of losing a friend.

One part of my life didn't change at my new unit-I still was hungry most of the time. Then I discovered that after everyone had gotten his portion at the chow line, there were always some leftovers. So I tried to be one of the first in line, gulped everything down and hurried to get back in line as fast as I could. That worked out nicely. I still eat too fast today and sometimes wonder if this was the time when I started this habit.

The French toilets were quite a surprise. They had nice tiles, but had only a small hole in the floor and a handle attached to the wall on either side to grasp. I thought it was uncomfortable and messy. Apparently others had the same thought before and wedged a beam between the walls at all toilets. This way, one could at least sit down.

One day one of our cooks was killed when he fell from a truck. I didn't know the man but I was picked to be in the honor guard at his funeral. There were 12 of us in the guard. We were instructed on how to march and how to fire our salvo. The funeral took place in a French cemetery. We had to march slowly, dragging our feet purposely down a long path to the gravesite. Once there, we lined up in two rows and waited for our command to fire three salvos. When the first command came to aim our rifles in the air, everything clicked like clockwork. We knew the second command was going to be "Fire" but before it was given, one of us jumped the gun and pulled the trigger. The rest of us didn't know what to do for a moment but fired anyway. It was a complete disaster and some French civilians, who were watching, had a grin on their faces. Fortunately, the second and third salvos worked out all right. The lieutenant in charge wasn't very happy with our performance. He told us the first salvo sounded like a goat shitting on a drum skin.

We didn't expect anything like this to happen, but the commanding officer gave everyone in the squadron the chance to see Paris. It wasn't very far to Paris, only a three-hour train ride. The platoons had to go separately over a period of two days. When my time came I was very excited, because finally there was something worthwhile to see and to do.

After our arrival we were shown where we would stay, eat and meet for our departure. I was surprised that they let us go on our own; it must have been safe enough at this time. I joined up with another soldier and we didn't waste any time experiencing the city. As we left the building we got our first impression. A Frenchman approached and asked if we wanted to come with him and see women make love in 42 different positions. We politely declined and went our way. A short distance away we were approached by women who were carrying trays in front of them attached to straps around their necks. They looked liked cigarette girls in nightclubs. The difference was that instead of cigarettes they sold pornographic photos. I bought a few for kicks, but threw them away before I went to Russia. I was afraid if I should get killed they might be sent to my family.

The Eiffel Tower pulled us like a magnet. When we arrived there we were told that the elevators weren't working. We decided to take the stairs and walked up to the second platform. This is quite a climb as anyone who has done it can testify. I must say it was worth the effort. The view was impressive. We could see beautiful grounds below with people looking as small as ants, the Seine with its bridges and the city in the background. During our remaining time we saw most of the well-known landmarks, except for Notre Dame. We also rode the subway, something new to me. Our relationship with the Parisians was best described as impersonal, as we didn't pay much attention to each other. Aside from my impression that Paris was dirty, I have to admit it is a unique city, unlike any other city in the world. I was glad I had been given the opportunity to see it.

My stay in Mailly De Camp was short lived. The order came to pack our gear and move our vehicles to a rail yard. I had to drive the Bedford onto a flatbed railroad car. It wasn't all that easy for an inexperienced driver, like myself, but I finally succeeded. After the cars and trucks were in position and secured, solid wooden panels, about one foot high, were placed on all sides of the flat beds. My sergeant saw to it that the railroad car with the kitchen truck was hooked up behind us. I didn't blame him for this. I probably would have done the same thing. What I didn't like at all was the sergeant's dog. It was bad enough that I had to share the small car with the sergeant, but with the dog too.

I had no idea where we were going. When we started rolling I saw we were heading west; that was a relief. This wasn't the direction to Russia. After a while the sergeant told me to climb over to the kitchen truck and get something to eat. This meant I had to get down on the buffers, get a hold of the opposite panel and pull myself up on the other side. The train wasn't moving very fast but I thought this wasn't going to be easy. It was raining, the buffers were wet and shaky and I wore boots with nails on the soles, which made matters worse. In spite of all this I had to do it. I lowered myself down on the buffers without difficulty, but when I reached for the other panel, I slipped. Fortunately, I was able to hang on, but my feet were dangling just above the rails. The sergeant saw what happened and called me back. I was a little shaken. If I had lost my grip, it would have been the end. He didn't say anything, just gave me a strange look. He said he was going over there himself and I should watch his dog. He might have learned from my mishap because he made it safely to the other car. Since the dog didn't have a leash I had to sit in the car trying to hold him. This didn't work, because he wanted to go after his master and repeatedly snapped at me. I had no choice but to let him go. Somehow he managed to get on top of the panel and jumped trying to reach the sergeant. He missed and rolled down the embankment. He was all right, ran next to the train for a short distance, and then gave up. The sergeant saw it and got all excited. I felt bad, because even though I didn't care for the dog, I didn't want to see him harmed. I told the sergeant exactly what happened, but he didn't believe me and blamed me for his loss.

It took about two days to get to our destination, St. Sauveur Le Vicomte, a small town south of Cherbourg. We unloaded and moved into our new quarters, which reminded me of a warehouse with bunk beds. After just a few days, an alarm was sounded and everyone had to pack up and be ready to leave. We were told later that this had been only a drill and was meant to prepare us for an invasion by the allies. Interestingly enough, the actual invasion came two years later just a short distance away.

I had a toothache and went to see an army dentist in Cherbourg. This was quite an experience. It looked like he treated at least a dozen patients that morning. He didn't change drills or anything and when he treated me I thought there wouldn't be anything left of my tooth, but I have to say he must have done a good job. My toothache was gone and the filling lasted forever. Years later this filling puzzled many dentists because it looked like clay.

Before we could test our readiness for an invasion again, we had to leave permanently. I wondered about the short duration of our stay. From what I could gather our movements were part of a plan to mislead the allies about the German troop strength in France. We went through the same routine of loading once again. This time I had no problem getting my car onto the flatbed. As usual I didn't know where we were going, but I could tell it was again in a westerly direction. The sergeant didn't look too happy. I guess he missed his dog, and that made me a little uneasy. Fortunately, the kitchen truck was next to our car again and he spent a lot of time there.

After about three days we arrived at another small town named Chateau Gontier. It was a quaint looking place near a river and I hoped that we would stay for a while. While driving the sergeant around, I found that the gasoline gauge wasn't working. Afraid that I could run out of gas, I started to test the gas level in the tank with the branch of a tree. One day the car didn't want to start. I should have called a mechanic right then, but I made the mistake of trying to find the problem myself. To make a long story short, I found out that a bud from the tree branch had been lodged in the copper fuel line. After I had removed the bud I reattached the fuel line with two brass fittings. The car started and I was very proud of my accomplishment, which was a bit premature. The next day the sergeant wanted to go somewhere by himself and when he started the car he smelled gas. He looked under the hood while the engine was running and claimed a spray of gasoline squirted him. Apparently I had failed to attach one of the brass fittings properly. He was furious and told me I was unfit to be his driver. He meant what he said and by the next day I was back on a bicycle.

I was very unhappy about this development. All my efforts to get away from becoming a living target had failed. However, as many times in life, something good comes out of something bad, as a later event proved. We conducted some minor war games in the area and possibly worried the local population. Our outfit had finally reached its planned strength, and when we all lined up on the road with antitank guns, jeeps, motorcycles with sidecars, bicycles, radio cars, trucks, I must say we looked well prepared. It was clear that our time in France was coming rapidly to an end and we would soon be on our way to Russia.

One day I was called to the commanding officer and to my surprise was promoted to the rank of a corporal. This, I couldn't quite understand. Why me? The reason, I found out, was that I had been in Russia the previous year. That still didn't make sense since I had been in Russia with the Labor Company, not with the army. I didn't say anything and just accepted it. Incidentally, this was the only promotion I received during my army years.

There was somebody I should mention here, a corporal named Hauwie who had the duties of a clerk. He was probably the most disliked person in the whole outfit because of his arrogance and obnoxious behavior. What puzzled everyone was how he was always supported or backed up by our commanding officer. I later learned the reason for this mystery. Apparently his parents were owners of a grocery store and supplied the commanding officer's wife with food and other goods, something that was worth more than money at the time. I would not have mentioned Hauwie if it wasn't for the fact I almost killed him accidentally in Russia and had everyone fuming at me that I didn't.

When our departure day arrived we got a pep talk from a high-ranking officer most of us didn't know. We lined up in horseshoe formation together with some other units. The speaker was on a platform at the open end and all the soldiers decorated with medals stood in the front row. He was very pompous and the only thing I remember about his speech was that he assured us we were going to finish off Russia by the end of summer. After loading our vehicles and all our gear, we climbed on freight cars and started rolling.

We didn't know our exact destination and it didn't really matter. What began to matter was that the straw we were sleeping on was infested with lice. The lice especially liked our pubic hair and the area around our ankles. So most of the time we looked for lice and squashed them between our thumbnails. It certainly wasn't fun but it kept us occupied. The only amusing thing about this journey was when we found out that our pompous officer from Chateau Gontier had been infected with syphilis and was taken off the train in Germany.

During the final days of our ride we moved deeper and deeper into Russia and saw nothing but a bare landscape. I just couldn't help thinking, *what the hell are we doing here?* After seventeen days on the train going through France, Germany and Poland, we ended up in a small village near Stalino in southern Russia. Everything looked quite depressing, no paved streets, old shabby one story wooden houses and people dressed alike in gray, quilted clothing. The only positive about the place was that we were deloused in hot showers using a special soap and our uniforms were disinfected in a steam room.

After unloading, everyone packed his own gear and in my case that meant mounting it on a metal frame behind the seat of my bike. The weather was actually pleasant for Russia, blue sky and warm, as we started moving toward the front. Before we reached our destination we stopped for a few days about fifteen miles behind the front line. Finally the order came to move in and we were told we would take over a bulge in the Russian line presently held by the 9th Infantry Division. I definitely wasn't too anxious to get there, as we started moving forward one afternoon.

I liked to chat with our interpreter, Czisch, who spoke Russian and some other Slavic languages. I had always been interested in learning other languages and thought that Russian certainly would come in handy under the circumstances. What I had not anticipated was that this relationship could have cost me my life. While we were moving along, Czisch had a flat tire and I stayed with him to keep watch. We were supposed to do this on account of Russian guerrillas. It could have had grave consequences for anyone to stay behind by himself.

A half hour later we took off after the others and came to a fork in the road. At this fork was a building which resembled a stable and there were approximately a dozen Russian civilians standing in front. Czisch wanted to go over to ask them which direction our troops had taken. I told him that wasn't necessary since one could see all the tire tracks in the sand were going to the left. Well, he didn't believe me and went over and asked them, and as I had expected, they told him our troops had gone to the right. I argued with him but did not get anywhere; he said since he talked to them in Russian, they wouldn't lie to him. Because he outranked me I had no choice but to follow. After about an hour of fast travel we hadn't caught up with our outfit and Czisch realized that he had made a mistake. In the meantime it had moved toward darkness and he had the stupid idea to go back to the fork in the road. That is when I rebelled. I told him there was a good chance that those people were waiting to ambush us. I suggested that we turn to the left and move toward the road we should have used to begin with.

This time he listened and we went across a desert like area of sand and small bushes. While we never found that road we knew we were getting close to the front. We could see flares going up and heard the sound of artillery fire. We decided to stay and wait for sunrise instead of possibly ending up behind the Russian lines.

The next morning it was very quiet and we proceeded cautiously in what we thought was the right direction. We eventually came to some houses that seemed deserted, but from between two of the houses some men emerged who looked like Martians. We found out they were German Infantry with mosquito nets over their helmets and faces. We were relieved to see them. They even knew about us being missing; as a matter of fact, they said our people had given up on us. They showed us the way to our behind-the-line support unit who were also surprised to see us alive. They explained that our outfit had moved into position last night and had already suffered casualties. Then a sergeant led us to the front the same morning. We crossed some open ground through the ruins of some houses, and then trudged through a swampy area into a small village. He had only been to the front in the dark on the previous evening and didn't know much about the situation. However, we were to find out quickly. While we stood with our backs against one of the houses, right over our heads we heard clack, clack into the woodwork, bullets from a Russian sniper. We hit the dirt and then we saw one of our guys waving at us from a basement window. Not knowing what to expect, we crawled over and into the basement. The chilling thought crossed my mind, if the sniper had aimed just a hair lower, I might have entered the happy hunting grounds.

We heard that it wasn't too dangerous to be out in the open as long as one stayed low to avoid the sniper fire and was aware of sporadic mortar and artillery fire. This applied only to the daytime hours, at night all hell broke lose! We were entrenched behind barbed wire; I would guess approximately three hundred yards from the Russians. In the daytime both sides only had guards manning the trenches, but at night almost everyone was on duty. I certainly didn't like the whole situation. Then, I don't know why, I was chosen to be in charge of four men to make supply runs. Every late afternoon we had to go back to our trucks to get food, ammunition and messages, a distance of two miles. That I came out of this assignment alive was a true miracle. Even though the Russians couldn't see us, they knew our path. I realized this on my first trip when I saw the shrapnel everywhere. There was the grave of a young soldier on the route; it had a primitive cross with his name and age; he had been nineteen years old, the same age as me.

For a few days our trips went smoothly. Then one evening on the way back we thought the devil was after us, as horrible screaming grenades exploded behind us. Luckily, we were near the ruins of houses and dove into them. I carried a metal canister filled with hot soup on my back that leaked and ran down my neck, but I didn't care. We learned rockets fired from launchers, in jest called "Stalin organs," had bombarded us. The following day we noticed the craters were only a few inches deep but the shrapnel tore off in all directions.

My next brush with death came just a few days later. A mortar shell exploded about 30 feet in front of me. I was carrying a metal box containing hand grenades and instinctively threw myself behind it, which, of course, was useless because it would have been too late. All of us stayed low for a while but nothing else happened. I walked over to look at the spot and saw that, possibly on account of the wet ground, the shell had exploded in an angle away from me and the grass was blackened and singed on that side. I knew that under other circumstances I might have looked like a sieve.

I don't remember the exact size of our outfit but I think there were one hundred and twenty men with four officers, one captain and three lieutenants. One day, a lieutenant wanted to try infiltrating the Russian side to blow up one of their bunkers. I

Near the front line as a messenger
Russia 1942

knew what was behind this plan, namely to earn the Iron Cross, the German medal of bravery. This decoration was expected on every German officer's uniform. For this mission he wanted two volunteers to go with him. While addressing us he looked straight at me and I looked straight back. I was thinking *you are looking at the wrong guy*. I saw no reason for getting involved in this kind of undertaking and putting myself into more danger than I faced already. By the way, he did find two volunteers to go with him and supposedly they accomplished their objective. Luckily, only one man was slightly wounded in the leg from a trip wire.

Having been in the same location for about a month, something out of the ordinary happened. The Russians started to shell us with everything they had and our captain expected an attack. I had just arrived with my group bringing food, etc., when we were sent back to the trucks again to retrieve more machine gun ammunition and hand grenades. When we approached the front on our return it was nighttime and the place was an inferno; flares going up, grenades exploding everywhere as well as machine gun and small arms fire. I always walked in front of the other men and we were practically back at our base when I thought I heard someone calling "password." Even though I didn't see anyone, I yelled the day's password "Neuenburg" and this saved my life. Two German Infantry men stepped out of the dark, with machine pistols pointed at me, and told me that they had called before without getting a reply. If I hadn't answered they would have fired. I told them how glad I was and thanked them, but let them know that it was very hard to hear anything above all that noise. I found out that at this spot the infantry had a small artillery piece set up and that it had been done by request from our captain. The next day we learned that all the commotion had nothing to do with an attack, because of events along the whole front, the Russians had just used up their ammunition and withdrawn.

After the infantry cleared a passage through the former Russian lines, we started moving. We were ordered to stay within the staked out corridor to avoid being blown up by mines. What I didn't know at the time was that the 1942 German summer offensive had started on the southern Russian front with the intention to finish off the Russian Army. As it turned out, just the opposite was going to happen. Luck was on my side; our division was part of the army group ordered south with the goal of reaching the oil fields in Baku and the Caucasus mountains. If I had been with the army group ordered east to Stalingrad, I wouldn't be here today. Nearly all of the two hundred and fifty thousand men sent there were either killed in battle, or died in the ice and snow on their march to prison camps.

For the first time our squadron started to move in the correct order, which meant two guards on bicycles rode about two hundred yards in front of a squad of approximately twenty men on bikes. The rest followed in a staggered order with the trucks at the end. I was very fortunate to be a guard only once. I remember that it made me feel like I was on the way to my execution.

I had been trained on a fifty-millimeter mortar and was still under the command of a sergeant by the name of Geiler. Besides him and myself, there were two other men manning the mortar. We operated the mortar in the following way: I was the number one man with the bottom plate which I had to ram into the ground, then level the plate and adjust the distance and side angles. The number two man brought up the tube and loaded the mortar and the number three man furnished the grenades, which by the way were shaped like little bombs. In the field, the sergeant was always in front giving me the necessary distances and adjustments. Since the mortar only reached targets as far as five hundred yards, it meant we were pretty close to the enemy. In addition, with three men close to each other, we made quite a target. Before it became a worry I received a new assignment. One of the lieutenants wanted me as his messenger; perhaps he had noticed that I did a good job earlier when I brought messages to the front.

In a way, I was glad about this change; on the other hand, I had to take orders from his sergeant, named Richter, who didn't like

Crew manning a 50-millimeter mortar
Hans in center
Russia 1942

me. This bothered me quite a bit because I anticipated a lot of problems. He was also from Breslau, and usually the guys from my hometown were like a brotherhood. Unfortunately, he was an exception.

We kept on moving forward for several days without catching up to the Russians. The only things we found were awful smelling dead horses. I had to admire the Russians for the way they retreated; they left absolutely nothing behind. However, I didn't enjoy their small bombers flying overhead at night. They were rather primitive, their engines sounding like a hand cranked coffee grinder. When they wanted to release a bomb they turned off the engine, and I guess they dumped the bomb overboard. We always knew when the engine stopped the bomb was coming. One night, when we thought we were well hidden, one of the coffee grinders must have found us. Until then, they hadn't caused any damage, so we were not too concerned about their presence. I was sleeping in a tent next to a deep ditch and this probably saved my life, because a bomb landed in the ditch just a few feet away. Talk about a rude awakening. In a way it was a good thing it happened, because after that we paid a lot more attention to them.

Moving into the Donetz basin one afternoon we carefully entered a village, but found no resistance and the people quite friendly. They even told us that the Russian soldiers had departed shortly before we arrived. We continued and came upon an elevated railroad track with a big pile of coal beyond it. Expecting trouble, we spread out and approached it cautiously. Then we were fired on from behind the railroad embankment. Every one opened up and all we saw was a lot of black dust from that pile of coal. When we didn't receive return fire, we kept going and one brave soul looked over the tracks and didn't see any Russian soldiers. We ventured over the tracks and saw a number of small houses and a few civilians who came toward us. They told us that the soldiers had buried mines in the streets. We were very grateful for this information. It must have rained not too long before, and we were able to locate the mines by finding their outlines, which looked like fine cracked lines in the black dirt. Their size was similar to the shape of a brick but a little larger. We marked them with pieces of paper held down by chunks of coal.

We stayed overnight and our captain gave orders that no vehicles should get close until the mines had been removed. I didn't have to stand guard that night and slept in one of the houses. In the morning I heard a large explosion and thought someone had stepped on a mine. I was partly right, the sergeant who had released me as his driver in France, had disobeyed orders and had run over a mine with his Bedford. His driver was dead. Two guys carried the sergeant between them with his arms around their necks. He was blackened and bloody in the face and one of his legs looked like it was hanging on a thread. Our captain was furious and cursed him, but I guess the sergeant didn't care much in his condition. I felt sick to my stomach, because I knew if I had gotten along with him, I would have been the dead driver.

It seemed as if we were catching up with the Russians and every night almost half of us stood guard. We reached the Donetz River one evening and crossed on a pontoon bridge. The crossing went fairly smooth considering the moon was shining brightly and there were two or three coffee grinders bombarding us. One of our vehicles got stuck on the bridge, and we had to dump it into the river, which was probably better than wasting time and being hit by a bomb.

Not long after, we approached the Don River, which we also had to cross. At this time some other units of the German Army were near us. This was the home of the Don Cossacks, who hated the Bolcheviks with a vengeance. In fact, toward the end of the war, an army, which to a big extent consisted of Cossacks, fought on the German side. After the war, their general, by the name of Vlassow, was captured by the Russians tortured and hanged in Moscow.

With the German troops were some Austrian mountain units who probably were assigned to go to the Caucasus Mountains. One night as I stood guard, the full moon came up and looked

Russian villagers having fun on an outing
Russia 1942

incredibly huge, bright orange, the biggest I have ever seen the moon appear. I could hear singing in the distance, and could tell they were the Austrians and Cossacks, who were singing alternately their native songs. I never liked to stand guard, but this time I didn't mind. As a matter of fact, I wished I could have listened all night. I thought about this insane war and how beautiful the world could be.

The next day we were ferried across the Don River. The land was very green and quite different from what we had seen so far. We were heading south and into the unknown. As I understood the situation our tanks were ahead of us and the infantry was behind us. Our duty was to scout the enemy, get all the information and report it to the infantry.

It didn't take long to catch up with the Russians. They saw us and we came under heavy artillery fire. It was actually the first real experience of this kind for me. The old-timers had told me that when you're under artillery fire you could dig a hole in concrete with your fingernails. I had to agree, it was a horrible feeling. It taught me never to be without my spade. Even though the barrage lasted probably not more than ten minutes, it felt like an eternity. In the course of events we learned that the retreating Russians always kept either an artillery piece or a tank with their last few soldiers.

The following day it rained very hard and it felt good. The down side was the mud, which was almost a foot deep and clung to the spokes of our bicycle wheels, slowing us down as we continued onward. We were told a village was ahead and my lieutenant and about ten of us were ordered to go in front of our outfit and find out if the Russians had left. We approached the village very carefully and were lucky to find it empty. Most of the time I spent in Russia I felt like I was in a trance, detached from reality, but this was one of the moments when I fully realized that we were expendable. Since I was the messenger I had to go back and inform the captain. Because of the mud, I left my bike behind and walked. I had barely left the village, when three Russian soldiers with their hands up came out of a shack to my right. This startled me for a moment because we had been convinced that all the Russians had left. However, I had learned to always expect the unexpected, as well as never to let my guard down. I knew that in situations like these soldiers had lost their lives by being too trusting. With my finger on the trigger of my rifle I motioned them to walk in front of me. When we reached my unit I made my report and handed over the prisoners.

We kept going and the terrain started to look more barren. One day something almost comic happened. We saw a Russian half-track to the right of us, approximately 1500 yards away. There were about twenty soldiers on it. We set up one of our antitank guns and started to fire at them. First the Russians jumped off and ran over a hill, but when they saw we were unable to reach them, they came back, climbed on their vehicle and continued on their merry way.

Another funny episode took place in a village where we had stopped for the afternoon. We found a record player with records and started to play Russian music. There was also a speech by Tovarich Molotovo (comrade Molotov), their foreign minister. Some Russian civilians who were standing around started to smile and that was the end of our fun. Our captain came, broke the records and told us we were playing an anti-German propaganda speech.

In the meantime it started to get extremely hot, and we were still in our winter uniforms that, unfortunately, we had to put up with permanently. I mention this because it made us feel continually uncomfortable.

For a while there was the threat of Russian tanks and a crew with an eighty-eight antiaircraft gun was added to our outfit. It made us a lot safer because that type of gun was more effective than our antitank guns. The crew had it made on their big comfortable jeep, which pulled the gun. Their sergeant had a red beard, which he kept well groomed. We were not in the position to copy him, but this didn't stop some of us from growing a beard.

A Russian village after a rain
The mud was more than ankle deep

I had to admit that after a while we started to look rather rowdy with unkempt beards and hair, and some of us wore scarves of different colors around our necks or foreheads as bandannas. Because of the heat we rolled up our sleeves and kept our jackets and zippers open. One day our commanding officer called us together and told us to clean up or else. He acknowledged our circumstances, but said it didn't mean we had to look like Ali Baba and his Forty Thieves. His order helped somewhat; at least the beards disappeared.

Like most of the others I tied my steel helmet to my bike behind my seat. One morning after we had taken off, I lost my helmet and this turned out to be a day when I really was going to need it. Our guards entered a long village and were fired on. We dropped our bikes and the fighting started. My lieutenant was angry when he saw I didn't have a helmet. Immediately we lost two men, I should have taken one of their helmets but just couldn't do it. I felt it would have been a bad omen. The fighting advanced from house to house, with the Russians retreating. We finally managed to get all the way to the other end of the village. What I didn't realize was that with all that excitement we had lost one of our lieutenants. It bothered me because he had been the only one of our officers I liked. He did have the habit of wearing his steel helmet tilted toward the back of his neck, and I heard he had been hit in the forehead. If he had worn his helmet as he should have, it may not have happened. But then again, none of our officers came back alive.

We took positions at the end of the village with the Russians still in front of us. While we waited for the infantry to move up, Russian artillery shells exploded periodically around us. At this very inopportune time I had to use the bathroom and when you have to go, you have to go! The house I was in didn't have an outhouse, only a hole covered by four overlapping metal plates leaving an open square in the middle, in the back yard. I raced out to the hole and nearly died the worst death of all. When I stepped on the plates, they shifted, and I almost fell into that deep cesspit.

Miraculously, I caught myself and was able to finish my business.

Late in the afternoon the infantry arrived and shortly after attacked. I couldn't believe what I saw, these guys looked beat, as if they had been marching all day, which they might have. I thought if I would be one of them I wouldn't care if I were killed, just to get it over with.

While the infantry moved forward, we began to move back; then something happened I won't forget-ever. We had just climbed on our bicycles when diagonally from us, on the other side of the street, an artillery shell exploded. I looked right into it and it resembled the sun. I still don't know why none of us were killed or wounded. But, Carlson, the sergeant in front of me, ran at least a hundred feet out in the field to the right. I didn't understand why he acted like this; maybe it was a premonition, as he was killed two days later by our own artillery.

Our infantry had accomplished their task and we moved on the next day. Our trucks had caught up with us and I was able to get a new steel helmet. The following day we reached another village and after combing the place we decided to stay overnight. I noticed a house, better built than the others and neater looking. Curious, I went to take a closer look. By the photographs on the walls I saw the house belonged to a commissar, a member of the communist elite. I also noticed that it didn't have any religious pictures, candles or a crucifix like the other houses. There were books on shelves, some were school books printed in German. Going through the pages of one I saw a drawing that outlined Russia and Europe and said, "Europe is a Russian peninsula." Well, this was some food for thought!

I should mention at this point that the men on bicycles were divided in three groups; one was always in front and the other two somewhere in the middle of the entire unit. The groups rotated so each one would have the "opportunity" to be shot at first. I bring this up because of what happened the next day. We were on the heels of the Russians when we came under artillery fire from the rear. Our own artillery didn't realize that we were so far ahead.

We immediately shot white flares in the air, which meant, "We are here." The shelling eventually stopped, but it was too late. We lost three men, all from the group in front, Sergeant Carlson being one of them. I was lucky again, because I wasn't in the lead bicycle group on that day.

Shortly thereafter, late in the day we came to a safe village. I thought we might stay overnight. We had been without meat for a long time and when I saw a goose I decided to make it my dinner. I grabbed it, put its neck on a door stoop and chopped its head off with my spade. I still can't believe that I could do a thing like that. Anyway, I asked the woman of the house to fix it for me. Unexpectedly, around midnight, we had to move on. The woman was still cooking the goose when I told her in sign language to give me one leg. I got on my bike and tried to eat it, but found it to be half raw. I threw it away and that was the end of my gourmet meal.

We came to another village where the Russians had moved out without a fight. They left several trucks behind and a small artillery piece with grenades. We loaded the canon and grenades on one of their trucks and took it with us with the hope of using it someday. There were a few Russian soldiers who had deserted. We kept two of them as drivers and one of us sat next to each driver acting like a guard. Not knowing how long this arrangement would work, I felt lucky to be one of the first guards. It was great to get off my bike and driven for a day. I tried to use the few Russian words I knew on the driver, but found out that he spoke German. He told me he learned German from his grandparents who had immigrated to Russia many years ago. I forgot most of what he told me, except for a few things. He said before the war he and his brother worked in a factory and the rule there was that if anyone came late to work more than three times, the penalty was five years in Siberia. He told me it happened to his brother and by the time the war started his brother had been gone for eight years and he never heard from him any more. I also learned that every Russian company had, besides their military leaders, two commissars; everybody knew one of them, the other one nobody knew. This meant, of course, nobody could trust anybody, a very clever way to keep everyone in line. I liked the guy and again I was thinking how senseless this war or any other war really was.

I was barely back on my bike when we made contact with the Russians again. We couldn't see them but they must have seen us. We came under artillery fire on a road between fields resembling corn. The ground was soft and I was able to dig in a little; then I heard a sharp, metallic sound behind me. I found out later, a piece of shrapnel had cut off the front fork of the bicycle, just a few feet away from my legs. I began to wonder how much longer my luck would last.

Soon we entered the town of Shakhty. Our infantry and even their support vehicles were already there. Our entire outfit settled down between some long one-story buildings. A few things I remember vividly about this town: first of all, as incredible as it may sound, there was no water around. Then I saw at an intersection something strange in the dirt. A closer look revealed the body of a Russian soldier nobody had bothered to remove and now he was as flat as a pancake. The most memorable event, however, happened at night. I was standing guard with another guy. We had orders to shoot without warning, due to possible sabotage by the Russian guerrillas. The moon was out and we kept in the shadow of a building. Then, at the other end of the building I saw a figure crouched next to a small picket fence. I nudged the other fellow, raised my rifle and took aim. I was about to pull the trigger when I saw the person's cap with the round silvery German insignia. I called for him to come forward and identify himself. Well, he did and it was Hauwie, the guy everyone despised. I told him he was one second from being killed. He said he didn't mean any harm, and just wanted to see if we were doing our duty. Since this wasn't any of his business, he showed his true character again. He probably would have turned us in if we wouldn't have been watching, and would have made brownie points with his mentor; it also could have cost us our heads. When my buddy from this night told the others about this incident, they told me it was a shame that I didn't put him away.

After leaving Shakhty we drove on; hot, thirsty, dirty and miserable. One day we managed to get a little relief. We came to a small village and found an underground ice cellar made of clay and quite deep. The people had stored big blocks of ice and we chipped some small pieces off. In my eagerness to cool down, I took a piece of ice, wrapped it in my handkerchief and tied it around my forehead. This was a big mistake because it gave me the worst headache I have ever had.

Not too long after that we came upon some trees and bushes and were again under Russian artillery fire. Some shells exploded in trees near us and the branches made quite a noise crashing down. We made it unharmed through the trees and were told to dig in. Opposite us, perhaps a mile away, were some low hills and we found out that the Russians were holding out in these hills. We were ordered to stay in our foxholes overnight and that we would attack in the morning. This seemed quite wrong since we were not supposed to actually engage with the enemy. I felt this would be a very dangerous undertaking to cross this wide-open field. However, ours was not to ask and so in the morning we arose and began to advance. The commanding officer was to the right of me with the man who carried the radio transmitter like a backpack. Then I saw the radioman talking to the captain, and as it turned out, we were ordered to stay put and informed that the infantry would attack. This was quite a relief. We went back to our foxholes and I fell asleep and missed the slaughter.

Around noon, somebody kicked me in the helmet and told me to get up. It was all over. We got on our bikes and passed a horrific sight. Apparently, our infantry had suffered heavy losses and they had set up some sort of open operating room using four poles and a tarp for a sunscreen. Under it were tables with wounded soldiers and medics working on them. I had not seen so much blood in one spot before: it looked like a slaughterhouse. I wondered how many of the wounded might not have lost their limbs under different circumstances. Not that I put any blame on the doctors; they didn't have a choice.

One day, we stopped along the road and had the opportunity to rest and a chance to organize a few things. Our trucks arrived too and we got some decent food. We cleaned ourselves as far as this was possible, replenished our ammunition and even received some mail from home. Getting mail was a big event because it took a long time between deliveries. I was always glad to hear that everything was fine at home and that Breslau had not come under bomb attacks yet. I wrote home when ever possible, but we were not allowed to disclose our location, etc. In addition, I avoided mentioning what danger I was in. I also had a chance to observe our officers. It was astonishing what I saw. They were saluting each other and spoke in formal German to each other. I couldn't believe it; here we were on the brink of death and they acted as if they were home in Germany.

My leisure, if I may call it that, came to a rude ending. My sergeant, Richter, threw down a pair of his boots and told me to polish them. This was hard to believe, and I thought, *No way. I'm not your shoeshine boy.* I just left the boots where he had put them. When we were ordered to leave he came over to pick them up and saw that I had not touched them. I told him I didn't have time to take care of them. He gave me a dirty look and I knew more trouble lay ahead.

It came soon after our departure. There was a drop in the terrain and somewhat below was another village. When we showed up on the rim, we came under heavy mortar fire. We left our bikes behind and took orders to dig in. My lieutenant was at my left and Richter to my right. I was about finished with my foxhole when Richter told me to get his machine pistol ammunition, which he had left with his bike. I didn't believe he was without ammunition and suspected that he hoped to see me killed by going out in the open. All our bikes looked more or less the same: they were all painted black, but I found what I thought was his ammunition. I crawled back into my hole and threw it

Sergeant Richter (on left), Hans is second from the left
Russia 1942

over to him. He picked it up, threw it back at me, told me that it wasn't his, and called me a foul name. I crawled back again under fire, found his ammunition and this time hurled it at him. I was furious and to vent my rage I took my spade and started digging like a madman. The dirt was flying in all directions when my lieutenant told me to simmer down and that orders were orders. Richter didn't realize the danger that he could have put himself in; he wouldn't be the first one who was shot by one of his own men.

In the meantime, another outfit had moved up far to the right of us. What followed was almost like watching a movie. They sent an armored car toward the village, probably to test the Russian defenses. That didn't turn out too well. We saw the car get hit and men jumping out, some of them on fire. At this time two of our men, who thought they had enough knowledge to fire our captured canon started to open up on the village. Maybe they didn't know what they were doing or the different colored rings on the grenades had something to do with it, I don't know; but the grenades fell either too far or too short. They decided to give up. We were told we would attack at three o'clock in the morning, in tandem with the other group coming from the right. Every time we were ordered to fix bayonets it made me a little uneasy, but fortunately the whole thing turned out much better than expected. We made it into the village without a shot being fired and found out that the Russians had slipped out during the night.

While trying to keep up with the Russians, we moved in a southeasterly direction. The landscape became more desert-like and the heat worsened. The ground was so dry that there were long cracks, about three to four feet wide and just as deep. We saw for the first time some of the natives who wandered around in this desolate land. They were Kalmyks and looked like Mongols, with round heads, Asian eyes and pockmarks on their faces. They lived in very primitive wagons with wooden, spokeless wheels.

At this point, the infantry seemed to fall farther and farther behind which didn't surprise me. To march in their winter uniforms in this heat, carrying their weapons, ammunition and other supplies would slow down the strongest of all. I might add that during the entire time I was in Russia, I never saw one paved road. Wherever we went we always rode on dirt or sand. Since there was no opportunity to take a bath, I can say without exaggeration it was disgusting.

The day I had dreaded finally arrived: I was assigned as a guard. In the morning two of us rode in front of everyone else. We came up on a somewhat higher ground and there was a similar rise in the distance. Between and below there were only a couple of small houses. We stopped and saw what appeared to be Russian soldiers on the other rise. We didn't need time to find out, because there was a flash on the other side and an artillery shell came in and exploded in front of us. In the meantime the first group had caught up with us and we scattered. I saw a crack in the ground not too far away and went for it. Running and throwing myself down alternately between the incoming grenades I made it safely, but by the time I got there the firing had stopped. We continued to follow the Russians, but without making contact. I was thankful to have survived my day as a guard.

A couple of days later our captain split us into three groups, apparently to get a better idea of the overall situation. The main group stayed in the middle and the other two, consisting of about twenty men each, were placed on the left and right sides. I had no idea how far apart we were from each other and knowing wouldn't have helped. My group was on the right and we started moving ahead. We had a radio car and one of our lieutenants on a motorcycle. We came to a village and it appeared as if the Russians soldiers had just left. A few stayed behind and gave themselves up. We put them in a barn and left two guards with them. The Russians had abandoned some wagons and a few of us picked through their stuff to see if we could find anything of interest. I found a leather pouch that was stuffed full of brand new rubles; I guessed it must have belonged to their paymaster. I threw it away since it wouldn't do me any good.

We settled down overnight in the middle of the village, and

The Other Side of the Coin

since I didn't have guard duty I went to sleep. In the middle of the night I woke up to gunfire and tried to find my gun but was so sleepy I couldn't locate it. Fortunately the shooting stopped and I went back to sleep. The next morning I discovered what had happened. A commissar with one of his men, both on horseback, tried to ride through the village and our guards killed them. Apparently they didn't know we were there. The commissar had some red decorations on his collar that I removed and kept as a souvenir.

Later in the morning, we followed a road and soon after we saw German bombers approaching. Hurriedly we put a big flag bearing a swastika on the road to make sure they knew we were there. The planes kept coming and moments later we heard bombs exploding and the ground seemed to vibrate. We knew the Russians had to be right in front of us. I don't know where the orders came from, but we stayed put and then something incredible took place. The Russians came toward us in great numbers and I had no idea what would happen next. Our radio car took off: the operator told us later that he was under orders to save the car with its valuable equipment, which was probably true. He said he had radioed the main group about our situation and was instructed that we should fight our way out. What a joke. What I couldn't quite understand was that our lieutenant also took off on his motorcycle. Maybe he panicked or just wanted to save his skin. I personally thought he should have been court-martialed for that. Nevertheless, we set up our two machine guns and waited. We couldn't figure out why, but the Russians split up with one large group passing us to the left and the other group to the right. A smaller bunch came toward us without weapons and some had leaflets in their hands. We motioned to them to lay down with us and they did. Then something even more unreal happened-the big group of Russians to our left began to shoot over our heads toward the group to our right. I can guess only that because of the bombing, they lost their minds. After a relatively short time, it was quiet again and we didn't see them anymore. At the time I didn't fully realize what could have happened. They could have swatted us like flies.

We headed back to the village with about a hundred prisoners, including two officers, a small canon and a wagon with horses. Our men at the village told us the Russians came rushing through in a manic state. They kept out of sight, but managed to grab a few more stragglers. We told the Russian officers to get their men in order and that we were getting ready to move out. I have to say the officers didn't treat their men too nicely-more like dogs. When we finally were organized we looked quite unique: a company of prisoners, the canon, horses and us spread out among them. I thought we looked a little like Genghis Khan moving through the desert. We reached our outfit the same day, which made me feel a bit more secure.

About two days later we began moving out very early in the morning, when the sun was just starting to come up. Even though I had been very tired the previous night I hardly slept. Perhaps I was feeling a premonition of sorts. I was riding with my lieutenant in front of our group with only the two guards ahead of us. We saw a barn-like building to the right, about 300 yards away, with two men standing on the roof. With the sun shining into our eyes we couldn't make out if they were soldiers. Since our two guards kept on going, we followed. I smelled danger and crept over to the shallow ditch on the right side of the road, ready to drop. At this time the figures on the roof shouted commands in Russian and all hell broke lose. I was down in time but many of the others were hit. I'll never forget the horrible screaming of the wounded. I looked over the edge of the ditch and saw the Russians were coming at us from the front and both sides with their fixed bayonets. Bullets were flying everywhere and we were pinned down. I crawled back in the ditch toward the rear as fast as I could and thought I was going to make it when it felt like someone slapped me with a flat hand on my back. I didn't know what had happened, but then I felt my neck and it was badly swollen. I thought my jugular vein was injured and this was the end.

Incredibly my whole life rolled like a short film before my eyes. I prayed and I asked God not to let me die here. At this moment our other Bedford appeared from nowhere loaded with men, most of them wounded. I knew my only chance to get out of there alive was to get on this vehicle. I had already gotten rid of my helmet and belt with the attached gear, which helped a lot. I still don't know where I took the strength from but I got up and went for it. As I came closer the car seemed to accelerate and I yelled, "Hold it, hold it." The driver, ignoring the bullets whistling all around, actually slowed down so the others could grab me and pull me up on the pile of moaning and screaming wounded. Needless to say, we escaped and I am still eternally grateful to that driver for slowing down to save me. I know not too many others would have done this under those conditions.

After a while we stopped and the injured were spread out on the ground behind a building. I remember sitting and leaning against the wall. All I could see was a straight horizontal line with everything above the line snow white and everything below pitch black or vice versa, I'm not sure anymore. Even though I wasn't quite aware of what was going on, I still could feel a bullet under the skin near my right jaw. I don't know how much time passed, but eventually they put four of us in an ambulance and took us to some building. A doctor removed the bullet and showed it to me. It was dented and had to be a ricochet. He wrapped it in some gauze and put it in a pocket of my uniform. In my jacket he found a small hand grenade, which he carefully removed with two fingers.

They laid me on the floor of a tiny room and left me there overnight. I felt awful. I was very thirsty and flies were all over my face crawling in my nose and mouth, but mostly I was so weak I couldn't move at all. In the morning when they looked in on me I had the impression that they were surprised to see me still alive. I was loaded into another ambulance and while driving most of the day in the heat and on bumpy roads I drifted in and out of consciousness. In the late afternoon we finally came to a field hospital, and I believe I wouldn't have lasted too much longer since I could hardly breathe. The doctors there went right to work. They inserted a big needle into the right side of my chest and extracted what seemed like a bowl full of blood. Apparently, this didn't bring down the swelling in my neck and chest. They put me to sleep, and as I found out later, they had made four incisions, each about three inches long, in my neck and chest to relieve the swelling. They were nice enough to write to my parents telling them that I was in critical condition, but they would do all they could to save me.

Fortunately, the swelling of my neck and chest was gone and I was beginning to feel a little better but still couldn't move. After two weeks I was transferred by plane to a large hospital in Taganrog, Russia, at the Sea of Azow. This transfer didn't turn out too well. Another soldier and I, both of us unable to move, were laid on the floor of a Junkers 52 transport plane. There was an empty oil drum on the floor that kept on rolling around and bumping us. We couldn't call for help because the noise in the plane was too loud. We arrived a little more bruised than we started.

The hospital in Taganrog was wonderful; perhaps any hospital would have been great when coming from hell. Sleeping in a bed again with clean white sheets felt heavenly. There were even pretty Russian girls working as nurses. That I noticed them showed that I had made some progress. I found out that I had been wounded on August 8, 1942; until then, I had no idea what day or even month it had been. The doctor told me that the bullet had entered below my right shoulder blade, traveled inside my right lung and neck to my right jaw. He also expressed surprise that I had survived the injury and the whole ordeal.

Two weeks later I was told I would be transferred to Breslau by plane. I was excited that I would go home and be able to see my family. The day came, and early in the morning they took several of us to the airport. Most of us were on stretchers covered only with a light sheet. They put us down on the ground near the plane and started loading. This seemed to take some time. It was still dark and very cool being so close to the sea, so I called an orderly and asked him to put a blanket on me. He did it so well that I was almost completely covered. I saw that the loading was finished and I panicked. I wanted to go home! I yelled as loud as I could in my condition, and then somebody said, "Oh, here is one more." I might have been out of luck if it hadn't been for one of the wounded that went berserk from claustrophobia. They had to take him off and I went in. The plane was another Junkers 52 with bunk beds in the loading bay. Late in the afternoon we arrived in Breslau on a sunny afternoon. It was a beautiful feeling to be home again.

Looking back, my time in Russia had been a sad one, the pain, the suffering, the misery and all for what?

My return to Breslau wasn't exactly what I had hoped for. I thought my biggest troubles were behind me, but I was wrong. I was taken from the airport to a hospital and put in a big room all by myself. I felt frightened because I couldn't breathe and there was nobody around to help. My parents lived so near, if they just would have known. Finally a nurse showed up and administered a shot of morphine. They also notified my parents and they came to see me the next day. Despite my sad condition, we were glad to be reunited again. Afterwards my mother came regularly to visit, as well as my father and other relatives. My mother cut my finger and toe nails and washed me a bit. This alone made me feel so much better.

During the following days the room filled up with more wounded soldiers. In a way it helped, since I didn't feel so isolated anymore. In the meantime the doctor showed up too. Walking from bed to bed with a group of nurses, he kept on reciting rhymes he obviously had made up himself. He seemed very proud of his talent, not realizing that these rhymes were plainly idiotic. One nurse told me later that he had been a doctor in a mental hospital, which explained a lot. Word was that the best doctors were at the front, and I started to believe it. I could see and feel that the right side of my chest didn't move anymore. This came as a terrible shock. It gave me an idea how amputees must feel when they find out about their missing limbs.

I wasn't getting any treatment and didn't have any strength. I was injected with morphine regularly, which was beautiful because it made me feel like I was floating on a cloud. Then the doctor must have realized that he had to do something. They took me to the operating room, and I had no idea what was going to happen.

After lying there, which seemed like forever, the doctor told a nurse: "Puncturing, puncturing" pointing at me.

To my amazement the nurse asked me, " Where?"

I told her, "I guess my right lung."

They had to sit me up because I couldn't do it on my own and the nurse gave me a shot in the back. Then something happened which I wouldn't wish on my worst enemy. He stuck this long thick needle in my back to draw blood out of my lung. Talk about pain, I wished I would have fainted. He tormented me only one more time with the same negative results. I found out later, he probably knew what my problem was, but didn't know how to treat it.

After a while I was beginning to gain a little strength and was able to sit up. With some help, I could take a real bath, which I needed badly. It seemed the dirt from Russia was embedded in my pores. What happened next was an ordeal in itself. They started to wean me from morphine. I wasn't fully conscious, but vaguely remember that I was in agony, drenched in sweat, tossing and turning. The torture, which seemed to go on forever, probably lasted only a few days; however, I recall distinctly that my craving for the drug was so strong that I could have killed for another shot. I certainly can sympathize with drug addicts. In addition to this misery, I had reoccurring nightmares. A black object, like a bowling ball, came hurdling toward my face and woke me up in the cruelest way.

It took all my determination, but one day I forced myself to get out of bed and take some steps. I had lost a lot of weight and I still had a fever. I felt very weak, but I wanted to continue with my walking. It was now three months since I had been wounded, and I knew I wasn't making any real progress. I talked to my father about it, and I don't know how he managed it, but shortly afterwards I was transferred to another hospital. Even though I could hardly walk they put me on a passenger train and sent me off. On the train I became so sick I had to vomit out the window, which was embarrassing.

The new hospital was in the mountains and in a small town named Krummhuebel. Shortly after I arrived there they told me they couldn't give me the treatment I needed. They sent me to another hospital not far away in a town by the name of Schmiedeberg. This hospital was actually a nunnery and most of the nurses were nuns. The first morning after my arrival a doctor, by the name of Bittner, came to see me.

He examined me briefly and asked, "When did you get punctured the last time?"

This question gave me a cold sweat. I told him, "Three weeks ago but nothing was taken out."

He shook his head and said, "No, that's where your problem lies."

Later he looked at me through the fluoroscope and told me his diagnosis was correct. He took me to his office and sat me on a chair backward, told me to hold my right arm up and after counting my ribs a couple of times put the needle in my back. I couldn't believe it, I hardly felt anything. What followed was even harder to believe. He extracted so much pus it would have filled three coffee cups. I saw the pus in two glass cylinders on the table. He said they would give me the best treatment available, but if my body couldn't overcome the infection, there wouldn't be anything else he could do for me. I assume there were no antibiotics available at that time.

I was put in a nice sunny room with two other patients. Their names were Slebitza and Reimann. Slebitza had been wounded in the leg and it looked black. He was one of the few lucky ones who made it out of Stalingrad. Reimann had lost both legs below the knees, from frostbite he suffered in Russia. Two nuns by the names of Dionysia and Consulata looked after us. Dionysia was about thirty years old and pretty. She was our nurse but acted more like a mother. Consulata was very old and didn't do very much. She liked to talk with us and sometimes played a wooden flute. We didn't let on, but we thought it was funny.

I knew I was in bad shape but never believed that I could die. Maybe my attitude helped me to survive. I received the finest care they could give me: the best food, vitamins intravenously and even red wine, mixed with an egg, on a regular basis. Every week I was wrapped in a fur-lined sleeping bag and put outside in the fresh, cold mountain air. The only treatment I didn't relish was an injection of Campolon, which had to be injected into a muscle. Dionysia told me each shot was equivalent to eating twenty pounds of liver. I knew it was good for me, but the pain was terrible. I used to bite into my blanket to keep from screaming.

My mother came to see me on my twentieth birthday, and brought a cake. She didn't have to do this because we had cake regularly and at home they had to live on small food rations. I didn't tell her so because I was afraid I might hurt her feelings. She filled me in on what was going on at home. Breslau had not suffered from extensive bomb attacks so far. Sadly enough more boys from our neighborhood had been killed and apparently my friend Gerhard had been wounded again, this time shot through the arm.

The weeks turned into months and there wasn't too much to do. Fortunately I had Slebitza to talk with. He was very intelligent and I was happy for him that they had been able to save his leg. Reimann was a different story. He shaved three times a day, and to get to the sink, he lowered himself from his bed to a blanket on the floor and pushed himself along with his hands. Slebitza and I didn't dare to question him about his excessive shaving because he went easily into a rage. Sometimes, without provocation, he threw anything he could grab against the wall. I guess these were moments when he fully realized that he didn't have legs anymore. One day entertainers came to town and anyone, who was able to, went to see them. That left Slebitza and me out, but an orderly came in and said to Reimann, " I'm going to take you to the show tonight, so don't forget to wash your feet." We looked at Reimann, but he didn't say anything, and we all started laughing.

One time I was alone with Dionysia and sensed she had something on her mind she wanted to talk about. I didn't know how to react and started the conversation by telling her that I could hear the nuns singing at five o'clock in the morning. She became kind of serious and told me that she had made a mistake becoming a nun. She said she didn't have any privacy at all. The mother superior was reading all her mail, and if she wanted to buy a stamp she had to ask for a few pennies. I became encouraged enough to ask her why she had become a nun in the first place. She said she and her sister loved the same man and he married her sister. She couldn't bear it and thought to become a nun would be for the best. I felt sorry for her, but didn't really know what to say.

After about three months I could tell I was getting better and had begun to gain weight. Slebitza and Reimann had been discharged and I was moved to another room. I joined two other fellows who were both very outgoing. I still had to spend most of my time in bed, but could eat my meals in the dining room. That was a great improvement in many ways. I walked with the help of a cane because I felt very shaky. Sometimes I wondered if I ever would be able to be on my feet for a whole day again.

It was the beginning of March 1943 and I had spent more than four months in this hospital. I still felt weak but was finally able to take walks outside. This was an exhilarating feeling, like being born again. On one of my excursions I had a pleasant surprise. I stopped at a cafe for a cup of coffee and to enjoy the life around me. As a lady at my table got up to leave, I helped her with her topcoat. I couldn't believe it when a few minutes later the waitress brought me a plate of pastries, compliments of the lady. She must have either appreciated my good manners or felt sorry for me and the way I looked. Regardless, I enjoyed the pastries very much. Especially since I was unable to buy any myself not having the necessary food stamps.

Not too much later Dr. Bittner told me that he felt I was ready to be transferred to another hospital for rehabilitation. It was difficult for me to say goodbye. I knew he had saved my life. I had the feeling that I meant something to him too. I thanked him for everything he had done for me with tears in my eyes. I believe to overcome this awkward moment he said to me, "I liked you better when you were thin." I also said goodbye to Dionysia and Consulata and thanked them both. In leaving it really sunk in how fortunate I was to have been sent here; had I stayed in Breslau, the incompetent doctor would have cured me to death.

The new hospital was also located in the mountains, in a resort town named Schreiberhau. There was a large building for tuberculosis patients and two small buildings for patients recuperating from lung injuries. I was taken to one of the small buildings, which housed about twenty-five men. We had a nurse who stayed with us permanently and a doctor who came to examine us once a week. It was April and there was still snow on the ground here and there. It was cold at night but beautiful in the daytime. The pine forest was close by and very often one could see deer grazing. It felt like paradise. I spent a lot of time on the verandah, either playing chess or just reclining in a lawn chair enjoying the fresh air and sunshine.

One day in town I sat on a bench soaking in the action, when an officer in an Africa Corps uniform came toward me. At first I couldn't trust my eyes. It was my lieutenant from Mulhouse. We chatted for a while and I told him my story. He was on leave from Africa and he sounded quite depressed. Apparently the Allies controlled the Mediterranean by sea and air, and he was very concerned about his return. I wished him good luck, but never found out what happened to him.

I got acquainted with a patient from my building whose name

was Hans too. He was very funny and that was something I needed. All of us were happy to have survived, but some weren't exactly in a joyful mood. Hans was from a village by the name of Heuraffel in the Sudetenland, formerly Czechoslovakia. He was recuperating from shrapnel in his lungs. We enjoyed each other's company and spent most of our time together. We took some short walks and even had an occasional beer, something I hadn't had in a long time. He told me a lot about his home in the Bohemian Forest, and I could tell that he was as homesick as I was.

April 20th was Hitler's birthday and every soldier in the hospital received a bottle of claret and a smaller bottle of schnapps. This gave Hans the bright idea to take all of our bottles to a cozy inn we had discovered. The inn was located on a narrow quiet road about a fifteen-minute walk from the hospital. I was not interested in drinking too much, but made the mistake of going along with his suggestion. When we arrived we ordered some beer and the innkeeper had no objection to the consumption of our own alcohol. I do not know why it did not occur to me what disastrous consequences this foolishness could have. I can't remember how much we drank or how we made it out of the inn, only that it was very cold and dark, and that we didn't get very far before we collapsed. I do not think I exaggerate in saying that, considering the condition I was in, it could have been the end of me. Then, as many times before, help came my way. Some girls came by and apparently dragged us back to our building. They worked in the hospital kitchen and had been returning after a weekend at their village. After quite a tongue lashing from the nurse and a terrible hangover, I recovered and told myself, "never again!"

I knew my life of leisure was not going to last forever, but I had hoped it would end with my discharge from the army. Unfortunately, it did not work out that way. In May of 1943, after spending a total of ten months in hospitals, I was released with the order to report to my former unit at Oels in Silesia. I said goodbye to Hans and we promised to stay in touch. He told me if I ever wanted to visit him, he and his family would welcome me. I had no idea at the time what this friendship would mean to me someday. I think it was fate that we met.

I was surprised that my unit had been moved from Mulhouse to Oels, but was glad since Oels was only a few miles from Breslau. After I had settled down with my new outfit, I ran into a guy from my squadron in Russia. He turned pale when he saw me; he told me that everyone had thought I was dead. He had survived for a longer time than me in Russia, but then lost an eye. He said the day I was wounded they incurred close to thirty wounded and dead, including my lieutenant. He also told me that the last of our lieutenants was killed by an artillery shell while riding in the sidecar of a motorcycle. Our outfit moved somewhat farther into the Kuban desert, suffering more losses and eventually coming to a grinding halt. One night, when checking on some outposts, our captain and his aide were bayoneted by a Russian patrol. They found them the next morning. It all ended as I had envisioned.

My squadron in Oels was a reserve unit and a pitiful sight. All the guys were disabled. This became even more obvious at night when their artificial limbs were lying on the table and leaning against the walls. They couldn't really do much with us. After the roll call in the morning we were more or less on our own. Naturally I wanted to go home to see my family and finally got a weekend pass. It was a strange feeling coming home after an absence of seventeen months. Adding to that, my family had moved to a new apartment. I was glad to see that everyone was well and my father was behaving himself. Also, sleeping in my own bed and soaking in a tub was like being on cloud nine.

The right side of my chest had sunk in even more and looked hollow. I didn't feel very strong and easily ran out of breath. In the morning I always had dried blood on my teeth, which I sometimes scraped off with my fingernails. I didn't want to stay in Oels any longer than I had to and hoped that I would be discharged from the army. When nothing happened I decided to take things into my own hands, at least as far as leave was concerned. On Saturday mornings, after roll call, I removed my name from my bed and locker and hitchhiked to Breslau. It wasn't a problem as long as nobody missed me or I was caught out of town without a pass. One time, while riding in a civilian car, I had a close call. I had to get past a military checkpoint on the road. I was lucky they didn't ask for a pass and I believe they were looking for escaped Allied prisoners.

My stay in Oels came to a sudden end, but again not the way I had hoped. They had found out that I was a surveyor and I had to report to another outfit to become an artillery observer. I was angry; after all the misery I had suffered and ending up crippled for life, now I was assigned to the duty I should have had to begin with.

The new unit was located at a town named Schweidnitz in Silesia. This wasn't an easy-going reserve unit like the one in Oels. If I had taken notice, I could have avoided a big mistake. I was there only two days when our platoon had to go target shooting. Along with my inability to fire a rifle anymore, I was upset with the whole situation and just didn't go. To my surprise I was taken into custody, not by one, but by four sergeants and brought before the commanding officer. He shouted at me as if I had committed the worst felony. The way he put it, disobedience like mine eventually leads to rebellion and he sentenced me to fourteen days in the stockade. Luckily, he gave me a chance to answer him. I told him I knew what I did was wrong, but it was because I couldn't shoot a rifle anymore. I moved aside a little cushion my mother had pinned under my uniform and showed him my sunken right chest. I said the recoil from the rifle would put me back in the hospital or worse. He simmered down and said he still had to punish me, but would reduce the sentence to three days. I knew I had to control my emotions in the future, and was glad I got away relatively easy.

The next day I was taken to the stockade. Before entering I had to hand over my personal belongings, my belt, suspenders, even my shoelaces. I was taken to a cell that was about eight by twelve feet in size and certainly not the most desirable accommodation. It contained only a wooden cot, no pillow or blanket. My food consisted of bread and artificial coffee. There were two guards who were at least fifty years old. They looked pathetic and could hardly walk. When I had to use the bathroom or wash myself, they had to go with me across a yard. The hardest part came at night trying to sleep on the wooden cot. My chest hurt quite a bit. I tried to use my cap as a pillow, but it was useless. Each morning a lieutenant showed up to check on me. He treated me like scum and ordered me, among other things, to get a haircut. That wasn't easy in my situation, but of course, I answered each time, "Yes sir," which translates to, "You can kiss my ass."

When I had to use the bathroom again, I told the guards they could let me go by myself, because I wouldn't run away since I was getting out shortly. After that they let me go alone. I didn't know that this arrangement would pay out for me. The first time I went by myself I ran into a guy who looked familiar and sure enough we knew each other from Mulhouse. He asked me what I was doing here and I showed him my missing shoelaces. He asked, "You are in jail, aren't you? And you don't have anything to eat either?" He told me to meet him later at the same place, at a certain time. I was glad I had hidden my wristwatch above my elbow. I had done this mainly so I would know when my sentence was up, but it also came in handy at a time like this. He brought me some margarine and jelly for which I was very grateful. Too bad I never saw him again. I would have liked to repay his kindness.

After counting the hours, I was more than glad when my time was up and I could leave that wretched place. If anything good came out of my stay it was that I had a lot of time to think. I came to the conclusion the only way to get out of the army would have to be with the help of a doctor. I could have kicked myself that something so obvious hadn't occurred to me from the beginning. I didn't look forward to going back to my present unit, but luck was with me. I had a transfer waiting for me to another reserve outfit at Goerlitz in Silesia. I got my belongings back and was on my way the same afternoon.

When I arrived in Goerlitz I could see right away that it resembled the reserve unit at Oels. The guys looked just as pitiful and business, so to speak, was the same. At the first roll call, a fellow behind me answered to the name of Jessenberger. He was wearing a neck brace, and as I learned later, without it couldn't hold his head up. I asked him if he had a brother named Hubert, since I had been good friends with a guy by the same name in the Labor Company. He told me it was his brother and that he had been killed. It made me very sad to hear that.

In order to keep us occupied, in the morning we were split up in two groups, one with men who could walk normally and the other with those who couldn't. Because of my shortness of breath I ended up with the latter and it was almost like a stroll through the woods. I noticed that it paid to have the top bunk bed behind the door. Usually, a sergeant came in pointing his finger at whom he saw first and would say, "You, you, you come with me." To avoid being caught to do work in the kitchen, yard or the like, I was able to bribe, with my cigarettes, the guy in that particular bed to change places.

Before I had a chance to go ahead with my plan to see the doctor, I was ordered to go back to Schweidnitz. They wanted me to become a motorcycle messenger. I thought it was getting more ridiculous every time. I was even too weak to hold on to a motorcycle. At least the company in Schweidnitz saw that I couldn't handle this duty and sent me back to Goerlitz.

In August, judging by what I could see, the army was beginning to scrape the bottom of the barrel. The battle of Stalingrad had ended six months prior with the loss of a quarter million men. My mother told me that in almost every apartment house in the neighborhood someone had been lost at Stalingrad. I thought that this had to be the beginning of the end for Germany.

Back in Goerlitz I didn't wait any longer and went to see the doctor. I let him know I felt very weak and needed better care. He said he couldn't discharge me but would get me transferred to

Breslau, where I could spend some time at home. I was happy with his decision and had made a start on my quest to get discharged. I remained in Goerlitz another three weeks and then was ordered to report at a motor pool in Breslau.

After my arrival there I was ordered to join approximately thirty Russian prisoners who were washing out gasoline and oil drums with water hoses. I was handed two cans of paint, one white and one pink, and I had to paint the letters "O" for gasoline and "D" for diesel on the clean drums. The work was sickening; the fumes were so strong it took my breath away. This was about the worst situation I could find myself in. I went to see the doctor and didn't have any trouble convincing him that I was in the wrong job. He said he would get me placed in a clerical position.

He kept his promise and I started to work in an office. My new assignment turned out to be the best yet. In charge of the unit was a warrant officer by the name of Schlaeger. He was from the Rhineland and a very pleasant person. There were also two soldiers working as clerks and two female typists. The office was responsible for receiving all vehicles coming to Breslau from the southern Russian front, as well as their distribution thereafter. Cars were either sent to repair shops in Silesia or taken apart by Russian prisoners at the motor pool. For an unknown reason the latter received exactly fifty vehicles at a time for scrapping. For the incoming tanks, the decision where to send them had to be made by the Army Headquarters in Berlin.

My duty was as follows: whenever our office was notified by the railroad that a train had arrived with military vehicles, I had to drive to the railroad yard and take a complete inventory, in particular the year and model of each vehicle. For this duty I was issued a nice sedan. Back at the office I had to notify the railroad as soon as possible where to send the individual vehicles. I had a standard list of cars that had to be scrapped; that was easy. For the rest I had to go by the current lists of the different repair shops, which told me what kind of cars and how many they could accept. Each time tanks arrived, Gmuerek, one of the clerks, had to make a call to the High Command of the Army in Berlin. One time when asked to spell his name he became so excited he said, "G like Gustav, M like muerek." Schlaeger said, "What kind of animal is this? Kunert, you make the calls from now on." I felt sorry for Gmuerek, but didn't have a choice. When calling Berlin I usually had to speak with a colonel or higher and had to tell them, "This is Corporal Kunert requesting advice." I had the impression they didn't like talking to a lowly corporal, and I enjoyed their displeasure immensely.

I was very busy, but liked what I was doing. It built up my self-confidence again, which had suffered a lot. It was nice too that I could go home once in a while. On the negative side were the army meals, which consisted mostly of cabbage soup and bread. I lost most of the weight I had gained in the hospital. What was senseless was that we had to get up every morning at five o'clock. At six o'clock we assembled in a large hangar that was extremely cold. A sergeant named Bunk, that was his real name, made the roll call. He sort of jumped back and forth in front of us like an idiot telling us that we had to win the war. Here we were a bunch of sick, crippled and hungry guys. What could we do? It was nauseating. Then we would go back to our rooms to sit around for another hour waiting to go to our work assignments at eight o'clock. Why didn't they let us sleep another hour? I still kept going to see the doctor. I knew he couldn't or wouldn't do anything, but I wanted it to be on record.

One time I put another fifty cars together for scrapping, but discovered one car was missing. Conscientious as I was, I went on a Sunday morning to the lot to count them again. There I saw my superior, Schlaeger, stepping out of a trailer the Waffen SS had stored close by. On his shoulder he carried a box full of groceries. I saluted him and neither one of us said a word. He knew if I talked he would be in serious trouble. I didn't see any reason to turn him in. He had always been very nice to me, and had I been in his position, I might have done the same. For a while he didn't look me in the eye, but gradually he relaxed and we entered into a mutual trust.

Then, something of a different kind happened. Arriving at my barrack after work I needed to go inside to get the garage key. When I pulled my key out of the ignition there was a bright flash. I didn't know what to make of it and went into the building. Usually I stayed in there for a while to warm up; also, one of the guys played the accordion, which was fun to listen to. This time I went outside right away and saw my car lit up inside. I raced back into the building, grabbed a fire extinguisher and managed to put out the fire. The car was a mess, in particular around the dashboard. Even though it hadn't been my fault I was worried about the consequences. Fortunately, my good relationship with Schlaeger paid off. He took care of everything. I didn't even have to make a report.

Almost unnoticed 1944 had come and I had been performing my new duty for three months. I still liked my work and the people around me, but physically I was feeling worse. The cold weather and poor nourishment added to my already weak condition. Then I heard through the grapevine that one could be discharged at Freistadt, a city in Silesia. My desire to be discharged was so strong that I decided to take the chance and go for it. At the first opportunity I talked to Schlaeger. I told him how much I liked working for him, but here was my chance to get out of the army and I hoped he would understand. I asked him if he was in my place wouldn't he want to do the same? I could tell he wasn't too happy, but he agreed. He said he hated to see me go and, as he put it, leave him behind with those dummies in the office. We both had to laugh about that. He said he would talk to the doctor and see what he could do. I wasn't sure if my transfer to Freistadt would work out as planned, but then Schlaeger told me everything had been arranged. Before leaving, I thanked him for all he had done for me and that I hoped someday to meet him again under different circumstances.

Once again I was on my way and I was a little uneasy, not knowing if I had done the right thing. I certainly was going to miss the visits with my family. When I arrived in Freistadt I could see there was no difference between here and Oels or Goerlitz. All the guys were crippled one way or another, and there was a constant turnover. I was sent to a barrack that housed about thirty men. A lot of them played cards day and night and many of them smoked. It reminded me of a low class bar. Like any newcomer I had to be seen by the doctor. I told him that I had come here with the hope of being discharged. He didn't discuss that and I wasn't sure what to make of it. I also let him know that I wanted to get out of the barrack I was in, because the smoke was making me sick. He said he would take care of that. It didn't take long and I was called to the master sergeant. He told me he had an easy job for me and that I could share a room with another corporal. This worked out well, except for the fact that I didn't want a job. I wanted to go home. However, for the time being I had to go along with this arrangement.

My new assignment was similar to that of a doctor's assistant. I had to introduce all the new arrivals to the doctor. If they had medical records, I took them; if not, I had to prepare new forms. I had to tell them when and where to report in the morning. In the waiting room, I let them know in what order to come in and that they had to be in the nude. I also had to make sure their inoculations were up-to-date. In the examining room, the doctor sat in front of me and behind me was a medic waiting to administer shots. Before each man came in I handed the doctor his medical papers and told the medic if or which shots were required. This was a much easier job than the last one. Most of the time I had finished by eleven in the morning and could do what I wanted for the rest of the day.

After awhile I developed a friendly relationship with the doctor and one day I approached him again concerning my discharge. Along with my lung condition I realized I had another reason for a discharge. I told him as a trained technician I could contribute more to the war effort at home. I don't know if he bought this part. However, he told me a group of doctors came to the base at regular intervals to decide who would be discharged. He said he would make the recommendation to have me released from military duty. I told him how grateful I was. It seemed I finally was getting somewhere.

On one of my free afternoons I wandered around in town with another guy. We decided to go and see a movie and while there we got acquainted with two girls. After the movie we invited them for a cup of coffee and had a lot of laughs. By the time we left the cafe it was very dark; there were no lights anywhere because of the danger of bomb attacks. We escorted them to what we thought was the home of one of the girls. They invited us to come in and when inside, still in the dark, I said, "This smells like a butcher shop." They laughed and turned on the light and I had guessed correctly. Looking at all the sausages felt like being in heaven. I made sure that I ended up with the butcher's daughter. In this respect, it was just too bad that I soon had to leave town. Still, a few times I was able to get a taste of heaven, sausages that is.

The day came when the group of doctors arrived and I was called before them. They didn't examine me, only asked a few questions. I could tell they already agreed with my doctor's recommendation. The master sergeant was present and was told to arrange my transfer to the Army Discharge Center at Liegnitz. I was overjoyed and still couldn't quite believe that this was true. The looks I got from the master sergeant were hateful. I knew I had done a good job and perhaps he didn't want to lose me or he was envious. Whatever the case, I never thought he would sink as low as he did.

On my way to Liegnitz I was beginning to wonder where he was sending me; it didn't look right, but I had to follow orders. When I arrived at my destination I saw what he had done. Instead of the discharge center I ended up at another reserve unit. This was one of the biggest disappointments of my life. It made me very angry. The next morning, at roll call, reality hit me even harder. The master sergeant pointed at me and three other soldiers and said, "Oil transport, Romania." I told him there had to be a misunderstanding, I had been sent here to be discharged, and I wanted to see the doctor. That got me off the hook for the moment. The next day I went to see the doctor and I was fortunate. He seemed to be very understanding. After explaining to him what had happened, he said he would get to the bottom of the matter; in the meantime, he would put me on light duty. I found out quickly that light duty meant peeling potatoes. I have to laugh about that now, but at the time I didn't think it was funny. At least it turned out not to be as boring as I had anticipated. There were about six of us sitting around a mountain of potatoes peeling away and each one had war stories to tell.

About a week later I was called to the doctor. He said he had everything straightened out and had notified the office to send me to the discharge center. I felt like getting down on my knees thanking him. When I came to the office to pick up my papers, the master sergeant told me they couldn't let me go because I would be needed at the division headquarters. I felt crushed but there was no other way. I had to go back to peeling potatoes. When I mentioned to the others what had happened, one of them said he had been told the same story four months ago and he was still waiting. I knew I had to work the iron while it was hot. I had talked before with the doctor's assistant, also a corporal, and noticed that he smoked. I went to see him in the evening, taking all my cigarettes with me. He knew my story already and promised to help, if possible. I didn't waste any time and went back to the doctor the next morning.

When he saw me he said, "What are you still doing here?"

That was the cue for my fellow corporal; he said to the doctor, "They don't pay much attention to what you tell them."

As I waited in another room, I could hear the doctor talk in a very loud voice. I don't know what he told the master sergeant; maybe he threatened to send him to the front. In any case, when I came back to the office my transfer was waiting and my bed had already been cleared. I had never seen anything happen this quickly before.

The Other Side of the Coin

When I saw the doctor at the discharge center he looked at my medical history and said, "What took you so long?" I told him it hadn't been up to me. To tell him about my year of misery would have taken too long. I underwent a very thorough examination, which took two days. One of the tests was to determine what was left of my lungs. It turned out that my remaining capacity was sixty-one percent. To see my chest x-ray was interesting too; one side looked dark and the other light. Then the day came I had dreamed about for so long. On May 9, 1944 I was discharged from the army, a date I'll never forget. I was finally free!

ESCAPE FROM BRESLAU

The first few days at home I didn't do anything, just let it sink in that I had survived. My family was extremely happy to have me back, as so many young men never returned. My parents had moved into a new apartment. It was very modern, had a balcony with the view of a park in the distance and was located on a quiet street. They also had acquired some nice furniture. The downer was that Breslau had started to come under more bomb attacks and we didn't know how long we might be able to enjoy our new home.

On my first visit to the Office of Land Management I was surprised by how many changes had taken place. To save on heating, the office had moved into the courthouse. Wunnie, my supervisor, and the other old timers had gone into retirement. Only a few people I had known before were still there and some young men and women had been hired. I told the personnel office I would start work the beginning of June and they agreed.

My next visit was to Mrs. Weiser. With all my moving around I didn't have a chance to keep in touch. She was more worried than ever and for a good reason. Gerhard had been wounded for the third time and this time more seriously. He was being treated at a hospital in the Sudetenland. I tried, to the best of my ability, to make her feel better.

I hadn't seen a movie in a long time and one evening went to a theater. Even before the movie started the screen went dark and an air raid was announced. There were only a few people and no panic. I left the theater to find an air-raid shelter and found the streets illuminated with a strange light. When I looked up I saw all the flares in the sky that had been dropped by the advance plane. I knew they were to give the bombers a better sight of their targets. People had given the flares the name "Christmas trees," in my opinion, not a very appropriate name. I didn't have time to go anywhere because the first bombs were already whistling down. I ran back into the theater and was lucky, because it had a fairly solid basement. With so few people, all had a place to sit. Everyone was quiet and some looked pale. We could hear and feel the explosions, even though they were at a distance. Once in a while the light flickered. I had been under fire many times in Russia and had been able to shoot back, but this was different. One couldn't do anything, a horrible feeling. After about an hour we were allowed to leave and I rushed home to see if my family was safe. Fortunately, everyone was fine and they were thankful to see me again. At this point Breslau had not suffered the terrible destruction of other German cities. Incidentally, any bomb damage was always kept secret by the authorities.

On the bright side, I couldn't help but notice the great number of girls everywhere and very few men. I felt it would be my duty to take care of as many girls as possible to help keep up the morale at home. My good intentions almost ended before they started. I was notified by the army to come for another examination. There was no doubt in my mind that I could be drafted again. This upset me terribly, and I was determined to prevent it from happening. The morning I had to be at the hospital I smoked a cigar and took a very hot bath. By the time I arrived there I felt like fainting. I don't know if this had been necessary, but it didn't hurt. I was declared k.u., which translates into "unusable for war," for a period of twelve months. There was another guy examined the same morning who learned he was going to be drafted again. While waiting for the bus, he told me he had no toes, they had been amputated; without orthopedic shoes he was unable to walk. Water had to be withdrawn from his ribcage regularly. He said he would miss his wife and young child too. He had tears in his eyes. After listening to his story, I knew how lucky I had been.

Soon afterwards I was notified by the Veterans Administration that I had been classified as fifty percent disabled and was issued an identification card. Later on, this card helped me in many serious situations.

The invasion by the Allies had succeeded and one could see the war wasn't going very well for Germany. Nobody in his right mind dared to talk about it, but there were always exceptions. My father was still working for the company that built trailers. He told us the owner of the factory next to theirs had made the mistake of saying, "We can't win this war." He was arrested and executed because of his position; people looked up to him and this kind of remark undermined the war effort.

The way things were going became even more evident with the creation of the Volkssturm. These were units composed mainly of old men and some boys. They didn't have uniforms, but carried weapons. They looked pathetic. In my mind, I could see how they would be slaughtered facing battle hardened troops. In jest, people described them as our most valuable soldiers because they had gold in their teeth, silver in their hair and lead in their bones.

After I had started work I realized what we were doing was unimportant considering what was going on around us, but I didn't complain. I had introduced myself to the young ladies and one of them caught my eye. Her name was Irene, she was 21 years old, blonde, had the bluest eyes and a great figure. What really attracted me to her was her voice; never again in my life have I heard a voice as sexy as hers. I asked her for a date and she accepted. That was the beginning of my first love affair. I found out that she was engaged, but her fiancé was missing in Russia for almost two years and there was no hope for his return. She was living with her widowed mother and two younger brothers. We started to see each other regularly, and when we were together it was ecstasy. When I couldn't see her I was actually hurting.

A few weeks had passed when one of the other girls in the office, named Anneliese, was getting married to a young Air

Force doctor. She invited Irene and me to her wedding. Since Anneliese had three bridesmaids and no escorts for them, her fiancé asked the commanding officer for three young officers to attend the wedding. This worked out well and even the commanding officer came. The wedding day was bright and sunny and all of the couples walked arm in arm down the street to the church. Irene was all in white and looked like an angel. The officers looked very impressive in their gala uniforms and so did the bridesmaids in their pretty dresses. We attracted a lot of attention from people on the street and in passing streetcars. After the wedding many people waited outside the church. I had no idea that Irene's intended mother-in-law, a Mrs. Vogt, was one of them and what dire consequences this would have. She saw how happy Irene and I looked and didn't like it. She didn't waste any time and told Irene to move in with her. In a way, I could understand, as she still hoped her son would return. In addition, she lived alone in a big house. Irene told me she couldn't refuse, and we could continue to see each other. Unfortunately that didn't work for different reasons. Mainly, Mrs. Vogt kept a close eye on Irene and her house was on the opposite side of town. What really made it hard was Irene had been ordered to work in a defense plant located even farther away. It was too bad that I didn't have a car; it certainly would have made a difference. We saw each other a few more times, and I could tell the spark was gone. Irene had become depressed. She said it wasn't easy to live with Mrs. Vogt and her supervisor wanted to get intimate with her. In normal times I would have tried to cut through this Gordian knot, but this wasn't the time, everything was far from being normal.

Our food rations were getting smaller and smaller and meat was especially hard to come by. Then somebody in our house gave us a little rabbit. From the beginning it was understood that eventually he would become a meal. The problem was he was so cute and not only my sisters, but also all of us treated him like a pet. My mother didn't even get upset when he ate the flowers she kept in pots on the balcony. Since we were a "smart" family, we named him "Haesle," meaning "little rabbit." He liked my father and ran around his legs in a figure eight. When my father wasn't home and we wanted to lure him out from somewhere, we only had to hold up my father's pants, and here "Haesle" came making his figure eight around the pant legs. Eventually, he grew fat and thereby spelled his own death sentence. My uncle Kurt, my mother's brother, came one day during our absence and took care of things. All of us were in tears by evening. The following Sunday my mother fixed a great meal of potato dumplings, sauerkraut, gravy and roasted "Haesle." Despite our craving for meat, we didn't touch it, except for my mother. She didn't want to let it go to waste.

We scarcely saw hard candy anymore and my mother had the bright idea to make some. Using sugar and some secret ingredient she created a kind of toffee. It actually tasted very good but stuck to our teeth like glue. As a matter of fact, it pulled out one of my father's fillings. We thanked my mother for her good intentions but let her know once was enough.

After my discharge from the army, I had written to my friend Hans Pressl in Heuraffel, Czechoslovakia and finally received an answer. He was also discharged, living in Vienna, Austria, and enjoying himself immensely. He invited me to visit and mentioned he had two girls waiting, one for each of us. I was sorry I couldn't go. I couldn't ask for leave from the office, since I just had started to work. We decided to try again later.

I definitely wanted to further my education, but wasn't sure how to go about it. Then I learned the Nazis had changed requirements for admission to universities and colleges. In particular, disabled veterans would be accepted by taking preparatory courses. We had a very good technical college in Breslau where I could earn the degree of a civil engineer, and I decided to start school in spring of 1945. Unfortunately, circumstances were against me, and my plans never materialized.

To my big surprise Gerhard called me. He had been released from the hospital and was home on leave for two weeks. He had recovered from a nasty wound, which almost cost him a kidney. To see each other again was very emotional. We had a lot to talk about regarding our recent experiences. He also had a surprise. He had become engaged to a girl from the Sudetenland and she was staying with his parents. We couldn't avoid talking about our uncertain future. He had the rank of a sergeant and a chest full of decorations. For all his achievements, he had been offered to attend officer's school for a period of twelve months. He said he didn't want to go, because he despised officers. I tried to talk him into it, telling him it would get him away from the front and in a year the war might be over. I couldn't convince him, and it was too bad that he didn't listen to me.

I thought he would spend the few days allowed to him with his parents and his fiancée, but he wanted us to get together one more time. He said he would like me to meet his girl and asked if he could bring along his cousin, Irmgard, to make a foursome. I had no objections. I had met Irmgard briefly a few years before and remembered her as very pretty. It turned out to be a very nice afternoon. Gerhard's fiancée was very sweet and Irmgard was a lot of fun. In fact, Irmgard and I decided to meet again. When I said goodbye to Gerhard, he gave me a strange look, which I can still remember today. Maybe he felt that we never would see each other again.

I started to date Irmgard, and we always seemed to have something to laugh about. She was my age, had long blond hair and was usually elegantly dressed. There were still concerts and shows going on and we made the rounds, but mainly we liked to go to the outdoor pools. Breslau had some very nice outdoor pools surrounded by big grassy areas, trees, restaurants, etc., and one usually stayed the entire day. It was a beautiful summer and lying next to each other on a blanket brought us even closer. I just couldn't help thinking this is too good to be true. One day, I noticed a Band-Aid on her arm and asked what happened. When I saw tears in her eyes I lifted it up and saw her teeth marks there. She said it happened last night when she was wrestling with her conscience. She told me she was married. This was quite a surprise, especially since Gerhard hadn't mentioned it. Apparently she had married her husband on the insistence of her parents because he owned a house and had money. He was drafted into the submarine service shortly after their wedding, and there was no true bond between them. She brought it all up now because her husband was on leave in Kiel, at the Baltic Sea, and wanted her to come and join him. She said she didn't sleep all night thinking about our beautiful time together and finally came to the decision to ask for a divorce. This shook me up. I liked her very much, but I didn't want to break up a marriage, especially when I thought about him being in a submarine. I couldn't let her do that, but didn't have the nerve to tell her. I just didn't go into it, and when she tried to reach me at the office, I asked the secretary to tell her I was busy. Later, Irmgard told me she went to Kiel to see her husband and he was behind a fence waiting for her with tears in his eyes. Losing her hurt me deeply, but in the end I knew I had done the right thing.

Whenever enemy planes headed our way, air-raid sirens sounded. Near our apartment was a loudspeaker column, a cone-shaped concrete structure, which gave minute-by-minute reports of approaching planes. One evening a warning was sounded, and I went over to that loud speaker to listen. I had just arrived when the first bombs started falling. I knew I wouldn't make it back to our basement and ran over to a ditch at the park, which had been dug for this purpose. It was about five feet deep and had a zigzag course. When I jumped into the ditch I landed on human waste. It was disgusting. Apparently the ditch had been used as a latrine by foreign laborers passing by. The bombs fell for a long time, and I couldn't get away from the mess. Along with the bombs, shrapnel were raining down from exploding anti-aircraft shells. They were red hot and bounced off the pavement into houses and trees with a loud noise. What worried me the most was it looked like our house was on fire. When the attack was over I found out that a structure behind our street had been hit, causing the fire I saw. I was glad nothing happened to our house and shuddered at the thought that I could have lost my family. With this in mind, it didn't bother me too much that I had to spend a lot of time getting my shoes clean.

Ever since my return from the army I had been thinking about the Oder River and how it would be nice to have a kayak again. So I went to the old boathouse. The owner was the same and he remembered me. We talked and I asked him if he had a kayak for sale. He didn't but gave me the addresses of people who hadn't paid their rent in a while. I was lucky; at the first address was a young lady who said she would sell me the kayak. It actually belonged to her brother, who was missing in Russia, and she didn't think he was coming back. With the sales slip I went back to the boathouse and was very curious to see what I had bought. I was in luck again; it was a beautiful boat: sleek, in perfect shape, and I even loved its colors of maroon and yellow. The following Saturday I went to the boathouse put the kayak in the water and took off. The moment I started going I knew I had made a mistake, as the memories of bygone days overwhelmed me.

At the end of September, I was at the office, when Mrs. Weiser came in. Her eyes were red and swollen and I knew immediately that Gerhard was dead. She grabbed me, pressed her fingernails into my shoulders and cried, unable to control herself. It was heartbreaking. When she had calmed down a little she told me Gerhard had been killed by a sniper's bullet on September 19th. Even though I had been aware that this could happen, I was overcome with grief. Gerhard had been my best friend. I wished that everyone responsible for this terrible war would burn in hell forever.

There was a very solemn requiem held for Gerhard. An empty coffin draped with a flag and a steel helmet was placed in front of the altar. I was too upset at the time to remember the sermon but most likely it contained the usual phrase: the fallen soldier gave his life for "Fuehrer, Volk and Faterland." A lie, Gerhard didn't give his life; it was taken from him.

The Other Side of the Coin

As in every dictatorship, the public is never allowed to hear the truth. However, it couldn't remain a secret that a major offensive by the Russian Army was expected. My sister Jutta was sent with her entire school class, of fourteen-year-old girls, to a town by the name of Freienwaldau, which was to the east of Breslau and close to the front line. There, together with old men, women and boys, her class had to dig a defense system of ditches and tank traps. It was in my opinion a useless undertaking. My parents and Gerda went to see her and found the girls living under deplorable conditions. For example, they slept on straw infested with lice. I have to say my father took a big chance, bringing Jutta home without asking anyone for permission. He most likely saved her from a horrible death. Ilya Ehrenburg, the prime Russian agitator, promised the German women to the Russian Army. This had not been necessary, as they raped and murdered without this promise. It didn't matter to them if it was a little girl or an old woman. Later I spoke with many refugees and saw photos, which I will not try to describe, only to say that they were sickening.

I was surprised when my parents received a card from Guenter Schiewani, my friend from Mulhouse. He didn't know if I was still around, but asked them to let me know that he was in a hospital in Breslau. When I went to see him the next day he couldn't believe I showed up so fast. He had been wounded by several small shrapnel in the upper spine. The doctors had removed all but one. They didn't want to touch it for fear it might paralyze him. This left him with a serious problem. He suffered seizures at irregular intervals, which lasted for a few minutes and left him weak and unstable. I felt very sorry for him. I had the chance to see him only one more time, because later he was transferred to a hospital out of town. He wrote to me that he was helping in the rehabilitation of blinded soldiers. I thought that this had to be a very difficult job; if I would have been blinded, I probably would have gone berserk. After that I lost contact, I never found out what happened to him.

I was at a cafe one Sunday afternoon, when my former sergeant

Richter came in. He was on crutches and I could see that he had lost one leg below the knee. Even though I looked quite different in my suit from my time in uniform, he recognized me and came toward me with a fake smile. I stared at him briefly and then looked away. Seeing him crippled didn't give me any satisfaction, but also, I couldn't feel sorry for him.

My intentions to make as many girls as possible happy hadn't worked out as planned, but I didn't want to give up yet. One evening, I went to see a show and met an attractive, very sporty looking girl. She was my age and her name was Margot. She had been engaged and her fiancé had been killed. Even though I didn't have the strong feelings for her as I had for Irene or Irmgard, I enjoyed her company. She was very mature and we had a lot in common. After a while, it became clear that she took our relationship too seriously. I didn't want this to happen. It wasn't easy to cool things down, but eventually I succeeded. I finally realized I had to put things on ice until life had returned to normal.

One evening, after my father had returned from work, he called us all together. In a lowered voice he told us he had heard from an electrician that they were killing people in concentration camps. He warned us not to say a word to anyone or all of us could perish. As we found out later, what my father told us was true.

The end of 1944 was near and the war looked grim for Germany. It didn't come as a surprise when my office informed me I would be temporarily assigned to the Volkssturm Headquarters. There I found out I was going to work together with a draftsperson, and a military officer would supervise her and me. Our job was to draw and plot defense positions, mine fields etc.; also, to make up organizational charts. The work was easy and there was no pressure. Actually, the officer only showed up once in a while to pick up or deliver our work. Most of the time we sat around and talked.

Christmas came and certainly there was no peace on earth. At least we had a tree and my mother was able to fix a nice Christmas dinner. Presents were scarce, since there wasn't too much anyone could get in the stores. We were glad that all of us were still together, but our mood was solemn. We had the feeling something bad was going to happen, but didn't know what to expect.

Shortly after Christmas I ran into a girl I had gotten acquainted with through Irmgard. She asked me if I was unattached and if so, would I like to go to a New Year's Eve party with her. I said I would. I wished I had stayed home. The party just didn't get going; none of us was in the right mood. They had the radio on and Hitler was making a speech, but nobody paid any attention. When walking home it was very cold and heavily overcast. The whole city was in complete darkness and the streets were deserted. Without exaggeration, the city looked dead. I thought of yesteryears when there was light, music and laughter everywhere. I became even more depressed.

Less than two weeks into the new year, the uncertainty about our future started to unravel. On January 12th the Russians broke through the German defenses and were approaching Breslau. Panic set in. My immediate concern was how to get my mother and my sisters out. I knew getting out on the road with all the snow and terrible cold would be impossible. It had to be done by train. My mother and sisters packed their most important belongings. For my sisters this included their dolls, but I took them out and replaced them with warm clothes. They were not too happy about that, but thanked me later.

I took a risk. I didn't go back to work; instead, I went to the train station to check things out. Trains were still coming, but there was no schedule. The trains that came through carried wounded soldiers or were full of refugees. In addition, the train station had become a madhouse, panic-stricken people everywhere. Despite all of this we had to try. Fortunately, some unexpected help came from Aunt Hildegard, my mother's sister. She was alone and wanted to go with my mother and sisters. Her husband was in the service and her only daughter had been evacuated. Apparently her husband had a lot of foresight, because several months before he had traded her sewing machine for two boxes of cigars. She brought one of the boxes along with the hope of bribing someone. This worked out perfectly and her cigars became a real lifesaver. Hildegard also proved invaluable in coming up with a destination. She said, "We will go to Aunt Marie in Goerlitz." Her aunt had raised Hildegard. Goerlitz is located west of Breslau and it was a safe place, at least for the time being.

At the railroad station Hildegard saw a railroad employee who looked like the right person to ask for help. She was lucky; in exchange for the cigars he told her at which spot to wait and not to move from it. After a while a military train came with three cars reserved for civilians. Hildegard, my mother and sisters all were able to get in before everyone else. They did not know where the train was going. Luckily, they ended up in Goerlitz. I had no idea that we were to become part of one of the most brutal and chaotic mass expulsions in history.

We didn't know if we would see each other again. A train was a favorite target of enemy aircraft, and my father and I faced an uncertain future. The next morning, posted at street corners, were large red declarations that read in essence, "Men of Breslau, as of today I declare Breslau as a fortress. Every man between fourteen and seventy has to stay and fight. Who cannot fight has to serve in support. Anyone who tries to escape will be executed," signed Karl Hanke, Nazi District Leader. I knew if I stayed I wouldn't survive; I had to try to get out. My father was still working, which was hard to believe. I only can guess he didn't fully realize the severity of the situation. I went to his office and told him I was going to leave for Goerlitz. He thought I was crazy and that I would be shot. I said goodbye to him and could only hope that some day we might be reunited again.

I didn't waste any time. I wanted to get out as quickly as possible. I locked things of value in the basement and filled a canvas sack with clothing, documents, photographs and some food. I took my sisters sled, tied the sack to the top and with a rope attached the sled to my bicycle. When I closed the door of our home for the last time, many thoughts went through my mind, but I tried not to let it get to me. I took off in the afternoon and headed for one of the roads leading out of town. Snow was falling and the temperature was below freezing. I found out right away that my plan with the sled wouldn't work. The sled swayed from side to side like a dog's tail. I threw the sled away and tied the sack to the rack, on the back of my bike. I was glad this worked. Then I saw the most tragicomic scene ever. A woman was walking in the middle of the street, with one hand pulling a sled with her belongings; in the other hand she carried a table lamp. She kept on calling out a favorite Nazi slogan, "Fuehrer, give the orders, we follow you."

It didn't take long when the moment of truth came. I found myself in the middle of a great number of frightened people, horse drawn wagons and other vehicles. Everyone was trying to get past a checkpoint manned by Field Police. This outfit was part of the German Army and roughly comparable to the American Military Police. They were better known as "Chain dogs," because they had half-moon shaped brass plates hanging on chains around their necks. Their reputation was similar to that of the SS. I worked my way closer to them, waiting for the right moment to slip through. Then I saw a small bulldozer taking off pulling an open trailer. I thought, 'this is it.' I stepped on my pedals and went after them. I was aware of the fact that at this moment my life was hanging by a thread, had they caught me I most likely would have been executed. I heard someone yelling behind me but I ignored it. I'm sure all that commotion going on helped in my endeavor but I believe it was more the help I got from above. I hung on with my right hand to the rim of the trailer and was guiding my bike with my left hand. It wasn't easy with all the ice and snow on the road. Also, my hands started to get numb from the bitter cold. I just hoped I wouldn't fall. I probably would have frozen to death, like so many others. After a while the two drivers stopped and I found out they were French POW's. I had no doubt they were afraid of the Russians like the rest of us. On the trailer, huddled under blankets covered with snow, were about twenty women and children. The two Frenchmen helped me to get my bike and sack on the driver's seat. Even though it was a very cold spot, it was a lot better than hanging on to the trailer.

After midnight, we arrived at Liegnitz, which is located about half way between Breslau and Goerlitz. I found a movie theater where I could stay the rest of the night. The place was full of refugees, cold and uncomfortable. I didn't get much sleep and in the morning I started to look for some other means of transportation. I saw several fire trucks ready to move out. I approached one of the firemen and asked him where they were heading. Fortunately, they were going to Goerlitz. I told him Goerlitz was the place where I hoped to find my family, and couldn't I sit on top of one of the trucks? At first he said no, but I didn't give up and eventually he gave in and even helped me load my bike. I made myself comfortable among the bundles they had piled up, and I was on my way again.

Shortly before Goerlitz we had to stop. A military column was slowly passing by in the opposite direction. I was curious and made the stupid mistake of looking at them. I should have kept my head down. A lieutenant saw me, came over, and started to question me in a very unfriendly way. After I showed him my disabled veteran identification he hesitated for a moment, then gave me a hateful look and left. I had the feeling he considered me a deserter and would have liked to drag me down and string me up.

Fortunately I made it without any more trouble to Aunt Marie's home. To my great relief, my mother and sisters were there, as well as Hildegard. We felt we had been blessed to see each other again; so many things could have gone wrong during our escape. Aunt Marie was quite old, which wouldn't have been a problem, but she didn't have all her marbles anymore. From the first minute on I couldn't walk upright in the house, because that scared her too much. So the rest of my time I had to walk crouched down. She liked my sister Jutta the best and said to her, "Jutta, you should die. You are too good for this world." By the way, she also slept with a hatchet next to her pillow. At least this gave us something to laugh about.

Two days after my arrival we had the biggest surprise. My father showed up. I don't know how he had managed to get out of Breslau, because he never told us. My relationship with my father wasn't the greatest, but I was still glad to see him. We all considered ourselves extremely fortunate to be together again. However, we were far from being safe. Even though the Russian advance had slowed down, it was only a matter of time before they would reach Goerlitz. We had to do something, but what? Then I thought about the offer from my friend Hans Pressl, to come and see him in Heuraffel. I told my family about it and suggested that we should try to make it there. I would go first and then let them know if they should follow; but if necessary, they should come anyway. Fortunately, at least for the time being, the mail was still working. We agreed and I got ready to leave. Aunt Marie gave me a suitcase to replace my canvas sack, which was a big help. I just wished she had given me the keys for the suitcase. Aunt Marie had no intention of leaving her home and Hildegard decided to stay with her, since she had been like a mother to her. Hildegard also didn't want to go much farther because her fourteen-year-old daughter, Ursula, along with her school class, had been evacuated to Dresden. Sadly enough the entire class perished during the devastating Allied air raid on the city.

Before I left, I looked at Aunt Marie's books and found an atlas with a map of Europe. I removed it and kept it with me for a long time; at least it gave me a rough idea in which direction to go. Once again we said goodbye, not knowing what might happen to all of us.

When I arrived at the railroad station, I was stopped by soldiers who informed me I needed a permit to enter. They sent me to the gymnasium of a school and there was a long line of people already waiting. At the far end I could see a fat Nazi in a brown uniform, sitting behind a table. To the left of him sat his secretary. It was obvious the Nazis had taken over here too, like in Breslau. Finally, I reached the beginning of the line, with only a lieutenant in front of me. He wore his uniform jacket and striped hospital pants. He was asking for permission to evacuate several amputees. The Nazi flatly denied his request and told him, "They (the amputees) still can sit in a trench and shoot." The lieutenant didn't say a word, turned around and left. I knew that I had to do some fast-talking and definitely wouldn't give up that easily. I stepped forward and saluted him properly with "Heil Hitler." I showed him my disabled veteran identification and asked him for a permit to enter the railroad station. I said to him I was alone and wanted to join my family in Heuraffel, which, of course, was a lie. He wanted to brush me off, but I didn't move. I told him about my lung and in particular that I still brought up blood from my wound, which was true. I added I badly needed care. For whatever reason, he said angrily to his secretary, "Give it to him." I was very glad to have passed this hurdle. With all the excitement of the last days, I hadn't paid any attention to what date it was. Then I saw on the permit that it was January 29th, 1945.

I had left the house in the morning and when I finally returned to the railroad station it was late in the afternoon. There were quite a few people, but still no train schedule. It was very cold standing on the windy and icy platform. I was fortunate; after about an hour, a freight train came slowly rolling into the station and close to where I stood. First there were mainly flatbed cars full of old men, women and children. They were sitting on the cold floorboards and under blankets covered with snow. Then a few boxcars came along and one of them had an open door.

Running next to the car I yelled, "Where are you going?"

People standing at the door shouted back, "We don't know, maybe Dresden."

Since I couldn't be choosy, and Dresden sounded perfect, I threw my suitcase into the car and jumped. Someone grabbed me and pulled me inside. Still today, I wonder how I didn't kill myself. While running on the ice-covered platform, I had to jump over the opening between the platform and the moving train. All this while being almost frozen stiff and wearing a long topcoat.

The train actually went to Dresden, which was great. With the help of my map I saw that I needed to go west to a city named Plauen and then south to Pilsen and Budweis in Czechoslovakia. I didn't know yet how to get to Heuraffel from Budweis, but I figured I'd find out when I arrived. I just started to look for the right train when the air-raid sirens sounded. Everyone tried to force his way into the nearest bomb shelter, and I managed to get in too. No bomb attack came and I went back to search out the right train.

I didn't know how fortunate I had been, because a short time later, to be exact, between March 13th and 15th, the city of Dresden was burned to the ground. For three days and nights American and British bombers hit the city with incendiary bombs, creating huge firestorms and killing about 200,000 people in the most gruesome way. In addition to the citizens of Dresden, the city was filled with refugees trying to flee from the approaching Russian Army. Since the city had no military value and the war was practically over at this point, I cannot understand this slaughter of mostly innocent women and children. The man largely responsible was British Air Force General Harris, better known as "Bomber Harris." The British erected a monument to his honor that I find hard to comprehend.

The atmosphere at the railroad station reminded me of the one in Breslau, frightened people everywhere. After a long search I located a train that was going to Plauen. Some of the train windows had been knocked out and people tried to get into the train that way. I decided to squeeze through the door, but afterwards was surprised that I still had all the buttons on my topcoat. On the train it was common to hear family members asking each other at certain stops, "Shall we get off here or not?" I personally thought it would be the best to go as far west as possible. I arrived in Plauen just after a bomb attack, because some nearby buildings were still smoldering. Fortunately, the trains were moving again.

I didn't have too much trouble locating a train going to Pilsen, and I even managed to find a seat. I arrived in Pilsen dead tired in the morning and was glad to find a small hotel. The rooms weren't heated, but I didn't care; I just went to bed with all my clothes on.

The train for Budweis left in the evening and when I came to the station I saw the passengers all huddled together. I learned the Czech Underground had started to take pot shots at Germans. Fortunately, nothing happened and I made it safely on the train. I found a seat and had fallen asleep when a flashlight shining in my face awakened me. It came from two Gestapo Agents, Nazi Secret Police. Even though I hadn't done anything wrong, it made me a little nervous. I had to identify myself and was glad I had the permit from the Nazi in Goerlitz. After that rude awakening I couldn't sleep anymore, but it didn't matter because Budweis was close, and I had to get off that stop.

No lights were allowed on the train and the train station was just as dark. When I saw who I thought was a train conductor, I asked him how to get to Heuraffel. He said he wasn't a conductor, but a naval officer on leave, and both of us had to laugh. However, I was fortunate again. He told me he was getting on the same train I had to use and I could follow him. It was a small train, which moved slowly uphill and stopped on top of a ridge. When we got off, the officer gave me directions and said it would take more than an hour of walking to get to Heuraffel. I couldn't carry my suitcase so far and he suggested I leave it at one of the houses near the station. He said the people here wouldn't steal anything. I thanked him and told him how grateful I was for all his help. I left my suitcase at one of the houses and started to walk.

It was a beautiful night. The air was crisp and clear. The Moldau River below looked like a silvery tape and as far as the eye could see were snow-covered evergreens glistening in the moonlight. It all looked so peaceful, and it seemed unreal that not far away all that killing and mayhem was going on.

I arrived in Heuraffel late at night and everything was dark. It took me a little while to find Pressl's house. I felt really bad waking everyone up and barging into their home at that late hour, but I didn't have any choice. I had hoped my friend Hans would be there to greet me, but instead I met only his parents and three sisters. They told me Hans had been drafted again and they didn't know where he was. I was very disappointed and sorry to hear this. I was only glad his family knew about me, which made me feel somewhat better. They said I could stay with them as long as needed. I let them know that I was sending for my family, and once they arrived, we would have to find a place for all of us.

The next morning, my priority was to retrieve my suitcase. Pressl's youngest daughter, who was about ten years old, came along with her sled. We picked up the suitcase and everything seemed to be in order. A few days later I found out that this wasn't so. The people had taken the box with my photographs. This hurt me a lot, much more than anything else they might have taken. The photos were irreplaceable. It was useless to go back; I didn't have any proof.

I had a better look at Heuraffel in daylight and should describe it because of the events that followed. Heuraffel was a small village whose houses were strung like pearls along a road, which ran parallel to the Moldau River. On the westerly side of the road, meadows rose up about 200 feet to where the forest started. On the easterly side were meadows and farmland stretching about 500 yards from the road to the river. On the other side of the river was nothing but forest.

My next task was to find living quarters for my family and myself. I had to talk to the local Nazi official. I went to see him, explained my situation and told him what I needed. He said he was expecting refugees, but the available living space was reserved for people from Vienna. That angered me. I told him we were already homeless, but as far as I knew nobody had arrived yet from Vienna; besides, we didn't intend to stay there for long. He finally gave in and promised to take care of us. I have to say, he kept his word. I didn't waste any time and wrote to my parents to come, along with a description of the route I had taken.

The following days I tried to become more familiar with my surroundings. Since I was like a red dog in the village, I didn't have any trouble getting acquainted with people. Like the Pressls, most of the villagers owned a small farm and certainly weren't wealthy. However, that didn't seem to bother them-they looked happy. While wandering around I met a very pretty girl named Maria, who was my age. As it turned out, she was Pressl's neighbor. We would go for walks and afterwards her mother served us sandwiches. This was great, as I hadn't had enough to eat for a long time and was always hungry.

One morning, something very disturbing happened. I was at the Pressl's house looking out the window when I saw three SS soldiers with approximately thirty men walking by. The men were clad in what looked like gray striped pajamas, and I thought these must be concentration camp inmates. By this time Mr. Pressl had seen them too and went into a rage. He grabbed a hatchet and wanted to go after the SS soldiers. His wife and two of his daughters hung on to him like burdocks, and I got into the act too. Luckily, we managed to calm him down. It would have been useless to attack three armed soldiers and could have gotten all of us killed.

I didn't quite understand why Mr. Pressl became so infuriated. The first chance I had I asked Mrs. Pressl about it. She told me her husband had been a soldier in the German Army during World War I and was captured by the Russians. After the war ended, he stayed voluntarily in Russia and became a communist. Eventually, he returned to his home in Heuraffel. When Hitler invaded Czechoslovakia, Mr. Pressl helped communists escape to the Soviet Union, which proved to be costly for him. The Germans found out about his activities and put him into a concentration camp. Apparently, he suffered dreadfully during this time. Once, in winter, he and others were taken outside, stripped naked and had water poured over them until they turned into living icicles.

Most of the men died, and it was a wonder that he survived. After hearing his story, I could understand why he acted the way he did.

Not too long after this episode, another group of people came walking down the road. They were Hungarians fleeing from the Russians. They had horses and wagons, but most of them walked. Their women were extremely attractive, and most of them wore expensive fur coats. After two days, they came back again, apparently not knowing where to go. I felt very sorry for them. Even though my own situation wasn't much different from that of the Hungarians, my thoughts were on my parents and sisters. The days went by and I didn't know if they had received my letter and hoped if they didn't, they would come anyway, as we had planned. Then something completely unexpected occurred, a policeman came and handed me an order to come for a medical examination at a military hospital in Budweis. I couldn't believe that. How could anybody know about me in this little corner of the world? The only explanation I could come up with was that somebody reported me to the authorities. No matter what, I had to go. This time I didn't have a cigar nor could I take a hot bath. I only could hope for the best. When I came to Budweis, I found out I had worried needlessly. The doctor seemed to like me. He looked at my papers from Breslau, which showed I was classified as "k.u." for twelve months. He gave me a quick check-up and sent me home. I had the feeling, regardless of my condition; he knew that for all practical purposes the war was over.

One afternoon, in the middle of March, my family arrived. We were overjoyed to see each other again! They said they never received my letter and waited; but then the Russians came very close and they decided to come anyway. Also, their trip took longer since their train was re-routed to the city of Bautzen and stalled on account of the air raid on Dresden. At night they could see the glow of the burning city. Once again we counted our blessings; all of us could have been incinerated there.

I went back to the Nazi official, and he saw to it that we could move in with a couple by the name of Lebke. They were kind people who seemed to have an understanding for our predicament. We moved into the second floor of their house. The whole floor consisted of one big room with no furniture, only a wood burning stove and some shelves. It didn't bother us. We were happy to be together again and safe for the time being. I picked up my belongings at the Pressls and thanked them for their hospitality. They said as soon as they heard anything from Hans they would let me know. I knew they were very worried; he was their only son.

We had a place to stay, but we needed about everything else. Mr. Lebke gave me a few boards and loaned me some tools. I built frames for beds and filled them with straw. The Pressls and Lebkes loaned us a table, chairs, some pots and a skillet. My mother was able to fashion curtains from paper we found. Our main problem was to find food. We still could get a few groceries from the store, but this wasn't enough to live on. My father surprised me; he was able to acquire some food from the farmers. He wandered all over the neighborhood, and it was ironic to see him go begging in his sharp looking topcoat and his stiff Homburg hat. I did my part too, which included learning to catch fish.

There were "L" shaped jetties in the river, and the water between the shore and the jetties was less than two feet deep. Mr. Lebke had a flat-bottomed boat tied up there, which I was free to use. I found a three-pronged fork with a long wooden handle I could use as a spear. Lying on my belly, I gave the boat a push and it glided slowly enough so I could spot fish hovering on the sandy bottom, usually next to a rock. Spearing them was no problem, but since the fork didn't have any barbs, I had to keep the fork with the fish firmly in place against the river bottom and then reach down into the cold water with my other hand to bring the fish up. This was tricky, since the boat didn't always remain in place. After a while I became quite skillful and brought home three or more fish each time. I have to say the fish were usually not longer than twelve inches, but it helped to put food on the table.

We could tell the war was getting closer. A couple of times very fast, low flying American planes whizzed over our area, and we could hear them shooting at something in the distance. One day, my father and I had quite a scare with one of these planes. It sounds strange perhaps, but there wasn't a lot of firewood on our side of the river, and every week I paddled across the river to collect wood on the other side. That day my father was with me when one of the planes came at high speed down the valley. My father wanted to run, but I grabbed his arm and we remained next to a tree. I had heard the pilots had started to shoot at everything that moved, and I knew they couldn't make out a person standing still. On another day, when collecting wood, I found a small hedgehog and brought him home. He was so cute; we all fell in love with him. We wished we could have kept him a little longer, but he kept us awake at night. When he ran around it sounded like he wore wooden shoes; also, he made a lot of noise by playing with whatever he could find.

Then the inevitable happened, artillery fire echoing in the mountains, first from the west and then from the east. There was little doubt we had ended up between the American and Russian forces, and there was no way of escaping. All we could hope for was that the Americans would arrive first. For a couple of days it became very quiet and we could cut the tension with a knife. Then, looking out the window, I saw them-American infantry. What a relief! I felt like going out and kissing them. First the infantry came, then jeeps with mounted machine guns, followed by tanks with more infantry. They acted very cautiously with good reason. Not more than thirty minutes after they had passed, gunfire erupted. I later heard that they had run into a die-hard SS unit.

We considered ourselves very fortunate for the way things turned out. Then we found out we had been even luckier than we had realized, as the demarcation line between the American and Russian forces was at Friedberg, a small town, only two miles up the river. By a hair, we could have ended up under the Russians.

As many times before I thought a good angel must have been looking out for us.

The Americans started to set up a temporary prison camp between the road and the Moldau River. I don't know where all the German soldiers came from, but eventually there were several hundred of them. One day two American GIs came to our house with some German prisoners. They asked Mr. Lebke for a stack of long wooden poles he had leaning against the house. They needed them to outline the prison camp. One of the prisoners came over and asked me if I knew how far away the Russians were. I told him, and I could see how grateful he was for this information.

Interestingly enough, of all the people I knew, he was the only one I met later in Bavaria. He told me he and two other prisoners fixed their sleeping spot next to the river. In the middle of the night they put their clothes on top of their heads, floated down the river and escaped. I let him know that this saved his life, because the Americans handed over all the German prisoners to the Russians from the camps along the Moldau River.

I continued to see Maria and during a visit to her house, an American sergeant came in. Maria must have caught his eye and he asked her if she wanted to go with him for a ride. She definitely had no intention of doing this and asked me to get her out of this bind. I knew I had to be careful because I could tell he was drunk.

While I was talking to Maria he interrupted and said to me, "You, German?"

I said, "No, Slovak."

This was not the time to show true colors. I finally convinced him that Maria was my wife, and he left mumbling something. I was glad to have gotten out of this tight spot unharmed.

Another situation arose which was much more serious. My mother had made friends with the lady in the house next to us. She lived there with her old father and a fourteen-year-old daughter. She told my mother that on occasion, American soldiers came looking for whiskey and possibly more in the evening, and that she was afraid. So, my mother generously offered my services for

"Protection!" This might not have been too much of a problem, but the woman was hiding her eighteen-year-old son, a member of the former SS Division Hitler Youth, in the attic! I could hardly refuse, but I went there with mixed emotions. One evening three American soldiers came in looking for alcohol, and I was able to convince them that we didn't have any. During the entire time of our conversation I hoped and prayed the young man in the attic wouldn't make any noise. That could have gotten all of us into serious trouble.

One morning, we heard they were giving away sugar at the store, and I went there in the hope of getting some. As it turned out, there was no sugar or anything else. Walking home on the road, I saw a great number of GIs sitting high up on the edge of the forest. When I was in front of them, I heard a lot of shouting and then the soldiers began firing their guns over my head into the river. I hit the ditch on the opposite side of the road and crawled along until I was out of sight. I knew they weren't shooting at me, but I could have been killed just the same. When I came back to the house my family told me that the war had ended. That explained the shooting, their form of celebration. The date was May 8, 1945.

The following day I asked Mr. Pressl what he thought might happen now. He said with the German Army defeated, the Czechs are going to take over. He suggested we get out of Czechoslovakia as fast as possible. He added he wouldn't be able to protect us. I'm sure he knew, more than the rest of us, what to expect.

We didn't need to know more and started packing. Someone gave us an old wooden cart with oversize wheels to carry our belongings. In the morning we said goodbye and thanked everyone for all their help. I had the feeling Maria didn't like to see me go, and found out later I had guessed correctly.

We were now alone and on a journey into the unknown. We were worried about falling into the hands of the Czechs, where to find food and a place to sleep, but mainly we didn't know where we would end up. It was helpful that the weather was nice, but it was still a struggle getting up the mountains. As it always goes, on the first day our cart broke down, and we had to start carrying our belongings.

We found out we weren't entirely alone. We saw small groups of refugees here and there, all heading west. In the evening, we came to a farmhouse and the farmers let us sleep in the barn and even gave us some bread and water. This charity soon ended when more and more people showed up and farmers barricaded themselves. In a way, I couldn't blame them; not everyone was harmless. On our second day in the woods we met a former German soldier named Herbert. He asked if he could join us and offered to help carry our belongings. This helped considerably, since none of us felt too strong. The same day, we met a lady with a small daughter and they accompanied us for a while. She had escaped from Bruenn, a city in Czechoslovakia, and she told us about the atrocities committed by the Czech mob. Among other killings, she had seen how wounded German soldiers were thrown out of four-story high windows. In addition, she warned us about roving bands of released concentration camp inmates.

It became clear, under all circumstances; we had to avoid being caught in the open. The test for this came very quickly. As we headed west through the woods we came to a paved road we had to cross if we wanted to stay on our course. We couldn't see too far up the road in either direction, and I suggested we remain in the forest for some time to see if anyone passed. I was glad everyone agreed, because we didn't have to wait very long and a pick-up truck came along carrying Czech militia. They wore civilian clothing with armbands and they were armed with rifles. To play it safe, we decided to wait a little longer. It seemed the Czechs came by about every hour. Keeping an eye on the road from a safe distance, we searched for a crossing where the forest on both sides of the road narrowed. We found such a place and when the moment was right we hurried over a meadow to the other side and practically dove into the bushes and trees.

During the following two days we remained in the forest. We

were lucky again to find shelter and some bread. I honestly don't know how we managed to keep going on an empty stomach. Also, without a map of the area, we probably walked a lot farther than we actually had to. Sometimes we joined up with other refugees, many needing assistance. We helped whenever we could, like helping a mother push her baby's carriage. It was always sad to hear the different stories people had to tell. Most of them were about rapes and killings, losing loved ones and not knowing where to go. One time a woman asked us if we wanted a nine-year-old boy who had been separated from his mother. She said she wouldn't abandon him, but she was struggling to keep herself and her own children going.

We had one more road to cross under conditions similar to the previous ones. It sounds perhaps selfish, but I was glad we were not with too many other people at the time, just with Herbert and two older women. We took our time again and made it safely to the other side. The only mishap we had, before we reached the other side of the forest, was that one of the women lost her shoe in the mud. She wanted to retrieve it, but we pulled her with us into the bushes. She said she needed the shoe badly, because it was one from the only pair she had. I took a good look around, and when I thought it was safe, I ran back and picked up her shoe.

Shortly after, crossing one more road, we reached Austria. This was quite a relief. We left the forest behind, which made walking much easier. It took about two more days, and we entered the city of Passau in Bavaria. We were back in Germany. What a wonderful feeling. I only can guess that our trek had taken us eight days. At any rate, we were safe now, but our future looked uncertain.

The authorities in Passau had begun to help refugees the best way they could. We received some bread and soup, something which didn't happen a minute to soon because our hunger had become almost unbearable. After that we were sent on a truck to a former youth hostel about forty miles north of town. The effort of the authorities had to be more than appreciated, because this was only two weeks after the war had ended and Germany had been destroyed like no other country before. Considering how we had lived the previous weeks, the youth hostel was paradise. We could sleep on a mattress, take a shower and got a little to eat without having to beg for it. There were already other refugees present. Most of them were from the Ukraine and all highly educated people. My thoughts went back to Lvov, and I could understand why they had run away from the Russians.

All of us questioned each other as to where they were from and if they knew anyone from the other's hometown. It was astonishing how much valuable information was exchanged this way. Somehow we found out that two of my mother's sisters, Gertrude and Erika, had made their way to a village named Grottenholz, which was located only about twenty miles away. This was just mind-boggling.

We knew we couldn't stay at the youth hostel forever. So I decided to be a scout again, to check out Grottenholz and, of course, surprise my aunts. Herbert wanted to go with me and I was happy to have him along. We said goodbye, and were back on the road again. The population still had a heart for the army and because Herbert was still in his uniform, he didn't have much trouble getting something to eat. In contrast, I didn't fare that well with my unkempt appearance. Herbert handled that problem in a funny way. He begged first for himself and after he had gotten some food, he asked, "Don't you want to give some to my brother too?" This worked most of the time. It was too bad that soon I was going to lose Herbert for good.

The first evening we came upon a village where we hoped to stay for the night. As we approached we met an old man and asked him for advice. He was very helpful and even offered to let us stay in his barn. On the way to his farm he pointed out a large square-shaped grave that was covered with evergreen branches. He told us we had been very lucky that we didn't come three days earlier, the reason being that nearby the American Army had found the bodies of concentration camp victims. The SS had tried to burn the corpses but hadn't succeeded and only managed to cover them lightly. The Americans stopped all the male refugees coming through and had them clean the bodies and rebury them in this mass grave. In the process, the refugees were kicked and beaten by the GIs. There was very little justice in this world, I thought, as once again the wrong people were being punished.

It was a beautiful spring day when we went on our way in the morning. The sky was blue, birds were singing and everything looked so peaceful. Unfortunately, this tranquility didn't last very long. We had been walking along the edge of a forest and, when we came to the end, we were looking into the barrels of machine pistols belonging to two GIs. They told us to strip down to the waist so they could look under our upper arms. I knew the reason for that, because the SS had their blood group tattooed there. When they didn't see anything, they let us get dressed again; however, they checked our belongings. Nothing was taken from me, but they kept two or three small items from Herbert. After that they let us go on. Even though my pretty spring day was ruined, I felt very lucky to have gotten away unharmed. Herbert was angry that these gangsters; that's what he called them, had taken some of his things. I told him he should realize that they could have shot us on the spot.

In the afternoon, as we walked on a paved road, we found a dead rabbit. It was still warm, so we carried it with us in the hope of making a meal of it. This turned out to be a good idea. Down the road we came to a picturesque farmhouse. It was white with a red tiled roof, sitting on a hill with a lake below and surrounded by forests of evergreens. The whole scene looked like a beautiful painting. We went inside and asked if we could stay in their barn overnight and roast our rabbit in their kitchen. They said this was fine. Herbert skinned and cleaned the rabbit and I could tell he had done this before. The kitchen was spic-and-span, and the way we looked, we felt a little out of place. The couple that owned this farm had three children, two girls and a boy, all in their teens. The parents looked normal, but the two girls were mentally retarded and the boy's arms and legs were too short. Herbert fixed our rabbit and they let us eat it in the kitchen. This was the first time in weeks that I had some meat, and it seemed like a delicacy. We even had some entertainment, of sorts. The older girl looked like the main character of a German puppet show by the name of "Kaspar." Her skull was too narrow and she had a hooked nose. While we were eating she was sweeping the floor and off and on passed gas. Every time it happened, Herbert said to me, "Did you hear this? Kaspar farted again." Of course, I had to laugh and was afraid they might throw us out.

We left early in the morning and hoped to make it to Grottenholz the same day. Around noon we entered a village that reminded me of Heuraffel, because the houses lined both sides of the road. Since we were hungry, we went to the first house to ask for something to eat. The door was unlocked and nobody seemed to be home. We didn't want to go in and give the impression we were burglars. When we turned around we noticed a small brick smokehouse. Hoping to find some sausage, or anything edible, we looked in and saw a big basket full of eggs. Herbert raised his index finger and said, "Because we didn't find any sausage we are going to take some eggs." As we continued walking up the road we saw a group of people coming after us. We couldn't run with the eggs in our pockets. This situation could have been laughable if it wouldn't have been for that mob on our tail. At this moment, out of nowhere, an American officer appeared in front of us. He wanted to see our identification. After he had looked them over, he told Herbert that he had to stay and join some more POW's, whom we now could see behind some houses. I was allowed to leave. I noticed the officer's little dachshund had the German Iron Cross, the medal for bravery, dangling from his collar. I couldn't help thinking that this was adding insult to injury. When the people behind us saw what was going on, they turned around and left. I said goodbye to Herbert and we wished each other good luck. I never saw or heard from him again. Neither of us had an address.

I continued walking and hoped I would make it to Grottenholz that same day. I missed Herbert, not only that I was alone, but because I had lost a good friend. The landscape became more forested again, which made it a little harder to find my way. I had to ask for directions more often and got a kick out of the Bavarian dialect. I remember being told to go, "Umi, abi or fueri." Still today these words are like Greek to me, but I appreciated people's helpfulness. I must have understood enough, because I made it to Grottenholz in the evening.

I didn't have much difficulty finding my aunts. They were stunned when they saw me. Gertrude had her young son with her, and I knew that British forces had captured her husband in June of 1944. Erika was with her two young sons, but she had no idea what happened to her husband. We had a lot to talk about, mainly of our escape and how lucky we had been to survive. Except for Hildegard, none of us knew where the rest of the Heimlich family was. They mentioned how skinny I had become, which didn't surprise me. I believe I didn't have one single ounce of fat left on my body. I told them where we were staying and that we might want to come to Grottenholz. They thought that would be great, and they gave me the advice to contact the mayor.

In the morning I felt as if I was back in Heuraffel, as I tried to secure living quarters for all of us. The only difference was that this time I had to talk to a mayor instead of a Nazi. I didn't expect to find much cooperation, but was pleasantly surprised. The mayor didn't have the usual anti-refugee attitude. As a matter of fact, he said Bavaria needed fresh blood, but added I should keep his words under wraps. We both had to chuckle about that. He told me in most of the villages there were only two or three family names and there was too much inbreeding. Remembering the family I met the previous week, in their beautiful farmhouse, I had to agree with him. He filled out a form that I was to take to a local farmer. He said the man had a small empty house near his farmhouse, which we could use. I thanked him very much and went there.

I experienced quite a different reception at the farmhouse. The farmer, his family and laborers were having lunch at a huge table. Despite the great size of the table, there wasn't much space left which wasn't covered by food. I told him why I had come and gave him the mayor's paper. He stood up, raised both arms and lamented, "Us poor Bavarians, first you were real Nazis and now you come to us." I was in no position to argue with him, but couldn't help telling him that Hitler started on his road to power in Bavaria and not in Silesia. I had the feeling I should have kept quiet, because he probably didn't even know there was a Silesia. Looking with my empty stomach at the table full of food, I wondered who of us was poor? However, I was glad that he agreed to let us move into the empty house.

Gertrude and Erika lived in a house which belonged to a young widow who seemed to be a friendly person. I saw she had an old bicycle and asked if I could borrow it. She didn't have any objection, and I took off the next morning to get my family.

Even though it took me quite a few hours to get back to the youth hostel, bicycling was a lot faster than walking. I informed my family about what to expect in Grottenholz and everyone agreed we should go. They felt sorry to have lost Herbert, but we knew it would have happened sooner or later. Luckily we found a bus going to Straubing, a city near Grottenholz. I was able to tie my bike to the rear of the bus. We still had to walk another two hours. This wouldn't have been long under normal circumstances, but for us walking was becoming more and more difficult. Aside from being weak, we had to carry our belongings and our socks and shoes were torn and coming apart.

When we arrived in Grottenholz there was an emotional reunion of the three sisters, which lasted for a while. Then the farmer gave us the key and we moved into "our new home." Again, it was more or less like Heuraffel. The house had a stove, but that was about it. We slept again on straw, and my father and I made the rounds trying to find something to eat. For washing clothes and bathing ourselves, there was a clean small creek nearby. Since there were bushes one could strip down and be hidden from view. Somehow we found a cooking pot without a lid. This helped quite a bit, especially when we were lucky enough to get some potatoes, eggs, etc.

There were a lot of chickens running loose, and I tried to trap one. I collected kernels of grain and made a trail leading into the house, and as I had hoped, a chicken wandered inside. The problem was to catch it, because it fluttered around in the room making a loud noise, and I was afraid someone would hear it. I finally caught it, killed it with my pocketknife and my mother prepared it. It tasted good, but then again everything will taste good under the circumstances. We just wished we had a cover for our pot, as we often found earwigs and other bugs in our food. To make matters worse, we didn't have any shelves. Everything we possessed, including food, had to be left on the floor, and since we didn't have chairs, we also had to eat sitting on the floor.

The only one of us who had some fun was my sister, Gerda. She adopted four very small ducklings, or should I say the ducklings adopted her. They followed her around wherever she went, and she had names for each one of them. I was happy for her. Our whole life was pitiful, and I felt especially sad for what my sisters had to go through.

There was another refugee family by the name of Kersandt in the village, who had arrived before us. They were a husband, a wife and a teenage daughter. Mr. Kersandt looked and acted like a true gentleman and certainly was out of place in Grottenholz. He had been a dealer at different gambling casinos like Baden-Baden, Monte Carlo, etc. and hoped eventually to work in a casino again. We got together quite often and had some interesting conversations. One day he told me he was going to Straubing with his landlord and asked me if I wanted to join them. I was glad to get this opportunity, since I wanted to go there some day anyway and it spared me that long walk. It turned out the horse and buggy ride was fun and looking at the peaceful countryside made me forget my sorry life for the time being. Straubing was a nice little town, and I enjoyed my visit there. I checked out the railroad station, because I knew someday we would need to use it. I bought a newspaper to find out what was going on, since where we were living was like being on the moon. It was only too bad that being in town made me aware that we had run out of the money we had salvaged from Breslau.

Time just seemed to crawl, nevertheless it was already August 1945, and we knew we couldn't stay in Grottenholz any longer. According to the paper, as well as what we had heard from other sources, there was no chance of going back to Breslau at this time. We had to find a big city where we could work, make money and possibly start a normal life again. The question was where? I don't remember why we decided on Stuttgart. Maybe staying in Bavaria didn't seem to be a good idea, because the Bavarians always had hated the Prussians, or maybe we knew Stuttgart had a nice location and was a larger city. I still had it in my mind to get as far away from the Russians as possible, and Stuttgart was almost as far west as we could go.

We told Gertrude and Erika about our planned departure and destination and promised to let them know how things worked out. I said goodbye to Mr. Kersandt and his family and he asked me to keep in touch with him. We packed up once more, this time hoping to make it to Stuttgart.

In the morning we dragged ourselves back to Straubing and to the railroad station. There were a few more refugees, but no more panic like before. We hoped to get on a freight train, one that went in the right direction. After several unsuccessful attempts, we found an open boxcar on a train going to Nueremberg. By the time we arrived there it was very dark, and we ended up in a railroad yard. Someone had made a fire from old lumber and we settled down nearby, prepared to spend the night on the ground. If we hadn't been so miserable in every possible way, it would have been rather romantic. Then out of the dark appeared a woman, and after talking with us for a moment, she invited us to spend the night in her apartment. It felt like a present from heaven.

We followed her, and for the first time we saw the horrible sight of a bombed city. Breslau did have some damage from bomb attacks, but nothing compared to what we saw here. We walked down a street full of rubble. There was only a small path, and we were forced to walk behind each other. Once in a while we saw the forefront of a house. The moonlight shone through the empty windows and it looked ghostly. Except for a hungry cat, there was an eerie silence. Finally, we arrived at the lady's apartment. The house was one of the few still standing in the area. She had enough beds, which was wonderful after sleeping on straw for months and we had a chance to wash ourselves as well. In the morning we thanked her for her kindness and told her we were sorry that we couldn't show our gratitude any other way. I'll always remember her for what she did for us.

We left early in the morning and went back to the railroad yard. We were able to get on a train going to Frankfurt. This was a lucky break, because it was getting us closer to Stuttgart. This time we rode on a flatbed car, again with other refugees. It wasn't too comfortable, but we had an unobstructed view of the countryside. We stopped for a while in the city of Wuerzburg. A few more people came aboard; they told us about the horrific destruction of this historic city during the last days of the war and that still now, months later, more bodies were being found in the rubble.

We continued on our ride along the lovely Main River with the little towns and villages along its banks. Getting closer to Frankfurt, the train stopped near a grove of apple trees. Our stomachs were grumbling from hunger, and the apples looked so mouth watering, that a few of us jumped off and started to pick some. Because of what happened next, I really believe in my good angel. In my eagerness to get the apples and make it back to the train in time, I wasn't paying attention to anything else, and yet I turned around for no reason. Behind me stood the owner of the orchard with a wooden club raised in the air ready to hit me over the head. We looked into each other's eyes for a second, and he lowered the club and told me to get lost. I could understand his anger, but not to kill someone over a few apples!

It was nighttime again when we arrived in Frankfurt. This time there wasn't a good Samaritan to take care of us. We ended up in an empty building and had to sleep on a tiled floor. Since I was very uncomfortable, I woke up at dawn and walked around a little. Just then I saw a big suitcase standing near the railroad tracks. There was nobody in sight, and it was tempting to take it, but I decided against it. We probably could have used whatever the contents might have been, because we were looking more ragged by the day. My biggest problem was my right shoe. The sole had come loose, and to keep it in place, I had to tie string around the whole shoe periodically. This in itself was a problem, since I had trouble finding enough string.

After a long search, we found a coal train headed to Stuttgart. People were already sitting on top of the coal, and we were desperate enough to join them. I was glad it didn't take too long to get to Stuttgart, because we were hungry, dirty and near the end of our strength. I assume because of the number of refugees who had arrived before us, there was a Red Cross refugee assistance center. They gave us some soup and took us to a large, mostly empty five-storied building. We were placed in a room on the top floor. Everything looked very depressing, but no matter what, we were glad to have arrived at our destination.

THE EASTERN GERMAN PROVINCES

LEGEND
— Germany's Borders
▨ Territories taken from Germany in 1945

Note: The city of Breslau is now known by the name of Wroclaw

A NEW LIFE IN STUTTGART

The building we had been assigned to was all gray inside and out. Supposedly, at one time, it had been a place for homeless people. It couldn't have been more fitting. In any case, it matched our mood. Our room housed about a dozen people and we shared one bathroom and one toilet. The bathroom was actually a former kitchen, and we had to wash ourselves at a sink and there was little privacy. We slept on metal beds with mattresses, which were not very clean. The five of us occupied one corner of the room and we had to share it with a woman who was filthy. She was the only one in the room who made absolutely no effort to clean herself. We just hoped to get out of this dump soon.

Our building was one of three that were grouped around a fenced-in yard. As ridiculous as it might seem, there was a guardhouse. The guard's name was Rueckert. He was a native of Stuttgart and about thirty years old. There might have been other guards but he stands out in my mind because of his kindness. I was still wearing the same shoes with the loose soles. In addition, I had run out of socks quite a while back. One day Rueckert looked at my feet and saw my dilemma. He must have felt sorry for me and he brought me a pair of shoes. The shoes were black and had open cracks on the outer side of each shoe, which made my little toes visible. Even though they didn't quite fit, they were a vast improvement over my previous pair. Later on I found some black shoe polish and painted my toes black so my skin wouldn't show through.

What happened next had nothing to do with my newly acquired shoes. I knew I had an infection on the back of my right heel which, most likely, had to do with not wearing socks. Under the circumstances I was unable to do anything about the infection. Then I noticed a painful swelling in my right groin and to lessen the pain I started to drag my leg. There was a small hospital nearby, and I went there hoping to get help. To my surprise the hospital was empty, with the exception of a young doctor with one arm missing, and a nurse. When he saw my heel he told me I needed help immediately. He said it would be painful since he didn't have any anesthetic. I had to lay face down on a gurney, tied up with leather straps and given a napkin to bite on. He dug into my heel with tweezers and pulled out a solid clump of pus. I was glad he had given me the napkin. He gave me a little piece of soap and told me to put some soap shavings in water and bathe my foot. He apologized for not being able to give me something more appropriate. I must have had a strong immune system, because my heel improved.

By now there were at least some places where we could receive soup and bread regularly. It meant standing in line for long periods of time. No doubt, we had become the poorest of the poor.

The physical discomfort in our lives was bad enough, but what was even worse was the realization that our chances of returning to our home in Breslau seemed hopeless. Our feeling was best described by what Euripides once wrote, "There is no greater sorrow on earth than the loss of one's native land."

At the conferences in Yalta and Potsdam, Roosevelt, Churchill and Stalin had decided to divide Germany into four occupied zones: American, British, French and Russian! Berlin, the capital of Germany, located in the Russian zone, was divided into four sectors corresponding to the four zones. The East German Provinces of Silesia, East Prussia and Pomerania had been put under Polish administration. We couldn't believe that more than ten million East Germans would not be allowed to return to their homes or would be driven out from where their ancestors had lived for hundreds of years. It wasn't enough that over two million innocent women, children and old people had perished under the onslaught of the Russian Army-we had to be punished even more. I can't understand why this unbelievable cruelty inflicted on so many people is unknown in the United States. I only can think of the saying, "History is written by the victors."

On the broader scale, Roosevelt and Churchill gave Stalin control over Eastern Europe from the Baltic to the Black Sea. This meant putting tens of millions of people under Stalin's rule, a dictator even worse than Hitler. By conservative estimates Stalin already had the blood of twenty million of his own people on his hands. It didn't make any sense to eliminate one dictator and favor another. The consequence of this decision is well known-the Cold War.

Despite everything, we had no choice but to keep on going with our lives. I was surprised about my father and how he hung in there. Looking more like a skeleton, he was always trying to find a way to better our situation. I was trying my best too, but without success.

While walking in town one day, I was approached by a young lady. She asked if I knew how she could find out about locating her brother who was a POW of the French Army. I told her that to my knowledge there was a French Liaison Officer in Ludwigsburg, a town nearby, who might be able to help her. I showed her how to get there by commuter train. I only mention meeting her because of an incredible event, which took place a short time later.

Not a moment too soon we learned that the city of Stuttgart had opened an employment office and had begun to give out food stamps. My father and I went to register. We were told to come back every Friday, and if there was a job available we had to take it, otherwise we would not be eligible for food stamps. I have to add they were fair in the respect that they handled white and blue-collar workers separately.

My first job interview in Stuttgart was an experience I won't forget. I could feel the hostility from the interviewer before we even started talking. He let me know there was no way he would hire a "foreigner" and told me I should go back to where I came from. I know if I hadn't been in such poor physical condition, I would have punched him in the nose. Having lost my health, my home, my relatives, my friends, my job through no fault of my own, I had to listen to his insults. Later on I was glad I had restrained myself. I just told him I certainly wasn't here by choice and that he should consider himself lucky not to be in my shoes (literally).

Not too much later I had a similar experience. My father found out that the Stuttgarter Police Department was forming a new crime unit, which was going to consist of two detectives, a photographer, a fingerprint expert and someone who would take measurements and draw sketches of crime scenes. I was more than qualified for the latter and applied for that position. In contrast to my first interview, the man acted friendly and accepted my application. He told me to return in a week. The following week he said no decision had been made yet and I should come back the next week. I could read the handwriting on the wall, but went back again anyway. We sat down and before we could talk he was called outside the room. My folder lay open on the desk and I leaned over to read a remark in red I had noticed. It read, "Can not be considered; is not a child of this land." I just walked out; there was no doubt they didn't want us. I had already played with the thought of leaving Germany, but now it became my goal.

The food stamps we received weren't enough to live on but they were definitely better than nothing. With a little more food in our stomachs we felt somewhat stronger and started to concentrate on finding a better place to live. Stuttgart has a very unique and pretty location. The city is surrounded by high hills, and on account of this fact the bomb damage was relatively small compared to other German cities. This gave us hope that we might find something better than our current living quarters.

While we were still lingering at the shelter, I had something happen to me, which I'll never understand. I was in bed at night and was trying to fall asleep when I felt a gentle breath on my face, which seemed to come from very far away. It was so unreal; I had no idea what to make of it. Then it struck me, it was September the 19th, the day my friend Gerhard had been killed. Because of the dramatic changes in my life, I had not thought about Gerhard in months. In other words, I had no logical explanation for this occurrence.

Something similar happened to me about twenty years later. I was living in America and Gerhard was far from my thoughts. Then one night, while sleeping, the melody of the song, "I had a good comrade, you can't find a better one" came into my mind. In Germany it is the traditional song played at the burial of a fallen soldier. Still very sleepy, I tried to get it out of my mind and couldn't, which made me almost angry. Finally, I went back to sleep and had forgotten about it by morning. I remember it was a Sunday and while my family was still asleep, I sat at the kitchen table with a cup of coffee. Then I looked at the wall calendar and saw it was the 19th of September. The melody of last night came back to me, and shook me up so much that I had to cry.

My father's roaming around paid off. I don't know how he did it, but he managed to get permission for us to move in with a Stuttgarter family. We were all excited about getting out of the dismal place we had been forced to endure for three months. The new apartment was located on the fourth floor of an apartment building. It consisted of four rooms, a kitchen and one bathroom with toilet. We were allowed to move into two rooms; the rest we had to share with the apartment owners by the name of Greiff. We learned the man of the house had been a high-ranking SS Officer who was interned at a camp for war criminals. We were to share the apartment with his wife and three children. It certainly wasn't an ideal situation, nine people living together in such a small space, but we were glad anyway. In the following years there was friction, but we tried to get along with each other the best we could.

One time, while standing in line for soup, I became acquainted with a guy by the name of Horst. He had escaped from the

Russian Zone and both of us faced the same problems. We liked each other and started to meet regularly. Once, when discussing our circumstances and the lack of money, Horst had the bright idea to play postal service, because at the time there was only mail delivery within each zone. We followed up on the idea to deliver mail to the British Zone. A small cafe had opened in the center of town where with food stamps one could get some cake and a cup of artificial coffee. We got permission from the waitress to let people meet us there. I'm sure Horst's good looks had something to do with her approval. We pinned handwritten posters on strategic places downtown, which read in essence, "Two businessmen traveling to the British Zone will take and return mail. We can be contacted at Cafe "X" at a certain date and time." This worked out better than expected, as quite a few people showed up. The majority of them wanted to find out if their relatives or friends had survived the end of the war. We charged five Marks to mail a letter and one hundred Marks for a return letter.

If I had known how this trip would turn out I wouldn't have gone. I don't want to describe every detail of this undertaking, only the highlights. We started off one morning with the intention of taking care of our business and then coming straight home. Hitchhiking, we made it the first day to Heidelberg and the following two days to Frankfurt and Fulda. I believe it was on the way to Kassel that we had to cross into the British Zone. We didn't have a permit and had to circle through the forest around the British checkpoint. Once in the British Zone we faithfully mailed our letters. Our first stop for a return letter was Kassel and our next destination was Bielefeld. The trip so far had been a pain in the neck. Drivers were reluctant to pick up hitchhikers, and we had to sleep mostly in overcrowded and smoky former bomb shelters. In addition, there was the problem of finding something to eat.

When we arrived in Bielefeld we had to get a return letter from a man whose wife wanted him to come back to her in Stuttgart. He told us he had no intention of returning and asked us to wait outside for his reply to her letter. The man lived in an apartment house and Horst had been looking at the bell knobs with names at the entrance door. He said he recognized the name of a girl living there he knew from the Air Force and he went to find out. When he didn't come back I checked and saw he was already in bed with her. This surprised me, but not so later on, when I found out that Don Juan had been a kindergarten teacher compared to him. Our two remaining stops were the cities of Hamburg and Kiel. Horst asked me to give him a couple of days and he would meet me at noon at the city hall in Hamburg; if this shouldn't work out, at the same hour and place in Kiel one or two days later. For more reasons than one I should have quit at this point and returned to Stuttgart. Most likely it was my conscience, which made me go on.

When I arrived in Hamburg I was surprised to see so much destruction and was told that during one air raid alone over 45,000 civilians had been killed. Hamburg was a larger city than I had expected and it took me a while to find the house where I had to go for the return letter. Consequently, I missed my meeting with Horst. This didn't bother me too much, because I had my doubt that he would show up. I thought to save time it would be better to go on to Kiel.

Kiel didn't look much better than Hamburg. Most of the inner city was destroyed but the city hall was one of the few buildings still standing. I took care of two more return letters and that concluded my task. Naturally I was curious to find out what had happened to Irmgard, my first girlfriend. I went to her house and saw it, as well as the prison, both still intact. Her mother answered the door and recognized me right away, but acted very cool. She said Irmgard wasn't home and she didn't know when she would return. I told her to tell Irmgard hello and left. I knew I didn't look very presentable, but still had hoped to be invited in for a moment. Well, that closed another chapter in my life.

It was too late in the day to go to the city hall and possibly meet Horst there, so instead I looked for a place where I could stay overnight. This turned out to be a real problem. There wasn't anything except the usual air-raid shelter and this one was a madhouse. It was full of drunken sailors and the smoke was so thick that one could have cut it with a knife. Since the curfew for Germans was 10 p.m. I needed to get off the street. That's when I had the idea to go to the nearest police station. That worked, as they let me sleep in a holding cell, but told me I could do this only once and try not to make it a habit. The next day I went to the city hall, and as I had expected, Horst didn't show up. As I walked down the street aimlessly I passed a girl and we both turned around at the same time looking at each other. I was amazed; she was the girl who had asked me how she could find her brother, just a short time before, in Stuttgart. This was unbelievable. Stuttgart and Kiel are both large cities and hundreds of miles apart. She told me that the advice I had given her had worked out perfectly and that her brother was coming home soon. She asked me where I was staying and after telling her I didn't have a place, she invited me to stay with her and her mother. Her mother didn't have any objections and even invited me for supper. This was very generous, especially since they probably lived on meager food stamps. When leaving the next morning I thanked them for their hospitality and gave them a kitchen knife I carried around with me. I couldn't show my appreciation any other way and thought this was something they could use.

    I decided not to waste time on Horst and I headed for home. Hitchhiking again, it took almost a whole day to make the short distance from Kiel to Hamburg, and I felt I could do better by going back on a train. I found out about a passenger train going to Hagen, which was more or less in the right direction. The ticket was very inexpensive and I soon could see why. People were even hanging on doors, and I had second thoughts about the whole idea. Fortunately, the British had a compartment of one car reserved for disabled veterans, and once inside I even found a seat. I was thankful to the British for doing this. In general I found the British

Troops to be polite and professional. Still it was amusing seeing them walking arm in arm with their German girlfriends and their shouldered rifles.

It was dark when I reached Hagen. For monetary reasons I decided to continue my trip on a freight train. I had gotten the direction to the freight yard and walked along a long dark street in the middle of nothing but ruins with not a soul in sight. I began to worry about going in the right direction when I saw the light of the one and only house in the area. I knocked on the door and got the surprise of my life. There were about five scantily dressed girls all laughing and urging me to come in. I had no doubt that they thought I was a prospective customer. I was sorry I had to disappoint them, but they were very nice and told me that I was on the right course.

At the yard I found a train loaded with coal and supposedly going to Frankfurt. This was perfect and I climbed on. When daylight broke the train slowed down and started to make a wide left turn. Some fellow traveler said, "We are going to Hanau." I didn't want to lose sight of Frankfurt and made a snap decision, one that could have turned out disastrously. I threw my belongings off the train, climbed down the rungs and jumped. By that time the train had started to pick up speed, and I tumbled down the embankment like a sack of potatoes. I was more than lucky because I walked away without any injury, promising myself never to do anything that foolish again.

I made my way to a main road and was able to flag down a man in his car with an attached small trailer. I couldn't blame him for not letting me ride in the car, because of the way I looked, but he did let me sit in the trailer. The trailer consisted of a wooden box that had two wheels and apparently no springs; it rattled every bone in my body. I was very grateful anyway, because he took me all the way through Frankfurt and to the road exit leading south in the direction of Stuttgart.

I waited there almost all day before I caught another ride. Two guys in a small pickup truck let me get in the back of their truck.

They had mounted behind the cab a modified water heater and the truck was apparently running on steam. I had to sit close to the heater and on top of their "fuel," namely a pile of wood chips. The smell of the heater made me nauseous; in addition, it was raining, I was dead tired and hungry and wondered how I had gotten myself in this whole mess. Around nine o'clock we stopped in Neckarsulm, a small town close to Stuttgart. They invited me to join them at an inn and bought me something to eat. I was very thankful for their kindness. However, they couldn't take me any further, as they were driving on to Bavaria and had a permit that allowed them to be on the road after the ten o'clock curfew.

Since I didn't have a permit and didn't want to be arrested by the American Military Police, I resorted once again to seeking help from the German Police. This worked out fine but in a very unusual way. The police gave me a note and told me to take it to a nunnery. I thought this was something, as not too many guys can say, "I slept in a nunnery." When I arrived there a nun checked my paper carefully through a small opening in a very heavy door before letting me in. She led me to a room, which had two metal beds, one of which was already taken by another man. He was in his fifties and seemed to live there permanently. This puzzled me and I tried to start a conversation, but he didn't answer. The next morning the nuns gave me some soup and bread and I thanked them and went on my way. The sun was shining and after a good night's sleep I felt a lot better. Stuttgart was close by and I made it home the same day. Horst showed up about a week later. Even though he let me down I didn't harbor any bad feelings. Nobody had forced me to take this trip.

On my next visit to the employment office they had a job waiting for me. More refugees were coming to Stuttgart and the city needed to make a survey of the available living space. I joined a group of about thirty men assigned to a certain part of town. We set up headquarters in an empty store where we could pick up and return our daily assignments. Two man teams did the work. One did the paper work and the other took measurements and drew floor plans. Of course, I ended up with the latter. My partner was about my age and a good-looking guy.

It was interesting work, talking to the different people and more so listening to their stories. We worked fast, neither one of us wasting too much time on details. That meant we usually finished at noon with our assignment. Unfortunately, we had to deliver our work at five o'clock, and even though we took turns, it was inconvenient. Then I got a lucky break. One morning we climbed up the stairs to the attic of an apartment house and a girl was standing at her door waiting for us. She was very pretty and wrapped only in some silky garment. She waved her hand at us and said with a sexy voice, "Hello there." I could see my partner's eyes pop out and had an idea what might happen. My assumption was correct and from then on he went to see her every noon. He also volunteered to deliver our work in the afternoon, which meant I didn't have to come back at five o'clock anymore.

Another time we went to a mansion owned by an elderly lady who lived there with her maid. When she saw me she became very excited and told me I looked like her son who had been killed during the war. She ushered me to his room and showed me his photo. I didn't think I looked like him but didn't have the heart to tell her. Probably because of my appearance she asked if I needed anything. I needed just about everything but didn't want to take advantage of her. I only asked if she could spare some socks. She gave me three pairs, which were a big help, because I didn't have to darken my toes anymore. As I left she asked me to come back to see her. I never did and thought later that I should have. I knew it would have made her happy.

In connection with our job, we passed quite a few bombed out apartment houses, and as sad as it was, it was still funny to see toilets or even a bathtub hanging on a wall. A serious situation arose when adults as well as children tried to pull the copper pipes out of walls to sell to scrap dealers. It didn't take much for some of these ruins to collapse.

Our apartment was located on Rotenberg Street. We could see

all the way down Reinsburg Street, which was opposite the front of our building. By orders from the U.S. Authorities, the Germans living on Reinsburg Street were given two hours to move out, leaving all their belongings behind, so that concentration camp survivors could move in. It didn't take very long and the new residents started a black market business with the German belongings. I don't know what caused the following ruckus; I only can guess that it had to do with the ongoing black market. Anyway, we saw German Police on the street and all kind of objects raining down on them. Then shooting erupted and a man was killed. Eventually two American tanks with soldiers came and restored order. None of this made a dent in the black market business. As a matter of fact, with the American GIs and their cigarettes, it flourished even more.

I knew there weren't many men from my school class still alive, but one day while walking in town I ran into one of them. This was quite a surprise. His name was Bauer and he had lost one arm during the war. He seemed a little uneasy and I found out why. He took me to a secluded place and opened his briefcase. It was filled with sheets of food stamps, hundreds of them. He gave me a few and said not to tell anyone that I had seen him. I assured him he didn't have to worry and he disappeared. I never saw him again and assume he just had been passing through Stuttgart that day. I was glad to get the food stamps but sorry that we couldn't spend a little more time together.

Considering what our family had endured, all of us had stayed relatively healthy, although I could tell I was still bleeding occasionally from my lung. I didn't pay much attention to it because I felt there wasn't much anyone could do. Then one morning my sister Jutta felt sick and went to see the doctor. When she hadn't returned by late afternoon I went to the doctor's office. I learned she had been operated on for acute appendicitis. This made me furious and I let them know what I thought about their callousness by failing to notify her family. I raced to the hospital, which was underground in a former bomb shelter. She was in the

The Other Side of the Coin

only bed in a large, cold, musty smelling room with bare gray concrete walls. One dimly lit light bulb dangled on a cord from the ceiling. There was not a soul in sight. The whole scene looked almost surreal. I felt so sorry for her and also quite helpless. After her release from the hospital she suffered from complications for a long time, but eventually healed completely.

Christmas came and it was sad. We were thankful to have a roof over our head and something to eat, but our thoughts were with our home in Breslau and if we ever would see it again. It seemed our status had changed from refugees to expellees. We wished we would have had at least a Christmas tree, but this was impossible. There were very few trees available and people actually were fighting over them.

The small food rations we received for our stamps left us always hungry. That seemed to be a mass punishment for Germany. I can say this, based on my personal experience, I saw GIs burying their leftover chow while hungry children watched through a fence. Natives who hadn't been bombed out were the lucky ones, because they could trade their valuables for food. That of course, made the farmers very rich and cartoons of the day showed chandeliers and Persian rugs in cow stables.

The black market was already in full swing when I decided to become involved. My mother gave me her last piece of jewelry and I traded it for two cartons of Lucky Strike cigarettes. In the beginning I dealt with cigarettes only; later I added coffee, nylons or whatever, but never anything that could get me in serious trouble. I slowly built up my capital until I could skim money off and was able to buy some food at black market prices. For example, one could get an egg for 50 Marks, a loaf of bread for 500 Marks and a pound of butter for 1000 Marks. To put things into perspective, my father and I each received about 300 Marks unemployment money per month.

Then I got a real break. I found out that the U.S. Army had a personnel office. I went and applied for a job. To my surprise I was hired immediately; obviously the Americans didn't care that I spoke with a Prussian accent. My office was located in a U.S. Army base on the outskirts of town. The setting was very nice, mainly because it was surrounded by forest. Before I started working I was questioned intensely by three U.S. service men who seemed to be special agents. I wondered about this at the time but later understood the reason for the interrogation. I was paired with another German by the name of Lautenschlager. He was a mechanical draftsman, a native of Stuttgart and a funny guy. We worked directly for two colonels by the names of Willis and Rodgers and for a general. A sergeant by the name of Bernie Knowlton was the go-between. Occasionally we had contact with the two colonels, but never with the general. Colonel Willis had a blond secretary who was German and Colonel Rodger's secretary had dark hair and was French. Both girls looked more like models than secretaries.

I felt like I had entered a different world and it fortified my intention to leave Germany, hopefully for the United States. There were more military personnel on our floor, and there was discipline, but the whole atmosphere was very relaxed. This was all so different from the army life I had known. Every noon we were served a wholesome meal, which was fantastic. With my family being hungry I just wished I could have taken some food home. Unfortunately, it was impossible. When we left the base in the afternoon the guards at the gate frisked us, and if they found any food on us, we had to leave it at the guardhouse.

Our job consisted mainly of preparing maps for different purposes, designing charts and exhibits and a variety of related jobs. I began to understand why I had been so thoroughly interrogated. Many times we worked on maps needed for maneuvers in which American, British and French forces participated. One time we even made a map for General Lucius Clay, U.S. military commander of Germany. What was interesting were the orders for relatives of the U.S. forces telling them what to do in case of a Soviet attack; also, that every bridge in the U.S. zone, and probably in all of West Germany, had been prepared to be blown up. Even though all of this was unknown to the German population, everyone knew that there was no love lost between the West and East. Actually, we hoped that the United States would take on Russia because that seemed to be our only chance to go home again.

We must have been doing a good job because more than once Bernie told us that the General said, "This looks very, very good." This was probably to Bernie's benefit too because he brought us Coke, pastries and cigars, something he didn't have to do.

As far as eating was concerned things got even better. The cook had to make a drawing of the inner portion of a kitchen truck. He had no idea how to do that and asked if we could help him. We fixed him up with a nice layout and he was very happy. He wanted to pay us but we told him we would rather have something to eat. That worked out very nicely because we could come to the mess hall any afternoon and eat leftovers.

Getting all this food was great but didn't help my family. For this reason I continued to buy and sell cigarettes and coffee. I had established a certain number of steady customers, which made things very convenient. My friend Horst had caught on to the black market business, except that he went wholesale. He bought boxes full of cigarettes from a GI who even delivered them in his jeep. After packing them in suitcases he smuggled the cigarettes across the border into the Russian zone. He carried some vodka with him to bribe the Russian border guards in case they should stop him. I think he was lucky that he never had to test this theory. Once he made it to Berlin he sold the cigarettes to a German banker and made a profit of about 300 percent. Another guy went with him and Horst invited me to join them. I declined, thinking it was not a good idea. I didn't want to lose my job and especially didn't want to take the chance of getting caught by the Russians.

At work I became acquainted with a German janitor who had confided in me that he used to be in the Waffen SS. He told me he saved himself from certain death by burning his arm with a red-hot iron so his tattooed blood group wouldn't give him away. He showed me an ugly looking scar. One day one of my customers asked me if I could sell a ring for her and she asked for 2,500 Marks. It was a very pretty ring, gold with two rubies set on two snakeheads. I asked around and was lucky-the janitor said he knew the right person. Of all people, he took me to a Jewish lieutenant. I thought this was something else, a former SS man dealing with a Jewish officer. I could tell the lieutenant liked the ring but didn't want to give me the twelve cartons of cigarettes I asked for. He opened his officer's trunk and the top inlay was full of rings, bracelets, watches etc. He said he really didn't need the ring. Nevertheless, after a little more haggling we made a deal and agreed on ten cartons. Since he could get a carton of cigarettes for one dollar at the PX and I could sell one carton for 350 Marks on the street, we both were satisfied. I gave the janitor one carton and the lady the 2,500 Marks and both were happy. I cleared about 700 Marks in the deal, which wasn't bad considering my monthly salary was 500 Marks.

Horst was doing business with a storeowner in Ehningen, a small town near Stuttgart, easy to reach by train. I went with him a couple of times and was able to trade nylons for some bread and lard. I mention this because of what happened shortly afterwards, something that would change my life completely.

The war had ended a year before and life in general was getting better little by little. My sister Gerda had started to attend middle school and the students received a daily breakfast of oatmeal and cocoa. Churches were distributing clothing, which they had received from American churches. My mother was lucky and was given a winter coat, something she badly needed. In the pocket she found a note that said, "This gift comes from friends in America who have a heart for your suffering." It was signed, Henry J. Dirks, Minister of the Lutheran Church in Akron, Iowa.

Another cafe house by the name of Cafe West had opened near us. Horst and I decided to check it out. At a table near us sat a young woman dressed in black, obviously a widow. She was writing post cards and didn't pay any attention to her surroundings. I couldn't help looking at her because with her dark hair and blue eyes, I found her very attractive. Horst noticed her too, especially when she walked away, one could see her nice figure. Most likely I never would have seen her again, but fate must have played a part in the following events. When I met Horst a few days later he told me that he had gone to Ehningen again and had met the good-looking widow on the train. Knowing Horst it didn't surprise me that he managed to make a date with her. What surprised me was that Horst invited me to join them at Cafe West. I could only imagine that he had taken on more than he could handle, since he was already involved with a girl.

I went to the cafe but Horst wasn't there and as a matter of fact, never showed up. I introduced myself to the lady and learned that her name was Elfriede, like that of my mother. She didn't seem too disappointed about Horst's absence, only a little angry at being stood up. We talked for a while and I could tell that she liked me. I knew I didn't have to worry about hurting Horst's feelings when I asked Elfriede for a date. She said she would like to see me again and hoped that I would show up. We had to laugh and I assured her that I was not like Horst at all.

The following Sunday we met at four o'clock at another cafe and talked until closing. Having talked to her before made everything a little easier. I told her more about myself while gazing into her blue eyes. I also noticed that her complexion was darker than that of most Germans. I found this very alluring. She had been born in Stuttgart and had a brother two years her senior. Their parents were divorced when she was three years old. Apparently her mother couldn't take care of her children so, relatives in Herrenberg, a small town near Ehningen, raised Elfriede. She told me she had lost her husband the previous year and that she had a three-year-old daughter, who stayed with the same relatives who had raised her. That explained why Horst had met her on the train; she had been on her way to see her daughter.

She let me know that she had worked as a dental assistant before her marriage and seemed to be bitter that because of her situation at home she had been cheated out of a higher education. This story sounded similar to my own. She was a refugee herself. After having been under bomb attacks in Stuttgart for two years, she and her daughter were evacuated to the eastern Sudetenland. In May of 1945, after residing there a short time, the Russian Army was approaching and she decided to flee with her daughter. She joined a group of women and children, led by an elderly man, on their way westward in the hope of reaching the American lines. On the road, low-flying Russian airplanes strafed them and the man's head was partly blown off. Under constant attack, and without a leader, she traveled with the rest of the women and children until they finally reached the American forces. Their hopes of being rescued were shattered when the Americans turned them away. In time, the Russians caught up with them. Together with other refugees they were forced to linger on an open field, cold and hungry, subjected to the viciousness of the Russian soldiers. I sensed she didn't want to tell me more about this horrifying experience and I didn't want to know.

Eventually she and her daughter made their way to the home of her in-laws in Saxonia, Germany, which was at this time under U.S. occupation. Because of another hard to understand agreement by the Allies, the United States handed Saxonia over to the Russians. Unexpectedly, she found herself again under Russian occupation and decided to escape with her child into the American zone. Fortunately, she was able to join a group of people with a guide, but was forced to give the guide the rest of her money. He told her that he was taking a big chance by allowing a small child to go along with them, because a crying baby could give them away. Like myself she ended up in Stuttgart with only the clothes on her back. Despite all of this we both considered ourselves more than fortunate to have made it to safety.

By the time we left the cafe we felt very close. The similarity of our lives had something to do with it, but I think more so the physical attraction we felt for each other. I walked her home and I still remember the exact spot where I stopped and kissed her.

Elfriede, late wife of Hans
Stuttgart 1948

We started to see each other regularly and the more I saw her the more I liked her. She was sexy, intelligent, talented, compassionate and had a great sense of humor. One day, Elfriede brought her little daughter along. Her name was Hannelore and she was the cutest little thing with her blond hair and blue eyes. She was such a happy child and I liked her right away. Elfriede also introduced me to her mother who lived in Bad Cannstatt, across the Neckar River from Stuttgart. She had remarried and was raising two boys. Elfriede's father was German and her mother was a full-blooded Hungarian. I now could see where Elfriede's darker complexion came from.

I started to play with the idea of asking Elfriede to marry me. I felt we were made for each other, and I wanted to be with her all the time. The only problem was that despite my feelings for her I didn't want to give up my dream of leaving Germany.

I knew I had to find out now and asked her, "Would you like to live abroad?"

She smiled and asked, "Have you just made a marriage proposal?"

I answered, "Yes."

She said, "I would like to marry you and go with you wherever you want to go."

That made things perfect and I felt like I was in seventh heaven.

When I told my family about my plans everybody was very happy for me; only my mother wasn't overwhelmed with joy. I believe she probably felt like many mothers when giving up their son to another woman. In my case, it was even more so since most of the time I had been the man of the house. My next step was to find a place for the three of us to live. This was a problem as there were more refugees arriving all the time. Many of them had been temporarily assigned to cold, dark, former bomb shelters.

The City of Stuttgart had opened apartment referral services in different parts of town, and Elfriede and I wanted to try our luck there. The following Saturday I met Elfriede at seven o'clock in the morning and we went on our way. I told Elfriede I had a strange dream last night. I dreamed I had a patch on my upper left arm, which read, "Memento Mori" meaning, "remember death." I was wondering if this was some kind of a warning, not knowing that I was going to find out quickly. It was a beautiful morning and there was nobody around. We had just crossed a street and started to walk along a house wall when a truck came from the opposite direction. The driver was a very young looking man and he had an older man by his side. At this moment the driver wanted to make a left turn into the street we just had crossed, and turning too early, came straight at us. We didn't have time to do anything and I thought this is the end. Then, in a fraction of a second, I could see from the corner of my eye the old man grab the steering wheel and the truck ran over the curb across the sidewalk, barely missing the corner of the house. There again, I couldn't help thinking that I must have an angel shielding me.

The apartment service didn't have any vacancy for us and told us to try again. I thought we might have a better chance if we applied as a married couple. Not for this reason alone, but it seemed logical to get married. We loved each other and wanted to live together as a family. In addition, I wanted to get away from my overcrowded home and Elfriede wasn't much better off. She had rented a small room, which had enough space for one bed only.

After a courtship of six weeks we were married on July 1, 1946. It was a short civil ceremony at the marriage bureau with Horst and his girlfriend as witnesses. Elfriede wore a simple dress and I wore a suit Horst had lent me. I learned that Elfriede was born on March 20, 1920 in Stuttgart and that her maiden name was Ziegler.

Afterwards, we got together with our two families for coffee and cake at Cafe West. Elfriede's brother, Erich, was unable to attend, because he was still held as a POW by the U.S. forces in Belgium. I didn't think he missed too much. All of us got along very nicely, but since there was no food, drink or music, we split up soon. I'm not sure this was the way I had envisioned my wedding, but despite its simplicity, our marriage lasted for 42 years and I believe that a big amount of money spent on weddings doesn't guarantee a long and happy marriage.

With the help of some of Elfriede's distant relatives, we were able to secure a room in a quaint old inn for the weekend. However, our wedding night didn't turn out exactly as expected. We had contracted some kind of scabies and did more scratching than anything else. It was definitely memorable, and we laughed about it many times later on. Despite our dilemma we wished our honeymoon could have lasted a little longer.

Everything was perfect at the office. It felt good being appreciated, and as most of us know, that isn't always the case. Jeanette, Colonel Rodgers's secretary, visited us quite often in our office; maybe she didn't have much to do. She spoke German very well and particularly liked taking with me. After a while we became sort of friendly and she began to sell me cigarettes at a very low price. I had hoped to make this kind of connection ever since I had started to work for the American Army. This boosted my black market income considerably. I certainly didn't want to get rich this way and exclusively used the money to buy food.

I found out that farmers needed light bulbs badly and that gave me an idea. We had plenty of light bulbs laying around at work and nobody would miss one now and then. The problem was to get them past the guards who frisked us when leaving the post. Since they never touched us in our groin area I figured this was the best place to hide them and I decided to give it a try. Before leaving work I went with a bulb and some string into a stall in the men's room and tied the bulb near my private parts. I practiced walking like this and found out it worked quite well, if I was careful enough. I certainly didn't want to change my voice. When passing the guards I felt a little uneasy, but they didn't pay any attention; either they didn't notice it or thought I was very well endowed! Once outside, there was forest close by where I could take the bulb out and take it home safely.

Up to now, the only place where Elfriede and I had some

privacy was in her little room. Even there we had the suspicion the old couple, who owned the apartment, were spying on us. In order to see Hannelore we had to go to Herrenberg or bring her to Elfriede's mother's home where we could be together for a few hours. All in all not the ideal family life, but we hoped to change this soon.

We continued to go to the city apartment service and after quite a few fruitless visits were given the permission to move into some "living quarters." The place was in the attic of an apartment building and consisted of four compartments, which had been previously used for storage by the owners of the apartments. On the same floor were two regular apartments, and to the left of us were compartments occupied by a widow with a small daughter. On the floor was one toilet, which we had to share with the latter. Each compartment measured about 6' by 10' and half of the ceiling was slanted. This certainly wasn't what we had hoped for.

The walls separating the compartments were made of straw and plaster; there were no wooden studs. In order to make the place even moderately livable, I took out the wall between the two middle compartments, and cut a door-shaped opening from this new room into the compartment on the right. The idea was to use the two compartments in the middle as a combination living-dining-bedroom and the one to the right as kitchen. The remaining compartment I left untouched with the intention of using it as a buffer zone and for storage. This way the compartments at least resembled a place where one might be able to live.

In my eagerness to have a place of our own I probably made the mistake of not going back to the city apartment service and telling them the place wasn't livable. But hindsight is always easier than foresight. At any rate, my remodeling job upset the landlord. I received a letter informing me that he was going to sue me for destruction of property and theft. I couldn't do anything about the destruction part, but could about the theft. I took a gunnysack and went to gather the pieces of plaster, which I had thrown on the rubble of a destroyed building nearby, with the idea of giving it back to him. Unfortunately, that didn't work out, because the rain had turned the plaster to mush. All I could do was send him a letter of apology and to put the blame on the city for expecting us to live in those small compartments. I guess he simmered down, because I didn't hear from him anymore.

One day, while visiting my mother-in-law, I had the chance to meet Elfriede's brother, Erich. I had already heard that he was back and staying temporarily with his mother. He had been divorced during the war and was looking for an apartment or at least a room somewhere. I couldn't form an opinion about him, partly because he was talking in his Swabian dialect, which sounded like Watusi to me. I did notice that he and Elfriede weren't overly affectionate with each other. I assumed this had something to do with the fact that they didn't grow up together. Their grandparents had raised him.

Not much later we mentioned to my mother-in-law our need for furniture. Her parents had been evacuated during the war to a small town not far from Stuttgart. Her mother had died but her father was still living there in a retirement home. She said where her parents had lived the people had stolen their valuable belongings, but some furniture might still be present. She gave us the address of her father and suggested that we talk to him.

The first chance we had, Elfriede and I went to see her grandfather. We didn't have any trouble finding him and I really liked the man. He was very friendly, and one could tell it wasn't just because somebody had come to see him. He was in his eighties and still very active. He walked with us to a barn where his furniture was stored. It wasn't a pretty sight and one could see it had been ransacked. He said we could have whatever we wanted. Despite its condition, we told him we would gladly take it, and thanked him. On the way back to the home he pointed out some trees and said we should take some pears home. The memory of almost getting hit over the head because of a few apples was still on my mind, but we took a few pears anyway. After all, one couldn't get any fruit in the store.

The Other Side of the Coin

We were very happy about the furniture, but moving it to Stuttgart wasn't easy. I needed to find a truck and started to ask some of my black market customers, because some were business people and my best prospects. I was lucky; one man owned a pickup truck and was willing to get the furniture for us in exchange for cigarettes and coffee; incidentally, a lot of cigarettes.

One Sunday morning, Elfriede and I went with him and picked up what were the best-preserved pieces but mainly what we could squeeze into our "apartment." The man was very accommodating and helped us to carry the heavy pieces upstairs. Considering the way I had lived for the last year or more, my new home was an improvement. I still hoped we wouldn't have to stay there for too long, and I planned to continue my search for better place to live.

My father was still without work even though he tried hard to find a job. Despite the fact that I wasn't the head of the family, I felt guilty that because of my marriage I wouldn't be able to help much anymore. Then, luckily, my sister Jutta found a job with the American Army. She started to work in the kitchen of a snack bar. This made me feel better, because she had her meals there and later on was able to bring some food home. The snack bar was located in a wing of the opera house and, like in my case; all German employees were frisked when leaving work. However, they were able to find a way to smuggle out some food without being detected. They discovered a narrow passageway leading from the kitchen to the opposite side of the opera house. After having filled their bags with mostly ground beef and donut mix, they carried them through the passageway to a ticket booth. There, a guard kept an eye on their bags until they had made their way around the building and could retrieve them. I'm sure the guard profited from this arrangement.

The day came when Elfriede, Hannelore and I moved into our new living quarters. I had been successful in getting a small bed for Hannelore and a hot plate for our "kitchen" on the black market. This completed our immediate requirements, but we still needed a lot of odds and ends. Moving our personal belongings was not a problem since neither one of us had any possessions to speak of. Leaving my family wasn't too hard either, as we were living only ten minutes apart.

It was a good thing we weren't overly exited about moving into our new home, because we soon realized some unpleasant facts. For instance, there was nothing to keep us cool in summer or warm in winter. Also, the widow with the daughter living next to us looked like trouble. Nevertheless, we were happy to be together. We loved each other and that was what really counted.

Over the last months we had heard from different sources about the tragic end of Breslau. Shortly after our departure, the Russian Army completed their encirclement of Breslau and the remaining citizens within waited for the horror to begin. After three months of daily artillery fire and air bombardment, as well as heavy street fighting, the city surrendered two days before the end of WW II on May 6, 1945. The death toll amounted to more than 6000 troops and over 20,000 civilians. Large parts of this beautiful old and historic city were destroyed. Later we learned that my uncle Fritz, my fathers brother, my cousin Hardy's wife and my friend Gerhard's father, had all perished.

I read the book, "Inside the Third Reich" by Albert Speer, Hitler's favorite architect. In it Speer mentions Karl Hanke, Nazi District Leader, describing how he waged the battle of Breslau without regard for human lives and how he fled the besieged city in a small plane. All of this didn't surprise me, but made me realize again how lucky I had been to escape that slaughter.

We were given a more detailed description of what went on from Aunt Annie, my uncle Erich's wife. My grandfather and Annie were fortunate enough to survive the whole ordeal. During the fighting they stayed mostly in cold and wet basements and lived on whatever they could find to eat. After the shooting ended they found an apartment but were evicted from it, and later on from other apartments, by Polish people who were moving in and taking over. In order to stay alive my aunt earned food for her and my grandfather by cleaning houses for the new Polish "owners."

The Other Side of the Coin

One day there was a Russian holiday and no Germans were allowed on the street. Since she had no way of knowing this she went to work and was arrested by the Russians. She was thrown into a basement where there were other frightened people, many of them young girls. The next day she was brought up, beaten and kicked so badly that she lost the hearing in one ear. I should add that Aunt Annie was petite, which made this beating seem even crueler. She crawled home on hands and knees and she and my grandfather almost starved because she was unable to go to work. Eventually, in the middle of winter and together with other Germans, they were loaded on open freight trains and taken to Bavaria.

Among the many sad events of the war that occurred was the worst sea tragedy ever. The 25,484 ton German Luxury Liner *Wilhelm Gustloff*, a converted hospital ship, had sailed on January 30, 1945 from the port of Gotenhafen. The ship was overcrowded and had more than 6000 people on board. In addition to wounded soldiers, there were mostly women and children who were fleeing from the approaching Russian Army. While making her way through the icy water of the Baltic Sea, three torpedoes from the Russian submarine S-13 hit the ship. The *Wilhelm Gustloff* sank within minutes taking nearly all the passengers with her to a watery grave. Still today, it amazes me that there is nothing or only very little known about this terrible disaster.

We were glad to hear better news from my aunts Gertrude and Erika. Both their husbands had safely returned from the war and had joined them in Grottenholz. I never found out what Erika's husband experienced during the war, but Gertrude's husband had quite a story to tell. He had been a radio operator based in a large concrete bunker, which, together with four smaller bunkers formed part of the German Atlantic Wall. When the Allied invasion began, a bomb landed directly on top of his bunker, which resulted in a wide crack from one end of the bunker to the other. He said he was still shaking several hours later when British troops captured him. He considered himself even luckier when he saw that the four smaller bunkers had been completely destroyed.

Winter came and the attic became colder by the day. Elfriede and I took turns standing in line at the apartment referral service, but without success. Still more refugees were arriving daily and our chance of finding a better place to live looked hopeless. I tried to find a small stove, but didn't have any luck with this either.

I must have bumped my head too many times against the slanted ceiling or maybe the cold froze my brain, because I don't remember too much about that first winter, only that it was miserable. Hannelore stayed with my mother-in-law most of the time, and Elfriede and I visited friends or other places to keep warm. At home we lived in our topcoats or clung to each other.

Only a few minutes away from us lived a cousin of Elfriede's, named Erna. She was married and without children. Her husband's name was Kurt and he was quite an interesting person. He had the title of doctor, and even though he was smart enough to be one, we felt something wasn't quite right. Nevertheless, we visited them often for different reasons, one of them being our mutual involvement in the black market.

During one of these visits I was suffering from a very bad cough. Medicine prescribed by my doctor, as well as home remedies, hadn't helped. While at their apartment I began coughing terribly; Kurt said he would take care of my cough. He had a prescription form, apparently stolen from his doctor, wrote out a prescription in Latin and faked his doctor's signature.

He handed it to me and said, "Take it to the drug store."

I told him, "No, I'd rather keep on coughing."

I felt my answer had hurt his feelings because he said he would get the medicine himself. I went with him but kept a safe distance from the drug store. He actually did get the medicine and gave it to me with a triumphant smile. I was doubtful, yet curious enough to try it. To my surprise my cough was gone in no time. However, funny as it sounds, the first time I took the medicine I had difficulty lifting my arms. I suppose it contained a strong narcotic.

Somehow we made it through the winter and in spring of 1947

we began to discover more about our neighborhood. By orders of the American authorities, former Nazis had to temporarily take into their homes Jewish concentration camp survivors. This was the case in our apartment house too. Two Jewish men by the names of Boral and Greenspan lived with the families of former Nazis. I thought this was just amazing.

A Jewish couple by the name of Fuchs stayed in the house next to us. They had a little girl named Eva, who was about the same age as Hannelore. Elfriede became acquainted with Mrs. Fuchs and as a result, the two little girls started to play together. It didn't seem to matter that they didn't understand each other, since Eva only spoke Polish. In a way it was better that Hannelore didn't understand her because Eva had picked up some foul language from somewhere. Elfriede found out that she called the mailman, "You motherf......" It was probably a good thing that the mailman didn't understand Polish either.

Mrs. Fuchs and Elfriede became good friends, and she told Elfriede that this was also her second marriage. Her first husband had been a doctor, and when the Russians occupied Poland in 1939, they took him into the forest and shot him. Unfortunately, Elfriede's friendship with Mrs. Fuchs soon came to an end, when with help of the U.S. Displaced Persons Program, the Fuchs family moved to Detroit.

The murder of Mrs. Fuchs' first husband by the Russians was another example of the systematic liquidation of anyone who could pose a danger to the Soviet regime. One of the most dramatic examples was the massacre of Katyn. When in 1939 the Russian Army occupied the eastern half of Poland, they took thousands of Polish officers as prisoners. All of them were slaughtered on Stalin's order. In 1943 the German Army discovered a mass grave with 4,200 of the murdered officers at Katyn. After 50 years of denying this atrocity, in February of 1989 the Russian authorities finally acknowledged their responsibility.

Even though I was doing quite well in my black market business, there was always room for improvement. By accident, I hit upon a real gold mine in the form of a former classmate of Elfriede. His name was Robert and he lived in Goeppingen, a small town near Stuttgart. He had built a little distillery in his basement and traded with the local GIs, schnapps for cigarettes. He was so overloaded with cigarettes that he was glad when I took some off his hands, even at a very low price. The only problem we had was getting them back to Stuttgart since the German police periodically searched the trains for black market contraband. This was the time where Hannelore became very helpful. She wore a kind of jogging suit, the perfect place to hide quite a few packages of cigarettes. Luckily, we were never checked.

Summertime arrived and the heat in our apartment was unbearable. I hoped to find a fan somewhere but didn't have any luck. Once in a while we tied a wet bed sheet across the window, but this didn't help much either. The best thing to do was to get out of the house as often as possible.

One day, Maria, the girl from Heuraffel, came to visit my parents. She must have tried hard to find us. My mother told her that I was married and she seemed to be disappointed. Apparently, her family and the other German neighbors were forced to leave and to abandon their homes. She didn't know what happened to the Pressls or if Hans ever had returned from the war. I wished I would have had a chance to talk with her.

Then something very unpleasant happened. Elfriede's brother, Erich, came to see us. He had found a girlfriend and they were trying to furnish an apartment. He said to Elfriede in a demanding voice that half of our furniture belonged to him and he wanted it. Elfriede told him he wouldn't get any, because if it hadn't been for our initiative, there wouldn't be any furniture at all. He had the same chance to get it and he didn't. The argument heated up to the point where he insulted Elfriede and walked out the door. I had tried to stay out of the argument since I felt it was a family matter. However, when he insulted Elfriede I became upset. I went after him and told him to come back and apologize to my wife. He refused and said something to me I didn't like. This was a big mistake. I really let him have it with all the rage that had bundled up in me for a long time. Elfriede came running out and jumped on my back, which was probably a blessing because I might have killed him. Blood was everywhere, down all four floors and on the street. He ended up in the hospital for a couple of days, but wasn't seriously hurt. Of course, I got quite a tongue lashing from my mother and mother-in-law. I was sorry that I lost my temper and let this happen.

Some major events took place for my family. My father was hired as a statistician by the State of Wuerttemberg. The state needed qualified people for a new branch of the already existing statistical department; the reason being that the American authorities requested a monthly report of goods manufactured in the state. My father was very fortunate to get this job. It gave him the chance to lead a normal life again. I hoped he would realize that. Apparently he did and kept his employment with the state and eventually retired with a pension. This made me very happy for my mother, since she had suffered enough. However, she was wasn't entirely out of the woods because my father never gave up drinking.

Unfortunately, my sister Jutta lost her job in the snack bar. For whatever reason, all employees under the age of eighteen were laid off. This made a big dent in the food supply for all of us. In the past my mother had seen to it that my family received a share of the goodies Jutta brought home. At least Jutta didn't stay out of work for long. She found employment with an advertising agency. She liked her new job very much; not only for the people there, but that it gave her a chance to use her artistic talent.

My sister Gerda graduated from middle school and was very fortunate, too. Because of her better education, the employment office sent her to a company that was just starting to manufacture a variety of lamps. Gerda immediately liked it and completed an excellent three-year training in business, ranging from accounting to sales. Her training turned out to be invaluable in her later life.

I was doing business with a fellow by the name of Baldowski.

To be exact, I mainly bought nylons from him. One day, he asked me if I was interested in 3000 units of Salvarsan at the price of ten Marks per unit. I told him that I didn't want to get involved with anything of that sort; because I was sure it had been obtained illegally from an American source. It was just too bad that I made the mistake of telling Elfriede. She, in turn, must have told Erna and Kurt, because not much later they asked us if the Salvarsan was still available. They had made the acquaintance of a doctor who wanted to buy it for the price of fifty Marks per unit. He was treating displaced persons with venereal diseases who were afraid it would ruin their chances to immigrate. I told Erna and Kurt the same as Baldowski, that they should forget it. On top of that, I didn't quite believe the whole story. It was too bad that Elfriede was blinded by the thought that by splitting the profit she could make 60,000 Marks. She went to see Baldowski, and with this, a drama began.

The four of them met one evening and were going to meet the doctor at 8 o'clock at his hotel room. I stayed home and waited, wondering about the outcome. It was nearly eleven o'clock when Elfriede came home. She was angry and worried at the same time. Apparently, Erna and Kurt had not told the whole story; they had conveniently left out the fact that three other people were involved, two men and a woman. In any case, the four men proceeded to see the doctor while the three women waited on the street. She said the men never came back and she gave up and came home. There was no doubt; something had gone wrong, but what?

At about four o'clock in the morning, the police showed up and arrested Elfriede. I was glad that Hannelore was with my mother-in-law and didn't have to witness her mother being taken away. It looked rather ridiculous when the police, with revolvers drawn, led Elfriede out of the house. Of course, the whole neighborhood was awake and watching. With it we became kind of famous. Elfriede returned in the morning and I was anxious to find out what had happened the previous night. Actually, the answer was very simple-the so-called "doctor" had been an undercover detective.

This wasn't the end of the story. There was a trial. Elfriede was a nervous wreck, because she had never stood in front of a judge in her entire life. The judge must have noticed the condition she was in and probably felt sorry for her. She got away with a fine of 200 Marks. This was no problem since it amounted to a few packs of cigarettes on the black market. The bad part was that now she had a record. Incidentally, at the trial we learned that Kurt was not a doctor, which didn't surprise us. He explained when he was a POW in France he found out that as a doctor he would be released sooner, therefore he added "Doctor" to his name. He said that later he was embarrassed to confess to the truth. I didn't believe this story either, but it didn't really matter. Shortly afterwards, he and Erna moved into the Russian zone of Germany and we lost track of them. It always puzzled me why they wanted to move east when everyone else wanted to come to the West.

To my big surprise, Mr. Kersandt, the gentlemen from Grottenholz, came to see me. He had been offered a job in a new casino, which was to open within a year at Bad Homburg. He said it was going to be financed with German, French and Luxembourg money. He asked me if I was interested in becoming a dealer. He said I would make more money there than the Prime Minister of England. I believed him, but told him that I had made up my mind to immigrate to the United States. Elfriede also pointed out that with my damaged lung I might not last very long in a smoky environment. I knew he liked me and was a little disappointed. We parted as friends and I never saw him again.

The City of Stuttgart started to issue permits for the purchase of shoes and clothing, but only people in dire need qualified for a permit. We certainly fell into this category. Finally I was able to buy some clothing and, in particular, a pair of shoes. Elfriede applied for a slip, because she was in desperate need of one. After a lot of hassle she obtained a permit to buy a slip. By this time, we were short on food again and she sacrificed her slip by trading it for twenty pounds of potatoes.

Winter came and we still had been unable to find a stove. It was very depressing having to look forward to another cold winter in this pitiful dwelling. At least we had been able to acquire an additional feather bed and some warmer clothing. To find another apartment had become even more of a problem with the ever-increasing number of refugees arriving. Since we had a place, it made us feel almost ashamed to ask for anything better. But I swore that by next winter I would get a stove, even if I had to steal one.

To live the way we did was bad enough, but our problems with the widow next door made the situation even worse. I think she hated Elfriede from the moment we moved in for the reason alone that Elfriede had a husband. The parties living on each floor took turns cleaning their respective stairs for a week. In our case that included the toilet, too. When it was Elfriede's turn for cleaning, this woman dirtied the toilet and stairs in the worst possible way. When she knew we needed some rest or one of us was sick, she kept slamming her door as loudly as possible. Along with that, we caught her listening at our door and we found out that she went around the neighborhood telling all kind of lies about us.

In the hope of putting an end to this harassment, I took her to court. I presented my case and it was my impression that the judge didn't like me, perhaps because I didn't speak his dialect. However, his attitude changed after listening to the woman. She couldn't say anything in her defense, only that Elfriede had called her a malicious person. I was quite surprised when the judge said to her, "If I would be Mrs. Kunert, I would call you at lot worse than that." She started to cry when the judge asked me if I wished to see her punished. I told him I didn't. I only wanted her to behave like a decent person. She still had to pay the court costs, for an ad in the paper in which she had to confess to her lies, and to express her regret for the damage done to our reputation. This brought us peace, but not entirely, because a leopard doesn't change his spots. We just hoped to get out of this unpleasant situation soon.

At work, Lautenschlager and I had some bad luck. Our friend, the cook, had been transferred, which meant no more afternoon snacks. Still our daily lunch was grand, and I had learned how to smuggle out a little food now and then, such as a slice of bread, half of a lemon, etc.

One day, Colonel Rodgers came in and told us that the army had plans for a Christmas party for German children. He was wondering if we could put together a coloring book. Lautenschlager didn't think he had the talent for it, but I decided to give it a try. I had done quite a few drawings in school and thought I could do it. Here and there I found enough pictures of animals that I could use as patterns, and I was able to produce a nice coloring booklet. Colonel Rodgers was more than pleased with my creation. The only problem was after that he thought I could draw anything, which wasn't the case. At any rate, several hundred booklets were printed at the U.S. Army print shop in Heidelberg. Apparently this press was chosen because it could produce four different colors. The booklet must have been a success because I had difficulties getting one for myself.

Another Christmas came and I had wished I would have been able to buy some presents, but the stores were empty and our money virtually worthless. I felt especially sorry for Hannelore, because she was such a good child and deserved better. Then, two days before Christmas, a miracle happened. The two colonels came into our office followed by Bernie, who was carrying two beautifully wrapped packages. The colonels handed each of us a package and wished us a very merry Christmas, and told us we could start our Christmas leave early. It was hard to comprehend, two lowly Germans getting this special treatment. The funny part was that at first the MP's at the gate wouldn't let us pass because they suspected the packages were stolen.

That Christmas turned out to be the most memorable of all. The package contained so many things we hadn't seen in years, like cocoa, ham and so on. Even the smallest spaces of the package were filled with candy. I estimated everything was worth at least 9,000 Marks on the black market, but we didn't sell anything.

In spring of 1948, everybody thought something would happen soon, but nobody knew what. Our assumption had been correct. When we woke on June 21, our present currency, the Reichsmark, had become worthless and had been replaced by the Deutsche Mark. Every citizen received the same amount of money for transitional purposes, which I believe was DM 150. This event affected everyone and changed our lives completely.

The most visible and almost immediate transformation could be seen in stores; where empty windows and shelves used to be, all of a sudden one could find anything and everything. The thought of having made manufacturers and merchants rich by working for worthless money angered a lot of people. They felt cheated and riots broke out. In downtown Stuttgart show windows were broken and merchandise thrown on the street. It became necessary to call in American troops to restore law and order.

At first none of this excited me too much. I lost a few hundred Reichsmark, or my black market capital, but I was glad that we finally were able to buy some food and other things we badly needed. However, to my regret I learned that changing the value of our money meant the end of my job. The American Army laid off all German employees with the exception of the cleaning personnel. Lautenschlager and I said goodbye to everyone and thanked them for their kindness. Bernie walked outside with us and told us "Auf Wiedersehen."

I didn't expect to see Bernie again, but as incredible as it seems, I met him again exactly forty years later. I was alone at the time, living in El Paso, Texas, and had in mind to move to Santa Barbara, California. I contacted the Chamber of Commerce and, along with the requested information, received a letter from a real estate office offering their services. On the letter was a picture of the agent and I recognized Bernie almost immediately. I went to see him and when I walked into his office he couldn't believe it was me. We spent a very nice day together talking of our time in Stuttgart. I had to think about the saying, "Truth is stranger than fiction."

In June another momentous event took place. The Russians blocked all access routes leading from the West to Berlin, thereby breaking the agreement by which the Western Allies had free access to that city. This created a very serious situation and the possibility of war was real. As it turned out, the Western Allies decided not to let the confrontation develop into an all out conflict. However, they refused to be forced out by the Russians or abandon the people of Berlin. They started to supply the city by air. The airlift lasted for eleven months with a plane landing every three minutes. It was an incredible undertaking. It just seemed a paradox that a short time ago the Allies had bombed Berlin almost out of existence and now went to such unbelievable efforts to save it.

Mainly because of my marriage, but also for other reasons, I only saw my friend Horst once in a while. On one of those rare occasions he told me he was getting divorced. Even though he had never mentioned to me that he was married, I always had that suspicion. Apparently, his wife had succeeded in fleeing from the Russian zone and either knew or found out about his infidelity. She had gotten acquainted with a Greek who wanted to marry her. Her suitor manufactured all kind of zippers, a commodity in high demand. Based on the laws at the time, a divorce could drag on for years if one partner was uncooperative. It seemed Horst was using this opportunity to set himself up in business. He made a deal with the Greek in which he would agree to a fast divorce and in return would receive a car and unlimited credit toward his merchandise. Personally, I wouldn't even have thought about a plot like this, but then I wasn't Horst. When I met Horst later he told me he had succeeded with his plan.

I had no idea what had happened to some of my relatives and it was quite a surprise when my cousin Hardy, my uncle Emil's son, showed up. He had just been released from a POW camp in

Russia and was one of the few lucky German prisoners who came back. Upon his arrival from Russia he was informed by the German authorities about his wife's death in Breslau and was given our address. At first I didn't recognize him, because he looked like a shadow of himself. In the army, he used to be a warrant officer; incidentally, not the best liked people in the German Army. They were always far behind the front lines, acted like officers, and while the rest of us went hungry, had plenty to eat. Of course, I never held this against him.

He told us that in May of 1945 he was captured by Czechoslovakians in a city named Lauen. His captors beat him nearly senseless and then handed him over to the Russians. He was taken to a prison camp in northern Russia where the prisoners died like flies. The common procedure there was to form groups of five prisoners and to take them into the forest to cut down trees. Since all of them were malnourished and didn't have any protection against the sub-zero temperatures, hardly any of them came back. He knew he had to do some fast thinking to have a chance for survival. He decided to pretend that he was a furrier. He started to make vests, mittens, caps, etc. for the families of the prison guards. He was aware of the fact that he did a poor job and was surprised that they let him go on. The only explanation he had was that the Russians must have thought that the Germans weren't as smart as everyone assumed. Eventually he improved his work and earned a little extra food, but most importantly, it allowed him to stay in camp. Despite his advantage over the other prisoners he considered suicide many times. One thing that helped him to hang on were some small slides of pictures from home, which he hid in his shoe.

I wished I could have invited him to stay with us, but this was impossible. My parents weren't in the position to take him in either. Luckily, things worked out for him very quickly. More businesses started to form and the attitude of the natives had changed to some extent. Some had begun to realize that we were more of an asset to them than a burden. He found a job as supervisor with a fur coat manufacturing company, which had just opened a branch in a small town near Stuttgart. He was definitely qualified to run a business and it probably helped that he knew a little about fur. I was very happy for him; he had suffered enough.

My father had another surprise visit. His former bosses, the two brothers, came to see him. They had survived the fighting in Breslau and had managed to make it to the American zone. They had started a new business and wanted my father to work for them. My father told them that he was flattered, but wanted to stay in his present job.

They said they were more than fortunate to be alive. After the fighting in Breslau ended, they had been working as mechanics for the Russians. The first chance they had they went to see if anything was left of their factory. The place was close to railroad tracks and there were some Polish railroaders nearby. They started to talk with them and made the mistake of telling them that they were the owners of the factory. The Poles turned on them, called them "Kapitalistas," and forced them into a bomb shelter. They piled all sorts of heavy metal pieces in front of the door and left them in the shelter to die. Miraculously, the brothers found a wrecking bar in the dark and were able to open the door wide enough to squeeze out.

I went back to the employment office hoping to find a job in my profession. In the meantime I tried to comfort myself with my unemployment pay which was more than I had expected, it somewhat eased the pain of being out of work. I also was trying on my own and even had a couple of offers, but the work was not in my field. In addition, it wouldn't have made any sense, because the salary offered was barely above my unemployment pay. Since I was at home and could take care of Hannelore, Elfriede tried to find a job as a dental assistant. She didn't have any luck either; there weren't many dentists to begin with at this time.

Being unemployed gave me the opportunity to pursue my quest to make it to the United States. I went to the U.S. Consulate in Stuttgart to inquire about immigration procedures. I was informed it was presently impossible for a German to immigrate to the United States, with the exception of war brides. The German immigration quota was 26,000 persons per year based on the number of Germans who immigrated to the U.S., I believe, in 1883. At least the consulate accepted my application and I went on record as Number 686. It wasn't much but it made me feel like I had made a start. Most importantly I was informed that I was going to need a sponsor. I realized that this would be very difficult since we didn't know a soul in America. I was very glad that Elfriede was 100 percent with me on my endeavor; as a matter of fact, without her support we wouldn't have succeeded.

Even though it had become possible to buy a lot of things, some items were still hard to come by. Having time on my hands, I was able to find a fan. This didn't alleviate the heat in our apartment, but it made some difference. I was able to find a small stove and, after a lot of searching, acquired some pieces of stovepipe. The stove was in good shape and looked nice. The problem was getting it up four flights of stairs because it weighed a ton. Eventually, with the help of friends, we managed and were very glad about the prospect of staying warm during the coming winter.

Then, Elfriede fell ill. Her heartbeat was completely out of control and I had to rush her to the hospital. She had told me in the beginning that she had rheumatic fever as a child, which affected her heart. I wouldn't have known because she functioned like a healthy person. She remained in the hospital for three weeks, and the doctors believed she had a heart problem but were unable to determine the underlying cause of her illness.

I had no idea that these episodes were going to continue for the rest of her life and would hang over our heads like a thundercloud. At first I thought the doctors in Stuttgart lacked in knowledge, but later had to apologize to them in my mind. In 1970, after Elfriede suffered another period of her illness, she went for two weeks to St. Luke's Hospital in Houston, Texas. There, some of the best doctors in the world couldn't pinpoint her problem. They concluded that something was affecting her heart, but didn't know what. Personally, I believe that her actual problem was a very rare rheumatoid disease.

Again I had to leave Hannelore with my mother-in-law and was glad she hadn't started school yet. I visited Elfriede every day and otherwise just hung around. Since it was getting colder, I wrote my landlord a letter in which I asked him for his consent to let me connect a stove to a nearby chimney. This meant making holes through two walls, each hole six inches in diameter. I told him how cold and miserable we had been during the last two winters and hoped for his understanding. In his return letter he refused my request and warned me not to disobey him.

I was in a bad mood to begin with, but this made me furious. My chest was hurting, my wife was in the hospital, my daughter somewhere else; I had no job, little money and now faced spending another cold winter in that dump. Besides, I knew the landlord lived with his wife and son in a big villa.

When I had calmed down a little I went to the city apartment referral service. I explained the problem and that I needed help. I reminded them that they were the ones who had put us there. I told them I was at the end of my rope and something serious could happen. I don't know if I frightened them or if they felt sorry for me; regardless, I was given the support I needed. They gave me permission to connect the stove to the chimney and informed the landlord about their decision. I didn't hear from the landlord anymore, but neighbors told me, one day while I was gone, he came and pounded on my door with his fists. I was glad that he came at that particular time, because I knew if I would have been home I might have pounded him.

I was wrong assuming that my problems regarding the stove were over. I went to a tinsmith down the street and I gave him three pieces of pipe and a precise drawing. He promised to install the pipe in a few days. When he didn't show up I went to see him. He told me flat out that my pipe had been stolen and there was nothing he could do about it. I let him know that I didn't believe him and that I would get my pipe back one way or another. I was beginning to wonder if my problems would ever cease.

I thought the person who could help was Kurt the "doctor." I was right, and again I had to admire his talent. I told him my story and in no time he typed two letters, one to the police and the other to the newspaper. He accused the tinsmith of theft and fraud and of being of low character for the way he treated a disabled veteran and refugee. The letters worked like a charm, because the tinsmith "discovered" my stovepipe almost immediately. I located another tinsmith who did a perfect job and put the stove in working order.

After all that time and trouble we finally had heat and fully realized what we had been missing. However, there remained one more problem: firewood. During the previous years people used up all the wood they could find: in forests, bombed buildings, as well as park benches, railings, etc. Now everyone received an allotment of firewood, but it wasn't sufficient. Elfriede and I felt we had been cold long enough and decided to use the head, foot and side boards of our two beds for heating. I borrowed a saw and cut them up and this kept us nice and warm through the winter. It was easy finding bricks from bombed buildings on which to place our mattresses.

Just before Christmas my friend Horst came to visit us. He had been occupied with building up his business; in addition to zippers, he was selling Australian wool and Belgian lace. He had a very nice car, a Borgward, and he took us for a pleasure ride. One could tell he was very happy. He conducted his business by taking off on Monday morning and going from city to city offering his wares, mainly to department stores. He returned Friday night and over the weekend he packed his orders so he could mail them Monday morning. He said judging by the constant increase in orders he would need help soon. It didn't take long and he offered me to take over the northern German sales territory and he would take care of southern Germany. I declined and told him that I wanted to go to America and I was sure I had a better chance to achieve my goal as a technician than as a salesman. My refusal didn't bother him, but he told me I was passing up the opportunity to make a lot of money.

We spent a very nice Christmas. It was amazing how much difference a warm home made. With stores almost full of merchandise again, we were able to buy some small gifts. I even bought a wall lamp with a red shade, which made our room look cozy.

The New Year came and I was wondering what 1949 had in store for us and in particular for myself. Despite my ongoing visits to the employment office, I didn't have any luck finding a job. Like many times in life, when least expected, I got a break. I was hired by the City of Stuttgart as an engineering technician. After the removal of most of the ruins and rubble, the process to restore Stuttgart had begun. My place of work was in a newly created department that was appropriately called, "Central Office for the Rebuilding of Stuttgart." The head of the department was a professor by the name of Hoss. He was a very capable man and one who had a lot of foresight. He correctly anticipated that Stuttgart would grow much larger than most expected. In his plans for rebuilding the city his priority was the widening of streets in the destroyed parts of town, as well as a radical enlargement and improvement of the inner city street net.

The department consisted of about thirty people and I happened to be the only "foreigner." To my surprise everyone treated me like one of their own. Maybe it had something to do with the fact that I was married to a native girl; also, there were quite a few veterans in the office and we shared a common bond. I was assigned to a section with twelve men and a secretary. Our supervisor's name was Roth and, as I found out, he liked to get all of us together either after work or on trips with our wives. This sounded like fun and something I hadn't expected either. In any case, I was very happy to be working again and especially in my profession.

I had intended from the beginning to adopt Hannelore and since she was going to school soon I felt now was the best time.

She thought that I was her daddy and I didn't want her to have any doubt about it. I went ahead and completed the adoption. It made me feel good and I was proud to be her legal father. I was glad that our monetary situation had improved, and when school started she was as nicely dressed as all the other children. We were able to give her a pretty paper cone filled with candy, fruit and a present, a tradition in Germany on the first day of school.

There was one more predicament in our daily lives I hadn't mentioned and this was how to stay clean under the circumstances. The only available water faucet was located in the room with the toilet. To bath or wash clothing, water had to be carried from the faucet to our compartment and back again. Another problem was the shared toilet facilities were often occupied by the woman next door or her daughter. In addition, all we had was an all-purpose galvanized steel bucket, which my mother-in-law had loaned us. I had to admire Elfriede for the way she kept all of us so neatly dressed. This situation was another reason that we couldn't wait to move to a regular apartment.

One day I had another unexpected visitor. Kurt, my friend and former chess partner from Breslau, showed up, although I don't remember anymore how he found me. He had ended up in Forchheim, a small town in Bavaria. He was divorced, as I had expected, but otherwise fine. Like myself, he was happy to have survived. We had a lot to talk about and in the course of our conversation we talked about my friend Gerhard. He said he knew where Mrs. Weiser lived and would send me her address. Kurt told me that he had started a German-American youth club in Forchheim. Following an invitation to come to America and study the clubs there, he had just recently returned from a three months stay. Apparently, what impressed him more than the clubs were the banana splits and the girls in their short skirts at parades. Listening to him made me even more anxious to go to America.

Kurt kept his word and sent Mrs. Weiser's address. She lived in a small town near Forchheim. I contacted her and stayed in touch with her for a long time. She wrote about her husband's death in Breslau and that she was now living with a family who treated her like one of their own. I was very happy for her.

Some outdoor pools had opened up, and to escape the heat in the attic we spent a lot of time there. In addition we visited the surroundings near Stuttgart, the forests, lakes and vineyards, all of which were great for sightseeing, walking or picnics.

Later in the year, Elfriede introduced me to "new wine." People would go in large numbers to villages outside Stuttgart where they served the new wine. The wine looked a little milky but tasted fine and a big glass only cost a dime. The evening trains back to Stuttgart were a sight to remember. I had never seen so many tipsy people all in one place.

One night in fall, I had a dream I'll never forget. I dreamed I was lying in bed when at the door "Death" appeared in his black hood and cloak. I couldn't see a face. I grabbed a mug and threw it at him, but even though he was only a few feet away, the mug took a downward curve and landed in front of his feet. Then he was gone. The following week I learned that my Heimlich grandfather had passed away. I hadn't thought about my grandfather for a long time, because since his arrival in Bavaria we hadn't been in close contact. Still today, I am puzzled by this dream.

I liked my new job, probably because the work was very similar to the one in Breslau. Even the heated negotiations with the property owners seemed to be the same. Hardly any of them wanted to give up part of their property. One day we had a very special visitor and one who wasn't as irate as most of the others. He was Ferry Porsche, the man who built the sports car named after him. He was also the son of Ferdinand Porsche who developed the Volkswagen. Ferry Porsche came to inquire if we could help him with some land acquisition. He said to start he had built ten cars without knowing if anybody would like them. To his surprise the cars were gone almost overnight and more orders came in than he could handle. We couldn't help him, because we were not involved in this sort of land distribution.

My friend Horst was interested in buying a Porsche, but the trunk was too small to hold his samples. This was regrettable, because most likely it would have been my one and only opportunity to ride in a Porsche.

Winter rolled around again, but this time we were better prepared. We tried to make our place a little more cozy. Our two large beds were located at an angle along walls and in daytime we changed them into sofas. We bought blankets to roll our feather beds in and placed the rolls against the walls. This worked out nicely when we had company, as they felt very comfortable this way. We had acquired a radio too, something we had missed all along. At night, with the warmth, music and the soft light from the wall lamp, one almost could forget what a dreadful place it really was.

Christmas had come and gone and 1950 had started. Since our life had somewhat improved, I felt more relaxed and this might have been the reason that I became a little careless, because in January Elfriede told me that she was pregnant. To be honest, I didn't get as excited over it as I should have. All kind of thoughts crossed my mind, such as where to keep a baby, since we already stepped on each other's feet, and how a baby would affect our plan to go to America. But mainly, how it would change our life all together. I finally came to the conclusion that I should have thought about all of this before, and that eventually in life everything falls into place.

Elfriede shared most of my concern, but as time went on all of us looked forward to the arrival of the baby. I just felt sorry for Elfriede to be in her condition in the hot attic. I tried repeatedly to find better living quarters for us, but without success. Then I heard that the city was building apartment houses and was reserving ten percent of the apartments for city employees. I considered this to be my chance. I went ahead and submitted my application to the proper office. Afterwards I thought it wouldn't hurt to get some additional help in this matter, because too much was at stake. At the first opportunity, I approached Mr. Roth, my supervisor. I described our living conditions and how anxious we were to rent one of the new apartments. I asked him if he could help me with my plight. He was very sympathetic and promised to see what he could do. He must have put in a good word, because it didn't take long and we were notified that we could move into one of the apartments by the end of the year. What a wonderful Christmas present.

We visited my parents and sisters and they came to see us occasionally. Unfortunately, we didn't have the relationship I would have desired. My father was drunk quite often and I didn't care to see him in this condition. In addition, my mother still wasn't happy about my marriage and didn't hide her resentment toward Elfriede. During our visits I always felt like I was walking on a balance beam. I didn't want to hurt my mother while at the same time trying to protect Elfriede.

The summer seemed to last forever, maybe because we were so anxious for the baby to arrive and also to get out of the attic. Eventually the time came for Elfriede to go to the hospital. I remember it was on a Saturday noon when we walked, or in Elfriede's case waddled, about eight blocks to the hospital. As it turned out we came too early, but the staff was nice enough to let her stay. Nothing happened on Saturday or even on Sunday. Monday morning I thought I might as well go to work, but when I arrived at the office they told me to turn around, because I had become the father of a little boy.

I hurried to the hospital and was glad to find Elfriede feeling fine. Then I had the chance to see my son for the first time, and as every proud parent, I thought he was the most handsome. We named him Gerald Michael with the thought in mind that these names would be suitable in case we would make it to America. Interestingly, Gerald was born on September 18, 1950 my mother's birthday. When Hannelore saw Gerald she was all excited and couldn't wait to hold her little brother in her arms. I loved Hannelore; she was such a happy and pretty little girl. Looking at all of them, I felt very fortunate to have such a beautiful family.

Back in the attic Gerald had to sleep in a clothesbasket on a table in the "kitchen." It was really pathetic. Even the washing and drying of diapers was a chore; but there was no other way; we had to keep on going, again Elfriede was carrying the heavy load. Fortunately, it wasn't for too long. We were allowed to move into our new apartment in early December. Four years of suffering in heat and cold, and all the other aggravations were finally behind us.

Occasionally, we had gotten together with a young couple by the names of Max and Hilde. They were originally from the Russian zone of Germany. When they found out about our move they offered to help. I appreciated their offer very much, because amazingly enough we had accumulated more possessions than seemed possible. I rented a large pick-up truck and we piled and stuffed everything on it. Since nothing we had was of great value, it was no problem.

Our apartment was located on the second floor and looked like heaven to us. It had a hallway, living room with a balcony, two bedrooms, a kitchen and a bathroom with a tub. Even the view was pretty from all windows. The suburb we had moved into was known by the name of Stuttgart-Wangen. On one side of our building was the Neckar River with promenades and an outdoor swimming pool and on the opposite side were hills with vineyards, Schrebergartens and forests. Later on, when Gerald was big enough, we often wandered up the hills and through the forests. While Elfriede or I pushed the baby carriage, Hannelore was usually running back and forth, covering the whole way at least twice. Around noon we would eat at one of the small inns along the way where the food was always tasty and inexpensive. Life was good again.

I might sound prejudiced, but I can't praise Elfriede enough. I knew already that she had many fine qualities, but after moving into the apartment, she surprised me with many more. For instance, she was an excellent cook, given the opportunity; also, she was a great homemaker and had the talent to make something out of nothing. She even was a good artist, painting landscapes in oil. But more important than all of that, I knew she loved the children and me and was the best mother imaginable. As I had already found out, and more so later on, she stood by me no matter what. I'm just sorry that I took her mostly for granted and didn't always realize how lucky I was to have her by my side.

Considering the poor and hopeless situation I had been in barely five years before, I should have been satisfied with my current status and that my life was back on track. However, I was not. I still wanted to go to America. I wanted my own home, a car and a higher education for my children, things I couldn't imagine ever being able to afford in Germany. Also Stuttgart wasn't Breslau and I never would have felt at home there. I didn't think the natives would ever lose their antagonistic attitude toward us refugees. More so, I loved the cheerful, relaxed attitude of Americans, which was in sharp contrast to the serious, tense Germans.

One day, at my mother-in-law's, I ran into Erich, Elfriede's brother. It was an awkward situation. We talked with each other, trying to avoid what had happened in the past. I had the impression that he wanted to get together with us. We didn't have any objection to that, and I was sorry anyway for what I had done. We invited him and his new wife to spend Christmas with us and they accepted. It turned out better than I had hoped, and I could tell they liked being with us, particularly with the children. I was glad we had buried the hatchet.

Not long after we moved into our apartment, my parents and sisters found an apartment of their own. This was a blessing, because the situation at their former place had become unbearable. The owner of the apartment, Mr. Greiff, had been released from the internment camp where he had spent five years. After his return there were nine adults crammed in a small space sharing one toilet.

With Gerald growing up fast, I thought it was time to put out feelers for a sponsor in America. I began to write to any place I

Hans with Hannelore and Gerald
Stuttgart 1953

could think of, even to Hershey's Chocolate factory but in vain. In the process I found out that one could immigrate to Canada without having a sponsor. The only requirement was to accept work for one year in agriculture, forestry or industry. Since we didn't have the means to leave together, it would have meant being separated for a long time. Neither Elfriede nor I liked the idea, and we decided to wait for a better opportunity.

This opportunity was closer than we had imagined. While beating my brain out as to which way I might succeed in my quest, it struck me like lightning: "the minister from Iowa." I went to see my mother and she still had his address. She might not have given me the address if she had known the events she set in motion.

I wrote to Rev. Dirks and told him how much we would like to come to America. Surprisingly, I received an answer. He mentioned that he was an immigrant himself and was originally from northern Germany and had immigrated to the U.S. after WW I. He indicated that he might be able to help us, but didn't commit himself. Despite that, I felt I had my foot in the door. I hadn't expected to hear anything concrete from him so soon. We exchanged more letters and one day he let me know that he was coming to Hannover, Germany in August to attend a Lutheran Church World Convention. He asked me if it was possible to meet him there. This was exciting news and it sent my hopes sky-high.

I knew that my uncle George, my grandfather's brother, together with his wife and daughter, had ended up in Hannover. I contacted him and he invited me to stay with him. That helped a lot; however, because of our tight budget I still had to hitchhike. To travel this way certainly was no fun, but I finally made it. Like the rest of us, my uncle lost everything in Breslau, including his auto body shop; but his greatest loss was that of his only son, Herbert, who was missing in action. What made it even more tragic was that a comrade of Herbert told my uncle he had seen Herbert just a few days before the war ended. Nevertheless, it was a nice reunion with my uncle, his wife and daughter.

Then came the big moment when I met Rev. Dirks. He seemed

to be busy and we didn't have much time to talk, but he told me that he was coming to Stuttgart to meet all of us. After my return home, Elfriede told me that I had missed by minutes a postcard announcing his visit. It was unfortunate that I had left for Hannover a little too early, but I couldn't dwell on it. I had to concentrate on the task ahead.

Rev. Dirks arrived and we were prepared for him. He liked all of us and saw that my letters to him had been truthful. Of course, we talked about our desire to go to America and the need for a sponsor. He still wasn't willing to make a commitment and we soon found out one reason for that. After the second day of his stay, he had a real surprise. He said he was leaving for a couple of days and we shouldn't expect him back at night. He was going to see another family in Reutlingen, a town not far from Stuttgart. The family consisted of parents and two daughters and they had the same intentions as we had. He made it clear if he became a sponsor, it could be for one family only. He showed us one of their letters and by reading it we knew we would lose this contest. The letter was beautifully written and interwoven with religious expressions. I had never mentioned religion in my letters and thought I probably should have. In any case it was too late now. Rev. Dirks left in the morning and we didn't expect to see him again until the next day.

We were wrong. At about eleven o'clock at night the doorbell rang and it was Rev. Dirks. He looked as white as a ghost and we thought he had been in an accident or something worse. He told us that when he arrived in Reutlingen the husband wasn't at home and his wife acted somewhat strange. As it turned out the man was an alcoholic, who couldn't hold a job and on this day had collected his unemployment pay. This meant he was out drinking. That kind of story was so familiar to me. His daughters and even their landlord searched for him and finally found him and dragged him home. What followed must have been a horrible scene. The guy was on his knees hanging on to the minister and everyone was crying and lamenting. We felt sorry for this family, but it was fortunate for us and for Rev. Dirks as well, that he went to see them on this particular day of the week. I felt that my good angel had been looking out for me.

Rev. Dirks returned to the U.S. and we weren't quite sure what to expect. Then in October he wrote that he had secured a job for me with the Iowa Highway Department in Sheldon, Iowa. That sounded great and gave us hope again; after all, he wouldn't have done that unless he intended to sponsor us. Following his letter came the confirmation from the Iowa State Highway Commission in Ames, Iowa. They were offering me the job as an instrument man at a salary of $225 per month.

I thanked Rev. Dirks for his effort and help, but didn't pressure him in any way. I didn't think he would change his mind at this point. I actually needed some time to take care of a few important matters. I wanted to learn more English and started to take one English lesson per week. I wished I could have taken more, but this was all I could afford. A big help was the America House in Stuttgart with their publications in English. I never forgot a fictitious story I read there about homeowners. In essence it went like this: the wife was telling her husband that he couldn't play golf, because the hinge on the garden gate was loose, in the attic was a broken window, the kitchen faucet leaked and the lawn needed mowing. As I found out later, this story was hardly fiction.

In the meantime I had to deal with an entirely different problem. The German Veterans Administration had notified me that my disability had been reduced from fifty to forty percent. This upset me quite a bit, because I had met veterans who had one finger missing and were classified at thirty percent disability. The pension I received was very small and a ten percent decrease wouldn't have made much difference, but any veteran under fifty percent disability lost all kind of benefits, such as an income tax deduction, lower priced tickets to sports events, movies, etc. Since I wasn't sure that I would succeed in going to America, I decided to appeal.

I had to appear before a panel to present my case. The panel tried to convince me that my injury wasn't serious enough to justify a fifty percent disability. I couldn't believe my ears. I told them, considering that I had to live the rest of my life with only one lung and with a caved in right chest, it would be very unfair to lower my present disability percentage. I suggested they should take a closer look at my medical record and in particular my x-rays. I insisted that I wanted to have my case examined by a higher tribunal. They finally agreed and told me I would be summoned at a later date.

With my immigration to America being a strong possibility, I had to make some extra money in a hurry. Just the visas for the four of us amounted to DM 1200. In addition, we needed money for our voyage and for a number of miscellaneous expenses.

I looked around to find a part-time job and was lucky, or so I thought. The Soccer Lotto Organization hired me. My job was to sort out the winning numbers of Sunday's soccer games. I joined a large group of people working from 6PM until midnight. The pay was for piecework-to be exact, DM 3- for checking a bundle of 100 lotto tickets. The numbers themselves consisted of 0, 1 and 2 and there was a minimum of 20 numbers per sheet. Except for a short coffee break, we worked for six hours frantically and without looking up. I figured checking three numbers per second amounted to 60,000 numbers per night. It was no wonder I couldn't sleep that night. The two following nights I still dreamed nothing but numbers and before I knew it Sunday was there again. Despite this torture I continued the work, because I was able to add about DM 150 per month to my savings.

It was amazing how my sisters had matured in a short time. They had grown into pretty young ladies and were dating. I didn't see them too often since our jobs and private lives kept us busy. Jutta was dating a young man who was from Freudenstadt, a town in the Black Forest. Eventually, their relationship became serious and they were married in Stuttgart. It wasn't a big affair, because both of the families were small, but it was a festive wedding.

We spent an especially merry Christmas with Erich and his

wife, since we expected it to be our last Christmas in Germany. On New Year's Eve we went with Horst and his latest girlfriend to what probably was the fanciest restaurant in Stuttgart. After dinner, dancing and celebrating, we went to our apartment for coffee and cake. At about four a.m. Elfriede and I went to bed and left Horst and his girlfriend in the living room. When we opened the curtains in the morning we wondered why the people passing by were looking up to us and laughing. Then we saw the reason. Horst had taken our stripped Christmas tree, which had been on the balcony, and had stuck it in the balcony railing like a flagpole with some of Elfriede's and my underwear draped over it. We had to laugh about it too, but Elfriede didn't want to show her face for a while.

I didn't think that the RM 200 penalty Elfriede had on her court record would give us any trouble with the American Immigration Authorities, but I didn't want to take any chances. I went to see the judge and asked him if he could do us the favor and remove Elfriede's penalty from her record. I told him that my wife had never violated the law before or after and at that time had done it only to get money for food. I explained to him that we hoped to immigrate to the U.S. and that I would feel better if my wife had a clean court record. He said he would have to check the details, but didn't see any obstacle in fulfilling my request. We heard from neighbors that someone had been inquiring about Elfriede and shortly afterwards she was informed that everything on her record had been stricken.

By now it was 1953 and we were still waiting for things to happen. Then in March, I received a letter from the Iowa State Highway Commission in which they wanted to know if I was still interested in the job they had offered me. This inquiry made me very uneasy, because I felt that time was running out. I informed Rev. Dirks and told him that the time had come where I needed to know if he was going to sponsor us.

Again we waited, hoping that our dream would become reality. Finally, the waiting and uncertainty was over. We received from

Rev. Dirks the official papers of his sponsorship. He advised us to contact the Lutheran World Federation in the event we needed any help in our endeavor. I thanked him very much and assured him that we would never be a burden.

The biggest expense we faced were the tickets for the ship, which amounted to about DM 3000. I didn't waste any time and wrote to the Lutheran World Federation. I explained to them my problem and asked if they could help in any way. I was excited when they replied shortly after and even more so for their offer to provide the ship tickets. Their only stipulation was to reimburse them later on and to furnish a recommendation from our pastor. The latter requirement was a real dilemma, because we didn't attend church. No matter how uncomfortable I felt, there was no other way; I had to go and see our local pastor.

I tried to build up my self-confidence by thinking about the church tax being deducted from my paycheck every month, but this didn't quite work. When I met the pastor I felt immediately better, because he spoke my own Prussian dialect. He was an elderly man and he told me that he was from a small town in Silesia; also, that he was the only survivor of his family, all the others murdered by the Russians. There was no doubt that he understood better than the natives did what it meant to be a refugee. I told him about my own experiences, why I wanted to go to America and that I needed his help. He could understand my desire to get away from it all and promised to help. I thanked him for that and for how much his support meant to my family and me. On the way out he asked why he never saw me in church. I should have expected this question, but I didn't and it caught me off guard. I only could come up with the stupid answer that I always sit in the back of the church. He just smiled; he knew I was lying. Despite my obvious dishonesty, I was glad this encounter ended on a positive note.

Feeling that my money problem had been solved, I contacted the American Consulate in Munich. They informed me that we would have to furnish a clean court, police and political record, proof of employment in the U.S. and certification of sponsorship. We would be notified when to come for a medical examination and to be prepared to pay the fee of DM 1,200 for our visas.

I had no reason to be concerned about any of these requirements, except for my lung injury. I knew I couldn't hide it, but I wanted to make sure that the injury wouldn't be mistaken for a lung disease. As I found out later, I could have saved myself a lot of worry.

I went to the city health department and explained my plight. I asked if they could do an examination of my lung and furnish the certification I needed. They said this wouldn't be a problem, but I had to furnish my medical records from the veteran's administration. When I approached the veteran's administration with my request, I was astonished. I was told I could get my records only if I withdrew my appeal. I felt this was government blackmail! I gave it serious thought, because if I dropped my appeal, and for some reason we wouldn't make it to America, I would lose the chance to keep my fifty percent disability. I decided to be optimistic and gave in to their demand. The city health department examined me very thoroughly and I obtained the documentation I needed. However, it turned out that I went through all of this for nothing, because the American doctor in Munich shoved my health record aside with the remark, "No German stuff."

Another snag was getting our German passports. Elfriede didn't have any problems, maybe because she was "a child of the land." In my case, the passport office didn't want to acknowledge that I was a German citizen, despite the fact that I presented my German birth certificate, my parents' wedding license and proof that I had served in the German Army. They found it necessary to summon my father and had him swear under oath that he had served in the German Army during WW I. It was unbelievable.

Faster than expected we were called to the American Consulate in Munich. We went by train and had to stay overnight, because we had to be there early in the morning. Everything went smoothly, except, as I had expected, the doctor was not sure about the condition of my lung. He wanted a second opinion and sent my medical record to an American lung specialist in Paris, France. I wished this wouldn't have been necessary, but I felt confident that everything would turn out all right, especially since the Consulate collected the DM 1,200 fee for our visas.

On the way back to Stuttgart something funny happened. Trying to avoid having to stay another night in Munich, we rushed to the train station. Running along the platform, Elfriede lost her panties. She picked them up in a hurry and stuffed them in her pocket. We could see some people looking out the train windows and grinning when they saw what had happened.

It had come to my attention that disabled veterans could get their pensions in advance for a number of years, by taking a twenty percent penalty. The reason for this was to give veterans a chance to purchase things that required a large down payment. I thought I should apply for such an advance payment, so I wouldn't have to start my life in America with a large loan. I went to the veteran's administration and talked to the person in charge. I explained to him that I was going to immigrate to the U.S. and that I would like to get an advance payment to purchase ship tickets. I told him that was all I wanted, and even would be willing to relinquish any further claims. Based on my previous experiences I shouldn't have been surprised when he turned me down and said in his native dialect, "Yeah, you would like that, shove the money in your pocket and run off to America." I was aware, that my request was perhaps unusual, but he didn't have to be so rude.

By September we were still anxiously waiting to hear from the American Consulate in Munich and I decided to give them a call. Even though I had expected to receive good news eventually, it was a relief when I heard that everything was in order and our visas were on the way. I received a sealed envelope, which I had to present to the Immigration Service upon our arrival in the U.S.

I notified the Lutheran World Federation that we had all the necessary papers we needed to immigrate. I informed Rev. Dirks and the highway department that our arrival was imminent. It didn't take long for the Lutheran World Federation to reply; and after signing the required forms, they issued us the tickets for the ship. With the tickets came a letter in which they wished us a safe voyage and informed us that one of their representatives would be waiting for us in New York. This took a big load off my shoulders, because it hadn't been quite clear to me how to get from New York to Sheldon, Iowa. The cost of the tickets for the ship amounted to $720, and we would depart on November 17, 1953 from Bremerhaven and arrive on November 27 in New York. With this information at hand I was able to tell Rev. Dirks, as well as the highway department, the exact date of our arrival. I was very glad when the highway department let me know that I could start my job on the first of December.

The die was cast. We had a lot of wrapping up to do. We needed suitcases, some clothes and lots of odds and ends. It started to cost us more money than we had expected. This created one more problem. After considering everything, we came to the conclusion that we still needed about DM 200 for the train tickets, a one-night stay in Bremerhaven and a little pocket money.

Compared to the major obstacles we had overcome, it seemed unimportant; nevertheless, I had to find a way to solve it. One of my first thoughts was to sell our furniture, but this was hopeless; it wasn't worth anything. Trying to borrow money from my parents was just as useless; because of my father's drinking habit, they lived from one payday to the next.

In desperation, I went to the local welfare office. I really didn't like doing this and had little hope for success. For a change I found an official who showed compassion. After I proved that we didn't possess anything of value, he provided us with the train tickets, money for the hotel in Bremerhaven and some extra money so we wouldn't be completely penniless. I was so grateful to this man that I sent him a small "Thank You" package from Iowa. I would have liked to make it a big package, if I had the means.

My parents and sisters had been looking at my undertaking with mixed emotions and doubted that I would succeed with my plan to immigrate. Now that it was becoming a reality, I could only hope that they would understand my reasons for leaving.

I had tried not to let my office know about my intentions, but it had been impossible to keep it a secret. Despite that, I had the feeling that they didn't take me seriously and were surprised when I gave notice. We did have a very nice relationship with each other at work and socially. Years later when visiting Germany, I went back to the office and had a stirring reunion. It was just too bad that some of my co-workers had already passed away.

There were no regrets whatsoever when quitting my part-time job with the Lotto Office. Many times I had been afraid that this job would drive me crazy.

COMING TO AMERICA

The day of our departure came, or in other words, the moment of truth was here. I was very happy having achieved my goal of going to America; yet, I was overcome by a certain sadness. I didn't have much time to sort out my feelings, because our families, together with friends and neighbors, were waiting for us at the railroad station. Elfriede and I were remarkably calm and that reflected on our children. With the last goodbye there were some tears here and there, but considering we might not see each other again, our departure was easier than expected. It seemed my father was more aware of that possibility than the others were, and even though he had caused me so much unhappiness, I felt sorry for him.

We made it safely to Bremerhaven and boarded our ship the next morning. She was a brand-new, beautiful, 24,000-ton ship named the *T.S.S. Olympia*. Little did we know how much misery this ship had in store for us. Soon the visitors had to disembark and the ship lifted anchor. The band played the traditional German Parting Song, which was later popularized by Elvis Presley under the title "I Don't Have a Wooden Heart." There were a lot of tears shed by the hundreds of people on the ship as well as on the pier. Before long the German coast vanished in the distance and we wondered what lay ahead for us.

We hadn't expected first class cabins, but what we got was the next best thing to steerage. The cabins were located at the stern of the ship, on the lowest deck and were flanked by large luggage compartments on both sides. In addition, we were housed in separate cabins. Elfriede and the two children had to stay in one cabin together with two women and another child, while I had to share my cabin with three men. There wasn't anything we could do; we couldn't be choosy.

Our voyage was going to lead us from Bremerhaven to Southampton, England; Cherbourg, France; Cobh, Ireland; Halifax, Canada; and our final destination New York, adding up to a total of eleven days. Under normal circumstances this could have been an enjoyable experience, but it turned out to be a nightmare.

A few days into the Atlantic a severe storm developed with a bang. While eating lunch in the dining room a big wave hit, tilting the ship sideways and sending dishes, and food crashing to the floor. The ship started to sway so badly that the crew had to install ropes all over the deck to prevent people from falling overboard, although with the whipping icy spray no one wanted to venture out. Almost everyone was seasick, including the Captain. People were throwing up everywhere and there were very few stewards left to clean up. It was the biggest mess. When lying in bed, I had the feeling that I was either standing upright or standing on my head. Getting up in the morning was worse because I had to vomit at least twice before getting dressed. Elfriede looked as pale as a ghost. I had to admire her for the way she was able to care for herself and the children.

One night one of the luggage compartments sprang open and luggage, boxes, etc., came sliding and tumbling down the hallway past our doors. The thunderous noise lasted most of the night, as the luggage crashed from one side of the hall to the other. However, it didn't matter because we could hardly sleep anyway.

Another night, the engines stopped and we thought this would be the end of us; fortunately, after a while they started again. It probably sounds extreme, but I was feeling so lousy that I was at a point where I didn't care anymore. The next day crewmembers told us that we had been close to being transferred to the lifeboats. We told them we wouldn't have gone and they said emphatically, "Yes, you would have."

I was glad that the children didn't feel as poorly as we did.

Hannelore found some children her age and of different nationalities. They spent a lot of time together, mostly playing hide and seek. Gerald didn't say much and we assumed he was all right. One time he broke his silence when we passed another ship. He said, "I want to go on a ship," not realizing that he was already on a ship.

Although we didn't need to lose weight, it happened anyway. We found out that the only thing we could hold in our stomachs were dry rolls and beer. This meant spending some of the few dollars we possessed. To be exact we left Germany with thirty dollars and I had hoped to hang on to most of that money until we arrived in America. Nevertheless, unusual circumstances require unusual measures. It didn't really matter if we arrived with thirty dollars or nothing. With this thought in mind, I rented four deck chairs for five dollars each. This allowed us to stay on deck most of the time in the fresh air and to escape the awful stench below.

It seemed like our ordeal would never end. Finally, the storm subsided and not much later we arrived in Halifax, Canada. It was a beautiful day and the air was cool and refreshing. It was interesting to see how fast we recovered from our seasickness the moment the ship stood still, and how suddenly so many passengers appeared. The day also had a special meaning for me; we had arrived in the "New World" on the 25th of November, my 31st birthday.

While on deck, I had the chance to speak with one of the ship's officers. He didn't have anything positive to say about the *Olympia*. He told me that the owner was a Greek who had the ship built in England. He had allocated a fixed amount of money coupled with the request for a greater number of decks than normal. As a result the ship was out of proportion. This didn't surprise me, because it had been my feeling that the storm we encountered wasn't the only cause of the pounding we took. Years later I read that the *Olympia* completed only three Atlantic crossings before being assigned to shorter routes. It had been our bad luck to be on one of them.

The Other Side of the Coin

Before we left Halifax I wanted to have a little birthday celebration and invited two couples for a drink. I had only one dollar left and since the drinks cost fifteen cents each, it worked out perfectly. Unlike many immigrants, I can't say that I arrived penniless in America; I still had a dime.

Some of the mess below deck had been cleaned up, but not completely, so we decided to stay on deck overnight. We took our blankets and pillows and faced the cold and misty sea air. The following night, our last one on board, we had to stay below and prepare for departure. In the morning we knew New York was close and went up on deck as early as possible. Then it happened- out of the fog appeared the Statue of Liberty. The sight was awesome. I'll never forget that moment and could imagine how all the immigrants before must have felt.

We didn't have much time to marvel at the skyscrapers or anything else. The American citizens debarked quickly and then it was our turn. Everybody was very nervous and tense, including us. I had been told Ellis Island was in the process of being closed and that the Immigration Officials would come on board. The first official I had to face was the doctor. I whispered to Elfriede, "If he says 'no' I'll jump in the water." The doctor sat behind a desk with a green desk lamp in front of him. When I handed him the envelope from the doctor in Munich he took a quick look at me. Then he checked the seal on the envelope very carefully, opened it and looked at my x-rays. I thought everyone around could hear my heart pounding. After what probably lasted no more than two minutes, but seemed like an eternity, he signaled me to move on. This was a tremendous relief and I felt like hugging him. The other officials only asked a few questions and we moved along the line quickly. Next to the doctor, my biggest worry was if a representative of the Lutheran World Federation would be on hand. When we came to the last official he asked if there was anyone waiting for us and I told him whom we hoped to meet. He smiled and waved a young lady over and said to her, "Here are your people." I can't describe how happy I was to see her. No doubt, without her being there we would have been in big trouble.

She introduced herself and we were surprised when she spoke perfect German. We felt dazed with all the activities around us and were glad she took charge. She secured our luggage and took us by taxi to a cafeteria. Since some of the dishes were unfamiliar, Elfriede and I discussed in German what to select. To our surprise, the server tried to be of help and explained different items to us in German. Pointing at us, he called to a waitress, "Hey, Frieda, Germans!" I was beginning to feel more and more at ease. It was very embarrassing, but I had to tell the young lady that we were out of money. She laughed and said she was prepared for that and we shouldn't worry. She told us she would take care of us and see to it that we made it safely to Sheldon.

We had a little time to look around and found the skyscrapers, the traffic, the number of people, etc., overwhelming. I was very interested in observing the people and thought they don't look much different from Germans, except that so many wore eyeglasses and women had cigarettes dangling from their lips.

It was getting dark and we drove through a poorer part of town. I remember that I saw children playing ball amid big piles of garbage. We transferred to a bus and at first in the dark, didn't notice that the bus had moved on to a ferry. Looking back, across the water, we had a perfect view of New York at night. It was another unforgettable sight. Soon we arrived at a railroad station and our guardian was about to leave. She handed us railroad tickets and $20 and told us to change trains in Chicago. We thanked her for everything and told her how much she and her organization had meant to us.

We were about to get an idea of the size of this country. The train just kept on rolling. Fortunately, we had comfortable seats and were tired enough to sleep. We arrived at Chicago Union Station and found a place to eat. On the train there were still some people we recognized from the ship; now, for the first time we were completely alone in America. It was a strange feeling and difficult to describe. What made us feel somewhat better was a waitress who knew enough German to chat with us.

Then something incredible happened; a lady came up to our table and told us in German that the waitress had mentioned that this family, pointing at us, was going to Sheldon, Iowa. When we said this was true, she blurted out "So are we." This was hard to believe; Sheldon was a town of only 4,000 people and compared with the United States, a drop in the bucket. They also had been on the *Olympia*. When we told them that we hadn't seen them before, they said they were so terribly seasick, they hardly ever left their cabin. They were a husband and wife with two boys who were one year and fifteen years old. Their family name was Hahn and their former home was Berlin. His first name was Erwin and he was a bricklayer by profession. His aunt, who lived in Sheldon, had sponsored for them. I also noticed that he didn't know a word of English.

When searching for our train to Sheldon, I approached a railroad official for help. He showed us the way and said to me, "When you come back here, you'll be a rich man." I can say that I came back to Chicago years later, not as a rich man, but a 100 percent better off.

We were glad to have met the Hahn's and with all the talking the train ride went by fast. When we stepped off the train, Hahn's aunt was there to greet them. In contrast, we had a regular reception committee waiting for us. I assume The Lutheran World Federation had notified Rev. Dirks about the time we would arrive, because we had neither the money nor the know-how to do so. Besides Rev. Dirks, there was the local minister by the name of Schiffler and a few other people. They took us to an apartment they had rented for us. We talked for a while and I gave Rev. Dirks a token of our appreciation, a little coo-coo clock. Then they left and we were on our own.

Our apartment was downtown and on the second floor of an old building; we also shared the floor with a real estate office. The view from our windows was a brick wall, only a few feet away. The apartment was small, with no bathroom, only a toilet. A bathtub, a genuine relic with its curved legs, was located in the bedroom. All of this was tolerable, except for the barely working steam heater. This turned out to be a real problem with the bitter cold. Somehow the place reminded me of our time in the attic.

Our more immediate problem was money. I went to see Rev. Schiffler and explained my predicament to him. I asked him if there was a way of borrowing money from somewhere until I would receive my first paycheck. He offered to go with me to the bank for a loan. This worked out and I obtained a loan of $50. I thought this was quite a bit of money, but found out very fast that this wasn't the case.

I had to go to work the following day. The Highway Department was in a two-story building on the outskirts of town, about a ten-minute walk from where we lived. The main level of the building housed snowplows, trucks, etc., and the second floor, the engineering office. I met the head of the department by the name of Kowalski and had the distinct feeling that he didn't like me. My immediate supervisor was an engineer by the name of Dutch Stolmeier. He was in his thirties and a very friendly fellow. There were also some young guys around who worked as rod and chain men.

My first task was to get acquainted with the English Measurement System. Being used to the Metric System, I found the English System too complicated, in particular when working with architectural plans, which are loaded with measurements in fractions of inches. Of course, I was anxious to learn. However, Mr. Kowalski didn't give me much time for that and sent me out in the field almost immediately. Our surveying party consisted of Dutch as party chief, myself as instrument man, and a rod and a chain man. Our work was typical, namely providing the necessary measurements and drawings for the construction, improvement and maintenance of roads. Since everything was new to me and my knowledge of English was limited, I was glad to get a lot of help from Dutch.

In the meantime Elfriede had become acquainted with our

neighbor, the real estate agent, who was elderly and a fine gentleman. He liked to have us around and he helped with a lot of good advice. He enjoyed our children and occasionally bought chocolate for them, something we couldn't afford.

Hannelore had started to go to school and was learning English amazingly fast. Together with her books from school, she was able to help Elfriede and me learn English. In the process I noticed that there was quite a bit of difference in the pronunciation between the American English and the one I had studied at the Berlitz School in Stuttgart.

Besides spending time with our neighbor and playing with Elfriede, Gerald found a few ways of entertaining himself. We found a ball of twine somewhere and he spent many hours tying all the different pieces of furniture together. He also liked to walk around in Elfriede's high heel shoes. Unfortunately, this came to a bad ending. One time, when walking out the door, he stumbled and fell head over heels down the stairs. On the bottom he hit a wall and ended up with an ugly cut on the back of his head. I was glad that he didn't suffer a more serious injury and that he lost interest in wearing lady's shoes.

We were glad to have brought warm clothes from Germany, because the weather was getting colder by the day and it began to snow. I wore everything I possibly could to work, but it wasn't enough. The area around Sheldon is farmland and flat, and most of the time an icy wind blew. I felt like the wind was passing right through me and being out in the open for hours was torture. When I came home at night, the first thing I did was to sit on the heater. Even though the heater never did get warm, it helped me to defrost.

Elfriede must have mentioned this situation to our neighbor, because he offered to sell me an old fur coat for two dollars. I knew he could have just given me the coat, but he didn't want me to feel like a pauper. This was very thoughtful of him. The coat was like a gift from heaven and I don't know what I would have done without it.

The Other Side of the Coin

When I started working on the first of December I didn't know that I wouldn't get paid before the beginning of January. With the borrowed fifty dollars we couldn't afford anything, and we had barely enough for food. It was a wonder that Elfriede was able to feed us for five weeks.

Weather permitting we attended church in Sheldon with the Rev. Schiffler officiating. This was a real education. We admired the big, beautiful cars, the well-dressed people and especially the money and large checks in the collection basket. The majority of the people there were of German descent. Despite being newcomers, we were well known to the congregation since our picture and story had made the front page of the Sheldon newspaper.

It was a sad Christmas, especially for the children. We didn't have a Christmas tree or presents, actually nothing. An old man, who had a bedridden wife, came by and brought us some cookies. I'll never forget his kindness. What bothered us was that we had to lie in the letters to our families, but it was impossible to write the truth.

To our amazement, we were invited on Christmas Day to Rev. Dirks' house. He picked us up, since he lived about an hour's drive away. We were impressed with his beautiful home located next to his church. He introduced us to his wife and daughter and we were surprised that his wife, to put it mildly, acted impersonal toward us. In contrast, his teenage daughter was very friendly and took Hannelore right away under her wing. There were also two other ministers with their wives present.

Lunch was the principal meal of the day and sitting around a long table, I saw how Rev. Dirks was eating up Elfriede with his eyes. When I glanced at his wife I could tell that she noticed it too. I didn't like that at all, but the worst was yet to come. After lunch all of the men retreated to the study. I couldn't participate in the conversation and felt like a fifth wheel; but it was certainly interesting to listen to them brag about how many gifts they had received from their congregations.

Later in the afternoon we went to a church service with Rev. Dirks officiating. Shortly before the service Rev. Dirks handed me a paper, typewritten in German, and told me to read this to his congregation. He added that most of the people understood German. When I read the content I was astonished, to say the least. I had to say how thankful we were for having been invited to spend Christmas with Rev. Dirks and for all the things he had done for us and, in particular more than once, that it was only through his grace that we were in America. Using me to put him in the limelight bothered me. I couldn't help wondering what his true motive had been in sponsoring for us.

I was going to find out soon. Rev. Dirks had arranged for a German-speaking couple to give us a ride home. They owned a farm and it was interesting to hear about their life. I never knew how hard it was to own a farm, for instance, the long days starting at four in the morning, the never being able to go away for long. In the course of our conversation we talked about us and were surprised by how much they knew already. Then we learned that Rev. Dirks had published our story in many papers and magazines, and even broadcast it over the radio.

On the sixth of January I received my first paycheck in the amount of $180. This was exciting and certainly came not a moment too soon, but after we paid $60 for rent and made a payment on our loan, there wasn't much left to live on for the next four weeks. Also, I had to buy a cap with earflaps, gloves and galoshes, all things I badly needed.

Despite our tight money situation, we decided to afford ourselves a bottle of beer on Saturday nights. Buying some beer should have been easy enough, but it wasn't. I don't know about the rest of Iowa, but in Sheldon I had to first apply for a booklet, and if approved, I had to take it with me to the liquor store. There I could purchase a limited amount of alcohol that would be duly recorded in my booklet. When I told Dutch about it he said not to bother, and he would buy what I wanted. He added it was ridiculous anyway, because it was only a few miles to the border with Minnesota where one could buy liquor without any restrictions.

While mentioning alcohol, one Saturday our neighbor stopped by to tell us that our landlady intended to visit us. When he saw our beer bottles he suggested we put them away before her arrival. I was at a point again where it didn't take much to upset me. I told him that we pay our rent, don't bother anybody and we weren't going to hide beer bottles or anything else. I don't know if he said anything to her, but she never showed up.

Once in a while the Hahns came to visit. Their life was somewhat better than ours was, but not by much. Probably because of the cold weather, Erwin had been unable to find a job as a bricklayer and they depended entirely on his aunt. From what we could gather, she wasn't the most generous person in the world. He told us for Christmas she gave him two pairs of socks from her deceased husband. Also, in his aunt's house lived a man who made wooden duck calls, which he tried out late into the night. They said that because of these unearthly sounds they couldn't get enough sleep. We had to laugh about it, but they didn't think it was funny.

We could tell that Erwin and his wife lacked the talent to learn English. This gave them the feeling of isolation, in addition to their already depressing situation. It didn't come as a surprise when they mentioned they were homesick and wanted to return to Germany. We told them not to give up so fast and there had to be better times ahead for all of us. As I listened to them I felt so lucky that Elfriede never even gave it a thought to go back to Germany. She loved America from the moment we arrived and defended it against anyone who said otherwise.

The weather became so cold it seemed like Russia all over again. I don't know if it was really necessary that we had to go out surveying every day under these conditions. We couldn't accomplish anything; it was like we were beating a dead horse. To adjust the instruments I had to take off my gloves and after a few seconds my fingers felt like icicles. Driving under these conditions was another problem; for example, on one single day we passed four accidents. On another day, I had to stand with an instrument in the middle of an icy road with no markers to warn motorists. Cars were passing left and right and I told Dutch that the cars were getting dreadfully close. His only response was, "They do, they do." I had to laugh about this remark later on, but not at the time. I was also worried about what would happen to Elfriede and the children if I should get killed.

With every passing day it became clearer that I had to get away from Sheldon. This wasn't the America I had hoped to find; a tortuous job without a future, a sponsor who used me like a puppet, and being surrounded by overly pious people. I just didn't have any idea on how to go about finding a better place, especially without money. But as many times before, my good angel came to the rescue.

On the ship from Germany we had shared our cabins with another couple and their small son. Their names were Horst and Christel Raue. They had moved to El Paso, Texas and apparently had an easier start than we had. Their sponsor had made the down payment on a small house for them and Horst found a job in a motel. In contrast to our dishonest letters to Germany, we let them know about our sorry life in Sheldon. One day, unexpectedly, we received a letter from them in which they invited us to come to El Paso. They said the weather was beautiful, the people were friendly but, most of all, we could stay with them for a while. We hardly believed that we could be so lucky. We thanked them for their generosity and told them we would come as soon as possible. Knowing that our days in Sheldon were numbered helped me immensely to cope with what was still to come.

Rev. Dirks informed me that he wanted to take me to a church meeting the following Sunday evening. I certainly didn't feel like going, but couldn't refuse. He came and we drove to a place unknown to me. He introduced me to a great number of people all the while patting himself on the back. He saw that due to my limited English I couldn't enjoy the whole affair, but this didn't

The Other Side of the Coin

seem to bother him. The meeting was over at midnight and I assumed he would take me home. I was mistaken. He took me to a small railroad station, bought me a ticket and left. I was the only passenger waiting in the dimly lit and cold waiting room. Finally, the train came and it was almost five o'clock in the morning when I arrived at home, shivering from the cold. Elfriede said she hadn't slept either, because she had been worried I might have been in an accident.

One day I had the chance to experience my first blizzard. It was amazing. On one side of the street snow had accumulated almost up to second floor windows. Dutch came and took me to work, otherwise I couldn't have made it. There was no doubt Kowalski couldn't send us out in this kind of weather. We also needed some time to work on our survey data. Then something completely unexpected happened. Kowalski told me to get a bucket of water and wash the stairs. This left me speechless. Aside from the fact I was busy doing engineering work, the young men who worked as rod or chain men were sitting around smoking and killing time. I stood there for a moment staring at him with murder on my mind, but I had no choice. I had to follow his order.

I had judged this man's feeling toward me correctly and I'm sure that he had waited for a chance to hurt me somehow and in this case by humiliating me in front of the others. If I ever had the slightest doubt about leaving Sheldon, it had vanished. At night, when I told Elfriede, she suggested I wear an apron to work. I knew she was joking to make me feel better.

During this depressing time there was at least one diversion. One morning our crew was driving slowly down a country road when we saw a pheasant in the ditch on the opposite side of the road. He was easy to spot since the whole landscape was covered with snow. We stopped and Dutch grabbed a shotgun he kept in the truck and approached the bird. He was only a few feet away when the pheasant took off and Dutch blasted him. He said he wanted me to have the bird and I thought this was nice of him. Elfriede was very happy to get the pheasant, because as far as meat was concerned, all we could afford was one pound of cheap ground beef per week. The pheasant turned out to be a great meal, except for the large number of small pellets embedded in the meat. We sorted them out but also bit on them and probably swallowed a few. I had the suspicion that the numerous pellets had something to do with Dutch's generosity.

Dutch didn't know about my intentions of leaving and he wanted me to get a driver's license. I had no objection and thought getting the license would be an advantage in any case. I had to take the written test first and surprised myself by passing it. The next morning the driving test followed and that turned out to be a total disaster. As usual, the streets were covered with ice and snow when we started. Driving straight ahead was no problem, but when making turns the rear of the car went over a curb and another time made contact with a telephone pole. The officer was very sympathetic, but told me I needed to practice some more before trying again. I fully agreed with him.

I didn't get a chance to practice, because a few days after my driving test we were involved in an accident. Dutch was driving, with me sitting next to him. We were going downhill on a narrow road following a Cadillac at a safe distance. When the driver of the car slowed down for a right turn Dutch wanted to do the same and couldn't. I guess it was the ice on the road combined with the weight of our truck. In any case, we plowed into the other car. The driver was an older man and he had lost consciousness. Fortunately, he was up and about again by the time the sheriff arrived. When I saw our collision coming I had braced myself and was fine; so were the two guys in the back, but Dutch hurt his neck. After that, Dutch didn't say anything anymore about my driving practice. I assume he didn't want to take any chances at this time. This was fine with me, I actually was glad.

The time for us to leave was getting closer. It was the beginning of March and we had hoped to get going in early April. I wished we could have left even sooner, but our money shortage slowed us down. I only hoped that nothing else would interfere.

I wrote to Rev. Dirks about our intention to leave Sheldon. I avoided mentioning any personal feelings and told him that our decision was based mainly on my hopeless job situation. I let him know that we would be forever grateful to him and hoped that he would understand. I didn't expect him to be very happy that we were putting an end to his bragging, but had no idea that he was going to insult me like nobody ever before. In his reply he called me names, accused me of being ungrateful for leaving him and reminded me that he was the one who pulled us out of the gutter!!! It took me a moment to digest this letter; how could this come from a man of the cloth? I decided not to let him get away with these insults and informed him that I would forward the letter to his superiors.

A few days later when I returned from work, I was surprised to find him waiting in front of the house with another man. He apologized to me with tears in his eyes and begged me to give him his letter. I told him that we would always be thankful to him for helping us to come to America, but he should realize that from here on we had to do what was best for ourselves. I gave him his letter; I wouldn't have done anything with it anyway. We parted and that was the last I saw of him. Eventually I let him know our whereabouts and we exchanged Christmas greetings until he passed away.

Giving notice at work gave me a lot of satisfaction. Kowalski looked at me in disbelief, probably thinking he had me in a stranglehold. He just took my note without uttering a word. I would have liked to give him a piece of my mind, but wasn't proficient enough in English to express myself the way I would have liked.

The last days went by fast. We said goodbye to the Hahns, wished them good luck and promised to write. Leaving them behind made them even more depressed, if this was possible. We had been the only people they could talk and relate to.

We thanked our neighbor for his kindness. I asked him if he wanted his coat back, but he didn't. I gave the coat to one of the rod men, which made the guy very happy.

It was harder saying goodbye to Dutch because he had been a friend of sorts. I thanked him for everything he had done for me and wished him the very best for the future. I knew he disliked Sheldon as much I did.

After getting my last paycheck and having fulfilled my obligation to the bank, we were ready to go. We had exactly $200 at our disposal and I already knew that our train tickets amounted to $90; this meant we would arrive in El Paso with only $100.

The train ride lasted two days and was arduous, to say the least. The last part from Amarillo to El Paso was mostly desert and after hours and hours of seeing nothing but sand we couldn't imagine that there would be a town at the end of the line. It was late at night when like a mirage, the city lights of El Paso appeared in the distance. We had arrived.

It was about 2 o'clock in the morning when we stepped off the train. We didn't want to wake up the Raues in the middle of the night and remained in the waiting room until daybreak. As demanding as the recent past had been, physically and mentally, it didn't get me down, but the few hours we spent in the waiting room did. I was at one of the lowest points in my life. I had no money, no job, no security of any kind and Hannelore had a fever and was feeling ill. I was questioning myself if I had been too self-confident, or if I was reckless or maybe crazy. But whatever, I had to go on and I was so thankful for having Elfriede by my side; she always gave me strength and support no matter what.

Horst came in the morning and took us to his house. On the way we saw that El Paso was nestled at the foot of high mountains, which looked very impressive compared to the flat landscape of Iowa. All of the Raues were happy to see us, and I had the impression that they were a little lonesome, like the Hahn's had been. We were glad too, to be with them and to be able to take care of Hannelore.

We had a lot to talk about-our experiences in Sheldon and, learn a little more in detail about El Paso. We found out the city

Hans, Elfriede, Hannelore and Gerald
El Paso, Texas 1954

was located at the border with Mexico, the Rio Grande representing the dividing line between the two countries. On the other side of the border was the city of Juarez. El Paso had a population of over 200,000 people, always had sunny weather and, possibly because of the Latin influence, had a tranquil atmosphere. All of this sounded quite inviting to me, particularly the warm weather.

I had recovered from my slump at the railroad station and was ready for action. I didn't waste any time and took off the next morning in the hope of finding a job. I don't know why I didn't get the idea to look for an employment office; instead I visited one business after another. At the end of the day I had at least one prospect. An architect told me that a colleague was building a hospital in Roswell, New Mexico and would be happy to have me. I was glad to hear this, but still hoped to find employment in El Paso.

The following morning I went to the city hall. I thought maybe I'd be lucky and find an opening in their engineering department. This wasn't the case, but they suggested I check with the Public Service Board, Water & Sewer Department. There, the chief engineer, Johnny Hunsicker, hired me on the spot. It seemed like a miracle that I found a job that fast and exactly the type I had hoped for.

Johnny was the best boss anyone could have asked for and because of him life in the office was very relaxed. Later we even became good friends. I really enjoyed my job and that I was able to use my training and experience from Breslau and Stuttgart. In addition, I learned the design and installation of water and sewer systems.

In a short time I doubled my income from that in Iowa and felt that I finally had reached my goal. All the things I had dreamed about, like a home, a car and a better life for my children were at my fingertips. It had been a long struggle, but as Shakespeare said, "All's well that ends well."

EPILOGUE

With our finances greatly improved we went ahead and rented a house. This was an incredible feeling to be living in a house by ourselves for the first time. We felt rich; within a year I was able to buy my first car, a 1952 Buick Special, and we felt even richer.

I paid off my loan to the Lutheran World Federation and they thanked me profusely. I had the impression they had not expected that I would live up to my obligation.

In Stuttgart, my sister Gerda married and gave birth to a daughter, Elke. Eventually she divorced and never remarried. She remained in Stuttgart and took care of our mother. I'll always be thankful to her for that. My sister Jutta gave birth to a girl, Marion, and shortly thereafter she and her family immigrated to Canada and later on to the United States. My sister bore four more children, three girls and a boy, Susan, Debbie, Chrissy and Gene. They settled in Michigan and still reside there.

Our life was as I had dreamed about all those years, and seemed too good to be true. I had the premonition that something unpleasant might happen. My thoughts were correct; I just didn't think it would be of such a horrible nature. In July Hannelore fell ill with an incurable muscle disease. The doctor informed us that she wouldn't last more than two years. We were devastated. In a way it was a blessing when she passed away after only six weeks. She couldn't swallow anymore and suffered terribly. She died on the 12th of August 1955 at the age of twelve. Only someone with this kind of experience will know that there is no greater pain in this world than that of losing a child. Even after all these years it is still very painful for me to think about.

We had to go on and in January of 1956 we bought our first house for the unbelievably low price of $9,000. This purchase was a big event in our lives, the work on the house and yard kept us physically busy, and our minds occupied.

A few months later Elfriede gave me the great news that she was pregnant. We were both very happy being able to look forward to a new child. Time went by fast and on the 10th of January 1957, Elfriede brought our son Steven into this world. I had been a little worried about Elfriede's health but everything went smoothly. Gerald was just as excited to have a little brother.

In July of 1957 my father passed away in Germany at the age of 67. I was unable to feel much pain, since he had never been a real father.

It had never crossed our minds to return to Germany and we became U.S. citizens on the 9th of January 1959. It made us feel like we really belonged.

I liked my job with the Water & Sewer Department, but Johnny Hunsicker left and the office wasn't quite the same. So, in March of 1959 we decided to follow the dream of so many before us and moved to California.

I started to work for an engineering company in Sacramento, which paid extremely well and enabled us to buy a nice house in Citrus Heights. Everything had worked out great; I liked my job and we enjoyed the proximity of San Francisco and the High Sierras. Unfortunately, in winter Elfriede suffered from the dampness, typical of the Sacramento Valley, and after only two years we returned to El Paso.

I found employment with the International Boundary & Water Commission, an agency of the U.S. State Department. The purpose of the agency is to solve the water and boundary problems along the entire border with Mexico. The work was very interesting and versatile. I became a section chief and retired in 1984 after 24 years of service.

During these years a lot went on in my life. There was my constant worry about Elfriede with her strange heart condition, which periodically put her in the hospital. I was lucky that she was such a remarkable person who was always upbeat and didn't allow her sickness to get her down. I had a number of hospital visits myself, including a gall bladder operation that almost killed me when I went into anaphylactic shock.

Our sons grew up making us proud parents. We were very happy that they had the opportunity to get a higher education, something we couldn't have afforded in Germany. Gerald became a hospital administrator and Steven a university professor. Both married and we were equally happy that two such pretty and fine young ladies by the names of Laurie and Amy became part of our family.

In September 1975, Laurie, Gerald's wife, gave birth to our first grandchild, a boy they named Evan. I don't know why, but Evan's birth gave me a feeling of immortality.

After our return from California, we bought a larger home. I had a swimming pool built and all of us, particularly Evan, had a lot of fun for many years. These were some of the happiest years of my life.

Even though it wasn't unexpected, it made me very sad when my mother died in 1984. Ironically it happened on the 25th of November, my birthday. She was 88 years old and outlived my father by 27 years.

Despite Elfriede's heart problems, we enjoyed my retirement and the things we could do together. We didn't travel very far, but California and Colorado, in particular, had a lot to offer.

In 1988, Elfriede's doctor talked her into a heart valve replacement. Something went terribly wrong and she passed away 10 days after her surgery. We had been happily married for 42 years and had been together through good times and bad. The loneliness was almost unbearable. I thought my life was over and sometimes felt like killing myself.

After spending a very painful and difficult year, I realized that I had to do something with my life, but didn't know what. By chance, I heard about a dance club and decided to look into it. It

Kunert Family
From left: Laurie, Elfriede, Evan, Gerald, Amy and Steven
El Paso, Texas 1987

Hans and Cindy
Cruise 1997

turned out to be a real lifesaver. It brought me back into the mainstream.

I met many nice ladies, but none held my interest. It didn't bother me, since I had become comfortable with my new life. I had moved into a condo and besides dancing, I traveled a lot.

I had no idea that my life was going to change again. In December of 1992 I wanted to book a cruise and met a travel agent by the name of Cindy. She was very attractive and I liked her right away. She had been divorced for many years and was the mother of two grown sons, Bryan and Bruce. One thing led to another and we were married nine months later.

El Paso wasn't the city anymore it used to be. Our children and many of our friends had left so we decided to leave too. We both loved the water and chose Palmetto, a quiet little town on the west coast of Florida.

Since my marriage to Cindy I have traveled the world. All of our trips have been exciting, but three stand out. In 1993, the celebration of my birthday at the elegant Rainbow Room on top of Rockefeller Center, exactly 40 years after I arrived with ten cents in my pocket in New York; and in October of 1998, the wedding of my grandson Evan to his pretty bride Dana in Flagstaff, Arizona. The most thrilling trip of all was to Kingman, Arizona in 2005 when I held for the first time my handsome great-grandson, Aidan Hans Kunert.

Many who have written autobiographies have said it felt like living their life all over again. I have to fully agree with them, at times my memories overwhelmed me so much I hardly could control my emotions. Looking back at my life reminded me of how fortunate I was to have survived. In all sincerity, I thank my good angel for that.

INDEX

8th, Calvary Regiment 64 128 130-131
----, Anneliese 120 Aunt Anna 25 Aunt Marie 128 130-131 Bruce 231 Bryan 231 Chrissy 228 Contessa 14 Debbie 228 Elfriede (Hans' Aunt) 8-9 Elke 228 Erich 9 Erich (Elfriede's brother) 172 175 181 200 205 Erna (Elfriede's cousin) 179 183-184 Gene 228 Guenter 31-32 70 125 Herbert 142-143 148 Hilde 199 Irene 119-120 126 Irmgard 26-27 41 122-123 126-127 151 Jeanette 173 Kurt 34 40 45 47 179 183-184 193 195 Margot 126 Maria 136 140-141 181 Marion 228 Robert 181 Rudi 18 34 41-42 46 Ruth (Hans' Cousin) 8 18 Susan 228 Ursula 131 Willie 13-14 18 Wunibald 34 Wunnie 34 49 117
BALDOWSKI, 182-183
BAUER, 164
BAVARIA, Passau 143
Bicycle, Accident in Military Training 65 First One 18 Trip to Ketschdorf 31
BITTNER, Dr 101 104
Black Market, Getting Involved 164
BRESLAU, Escape From 117 Return After Wounding 99 Tragic End Of 177
Bullet Removed 91
Burning Up The Car 112
CALIFORNIA, Citrus Heights Arrival In 229
Chess, Club Founded 40 Learning How To Play 9 Playing With Uncle Walter 21
CHURCHILL, 154-155
COLL, Pedro 43
Coloring Book for German Children 186
CONSULATA, 102 104
Country Club 2
CZISCH, Interpreter 78
Dancing, 231 Swing Forbidden 46 With Rudi 41
DIONYSIA, 101-104
DIRKS, Henry J 168 Rev 201 203 205 209 216 219-221 225 Meeting With 202

Discharged From The Army 116
Driving, Army School 69
  Learning in Iowa 224
EHRENBURG, Ilya 125
Field Hospital 97
Fifty-Millimeter Mortar 82
FLORIDA, Palmetto Arrival in 231
FOCH, Marshal WW I 41
FOGGER, 39
FRANK, Hans 56-58
French Toilets 72
FUCHS, Eva 180 Mrs 180
Furniture, From Elfriede's Family 175 Erich Demands 181
GERMAN REPUBLIC, Attempt To Overthrow 17
GERMANY, Division Of 154
GMUEREK, 110-111
GOEBBELS, German Propaganda Minister 33 35 65
GOERLITZ, Arrival In 109
GREIFF, Mr 157 200
GROTTENHOLZ, Arrival In 147 Family Arrives 148 Leaving 150
HAESLER, 29 Mr Confrontation With Jutta And Gerta 40
HAHN, Erwin 216 221 225-226
HANKE, Karl 128 177
HARRIS, General 133
HAUWIE, Corporal 77 90
HEIMLICH, Annie 177-178
HEIMLICH, Charlotte 19
HEIMLICH, Elfriede (Mother Of Hans) 2
HEIMLICH, Erich

HEIMLICH, Erich (Cont.) Attacked By Kapp's Soldiers 17 44
HEIMLICH, Erika 23 144 147-148 150 178
HEIMLICH, George 13 19 201
HEIMLICH, Gertrude 16 144 147-148 150 178
HEIMLICH, Alfred 2 Grandfather 44 177-178 Death 196
HEIMLICH, Grandparents 12-13 16
HEIMLICH, Herbert 19 201
HEIMLICH, Aunt Hildegard 127-128 130-131 147
HEIMLICH, Kurt 18 121
HEIMLICH, Walter 21 30 40
HEURAFFEL, Arrival At 135 Family Arrives 137 Leaving 141 Trip to 131
HIRL, Konstantin 52 62
HITLER, 11 28 41 45 47 54 57 105 127 136 148 155 Adolf Becomes Reich Chancellor 16 Visits Breslau 38
Hitler Youth, Attending Meetings 29 March 13 Pressure To Join 25 Honor Guard At Cook's Funeral 72
HORST, 157-158 159-160 168-169 172 188 193 205
HUNSICKER, Johnny 227 229
Immigration, Decision Made 190 Preparing For 204
IOWA, Arrival Sheldon 216 Decision To Leave 226
JAEGER, Troop Leader 52 54
JESSENBERGER, Hubert 109

Job Center, Counseling And
   Registration 30
KAPP, Wolfgang 17
Kayak, Naked Swimmers
   44 Purchase 124 Purchased
   With Gerhard 35 Selling 48
KERSANDT, Mr 149-150 184
KNOWLTON, Bernie 166 187
KOTT, Sergeant 65
KOWALSKI, Mr 217 223 225
KRAEMER, Jr Troop Leader 60
   Troop Leader 53 55
KRUEGER, 23
KRUMMHUEBEL, Hospital 101
KUNERT, Aidan 231
KUNERT, Amy 230
KUNERT, Cindy 231
KUNERT, Dana 231
KUNERT, Elfriede (Mother Of
   Hans) 2 169 Death 230
KUNERT, Elfriede (Wife Of
   Hans) 169 171-173
   175-176 179-181 183-
   185 191-193 196-197
   199 201 205 207 211-
   212 214-215 217-219
   221-223 226 Death 230
   First Date 169 Gets
   Arrested 183 Getting
   Passport 207 Heart
   Problems 230 Marriage To
   172 Pregnant 197-198 229
   Record Stricken 205 Tries
   To Find Work 190
KUNERT, Emil 8 188
KUNERT, Erich 1 Death 229
   Hit By Streetcar 25 Loses
   Job 4 36 Return From
   Gotenhafen 39 Work At
   Gotenhafen 39 Working For
   City Of Breslau 22
KUNERT, Evan 230-231
KUNERT, Gerald Michael 198-
   200 213 218 229-230
KUNERT, Gerda 16 62 168
   Adopts Ducklings 149 And
   The Flasher 43 Birth 16
   Marriage 228
KUNERT, Great-grandfather 2
KUNERT, Hannelore 171 174
   176 179-181 183 186 190
   192 198-199 213 218-219
   226 Adoption 194 Death
   228
KUNERT, Hardy 177 188
KUNERT, Jutta 8 10 16 204
   228 Loses Job 182
   Operated On 164 Sent To
   Freienwaldau 125
KUNERT, Karl 2
KUNERT, Laurie 230
KUNERT, Steven 229-230
KURSAWE, 68
Labor Company, Airfield Work
   52 End Of Service 62
   Moving Bombs 53 Parade in
   Krakow 56 Service In
   Poland 51 Supporting The
   Air Force 55
LAUTENSCHLAGER, 166 186-
   187
LEBKE, 138 Mr 138 140
LENK, 50 In Charge of Labor
   Company 50 Top Leader 53
   57-58
Letter Before Congregation 220
LEY, Dr 57-58
LOENS, Hermann 20 27
Lost In Russia With Czich 78
LUTHERAN WORLD
   FEDERATION 206 208-209
   214 216 228

MOLOTOVO, Tovarich 86
Move To, A New Neighborhood 19 Outskirts Of Town 22
MULHOUSE, Relations With The Civilians 64
Nazi Regime, Early Effects Of 21 28
Nosebleeds And Cure 37
NOVACK, 66 70-71
ODER RIVER, 1 3 8 36 124 Ice Breaking 20
Office Of Land Management 33 117
Playing Postal Service 158
PORSCHE, Ferry 196
PORSCHE, Ferdinand 196
PRESSL, 135-136 138 181 Hans 121 131 Mr 136 141 Mrs 136
Promoted To Corporal 76
Rabbit, Haesle 121
RAUE, 226 Christel 222 Horst 222
Reconnaissance Outfit Observer 64
Reichsarbeitsdienst 48
REIMANN, 101-103
Released To Former Unit 105
RICHTER, Sergeant 82 92-93 126
RODGERS, Col 166 173 186
ROOSEVELT, 154-155
ROTH, Mr 198
RUECKERT, Guard 153
RUSSIA, Arrival At Front Line 78 Shakhty Arrival In 90 Taganrog Hospital 98 Transport To 77 Troops Withdraw 81
RUSSIAN, Move Into Donetz Basin 83 Prisoners 86 96

RUSSIANS, Advance On Breslau 127
SCHIEWANI, Guenter 66 125
SCHIFFLER, Rev 216-217 219
SCHLAEGER, 111-112 Warrant Officer 110
SCHMIDT, 68
SCHMIEDEBERG, Hospital 101
SCHREBER, 8
SCHREIBERHAU, Hospital 104
SCHWEIDNITZ, 107 109
SEIDEL, 33
Six Day Coma 17
Sixteenth Birthday 41
SLEBITZA, 100-103
STALIN, 154-155
STAUFFER, Teddy 42-43
Stealing Light Bulbs 173
STOLMEIER, Dutch 217 220 222 224-226
STUTTGART, Arrival In 152 Leaving 211 First Apartment With Elfriede 174 Looking For Work 194 Move To New Apartment 199 Trip To 150 Trouble With Widow 185
Supply Runs 80
Swimming, Inexpensive Tickets Under Nazi Regime 45 Lessons 14 Off Tugboats 15
TEXAS El Paso, Arrival In 226 Leaving 229 231 Return To 229
Time In Stockade 107
Transfer To, Army Discharge Center 115 Artillery Observer 107 Clerical Work 110 Doctor's Assistant 113 Freistadt 112 Motor Pool 110 Reserve Unit 106 114

Trip To, Ketschdorf 31 Kiel 26
   Paris 73 Winzig 21
Tropical Fish, Given Away 48
   Tank 31
TSCHIRSCH, 28
Veterans Administration,
   119 Reduction In
   Benefits 203
VLASSOW, Gen 84
VOLKSSTURM, 119 126
War, End Of 141
WEISER, Gerhard 35-36 38 40
   42 44-45 47-49
   Assigned To Panzer
   Grenadiers 48 Death 124
   Wounded 63 102 117 Mrs
   63 117 124 195
WILLIS, Col 166
WOLFINGER, Leslie 13
Work, Engineering
   Technician Trainee 33
   Hired By City Of Stuttgart
   194 International Boundary
   & Water Commission 229
   Iowa Highway Department
   217 Public Service Board El
   Paso 227 Soccer Lotto
   Organization 204 State Of
   Prussia Office Of Land
   Management 33 US Army
   166 US Army Laid Off 187
   US State Department 229
WEST PRUSSIA, 41
Wounded, 96

www.ingramcontent.com/pod-product-compliance
Lightning Source LLC
Chambersburg PA
CBHW071424150426
43191CB00008B/1038